Skills for Managers and Leaders

Text, Cases, and Exercises

Gary Yukl

State University of New York at Albany

PRENTICE HALL

Englewood Cliffs, New Jersey 07632

Library of Congress Cataloging-in-Publication Data

Yukl, Gary A.,
    Skills for managers and leaders : texts, cases, and exercises /
Gary Yukl.
        p.   cm.
    Includes bibliographical references.
    ISBN 0-13-556564-2
    1. Leadership.   2. Leadership—Case studies.
    3. Management.   4. Management—Case studies.   I. Title.
    HD57.7.Y853   1990
    658.4′092—dc20   89-26578
                                                        CIP

Editorial/production supervision and
    Interior design: Kathleen Peifer
Cover design: Diane Conner
Manufacturing buyer: Peter Havens

© 1990 by Prentice-Hall, Inc.
A Division of Simon & Schuster
Englewood Cliffs, New Jersey 07632

Printed in the United States of America
10 9 8 7 6 5 4 3 2 1

ISBN 0-13-556564-2

Prentice-Hall International (UK) Limited, *London*
Prentice-Hall of Australia Pty. Limited, *Sydney*
Prentice-Hall of Canada Inc., *Toronto*
Prentice-Hall Hispanoamericana, S.A., *Mexico*
Prentice-Hall of India Private Limited, *New Delhi*
Prentice-Hall of Japan, Inc., *Tokyo*
Simon & Schuster Asia Pte. Ltd., *Singapore*
Editora Prentice-Hall do Brasil, Ltda., *Rio de Janeiro*

Contents

Preface

This book is a collection of text, cases, exercises, and role plays dealing with management and leadership in organizations. The purpose of the book is to teach practical skills required for effective management at all levels of an organization, but especially skills needed by middle and lower level managers. The book was designed for use as a supplementary text and workbook in a course in leadership, management, organizational behavior, or supervision. The scope and price of the book make it appropriate for use as a supplement to a regular text. Most survey texts provide a broad review of the literature on a particular subject such as management or organizational behavior, whereas this book provides more detailed coverage of a limited number of key topics. Each topic is important for effective management and involves skills in which many current and aspiring managers are likely to be deficient.

The book is approximately half text and half experiential exercises. It is divided into twelve modules corresponding to the key topics. Each module contains conceptual material and experiential exercises to enable students to test their understanding of key concepts and to practice and develop their management skills. The experiential exercises consist of concept recognition quizzes, skill assessment exercises, short cases, and role plays. The short cases range from one to three pages and take fifteen to thirty minutes to discuss. Most are composite cases inspired by events that occurred in real organizations, but are modified to provide more coverage of basic concepts. Unlike the longer, more complex cases found in many casebooks, the ones in this book are not designed to test a student's problem-solving and analytical skills. Instead, the cases are designed to increase a student's understandings of key concepts and procedural guidelines presented in the text. Some of the cases contain obvious examples of ineffective behavior by a manager and require students to identify these behaviors and discuss how to handle the situation in a more skillful manner. Other cases provide examples of effective behavior and will help prepare students for the role plays. The role plays are for groups of two to six students and take from twenty to forty-five minutes to complete. The experiential exercises in this book encourage active involvement by students and the practice of either diagnostic or execution skills. Many exercises provide students with an opportunity to assess their individual strengths and weaknesses.

Most of the experiential exercises are original, but some of the cases are reprinted or adapted from other sources. Many of the experiential materials have been used before in MBA or undergraduate courses. Some of the materials have been used in management development workshops in large corporations and public-sector organizations.

There is an accompanying instructor's manual with detailed instructions on how to use the book. The manual contains answers to the exercises and quizzes, guidelines for analysis of the cases, and guidelines for using the role play exercises. The manual also provides additional exercises for skill practice in class and suggestions about activities that allow students to practice skills outside of the classroom.

Introduction

People in managerial positions face a variety of challenges, but the most difficult challenges involve dealing with people, including subordinates, superiors, peers, and outsiders such as clients, customers, and suppliers. Traditional courses in management, leadership, and supervision seldom do an adequate job of teaching the skills necessary to handle these challenges effectively (Finney & Siehl, 1985-86; Mandt, 1982; Mintzberg, 1975; Porter & McKibbin, 1988). Most management textbooks are biased toward concepts and theories formulated at a very abstract level. Students learn numerous theories about individual processes, group processes, and organizational processes. However, students are not taught how to extrapolate from abstract concepts and theories to practical applications. Furthermore, students have little opportunity to acquire the execution skills necessary to apply concepts and guidelines to everyday problems.

Students also learn some analytical and quantitative skills in management programs, most of which are highly specialized and technical such as calculus, statistics, linear programming, forecasting, financial analysis, and cost-benefit analysis. These skills are valuable in some situations, but students who move into managerial positions will find only limited opportunity to use complex, quantitative techniques for decision making. What most managers need more are simpler, easier-to-apply procedures and guidelines for analyzing problems, identifying solutions, setting objectives, planning how to implement them, and checking on progress. The immense expansion of management development courses in industry during the past decade is an effort to fill this need and teach practical skills not being learned in traditional business programs.

Research on the nature of managerial work and the position requirements for managers in work organizations (Kaplan, 1986; Kotter, 1982; McCall & Segrist, 1980; Mintzberg, 1975) provide insights about the types of skills needed by managers. Since the nature of managerial work is inherently hectic, fragmented, chaotic, and stressful, managers need skills in planning how to manage their time and delegate effectively. Since many decisions cannot be implemented without the approval and cooperation of others over whom the manager has no authority, managers need skills in influencing people. Influence skills include knowledge of different influence tactics, understanding of when each tactic is appropriate, understanding of the underlying motives of the person to be influenced, and skill in using influence tactics. Since many decisions are made by groups, managers need to develop skills in determining the appropriate people to involve in making decisions and how to lead meetings that will be effective. Since disagreements often occur about the proper way to handle problems and do the work, managers need skills in managing conflict.

Research on managerial effectiveness provides additional insights into the types of skills needed by managers (Bass, 1981; Boyatzis, 1982; Katz, 1974). This research shows that four categories of skills are relevant.

1. *Technical skills* include knowledge about methods, processes, procedures, and techniques for conducting a specialized type of activity such as accounting, marketing, engineering, product design, production, distribution, financing, and business law.

2. *Conceptual skills* include general analytical ability, logical thinking, proficiency in concept formation, creativity in idea generation, and ability to analyze events, perceive trends, anticipate changes, and analyze problems.

3. *Interpersonal skills* include ability to understand the feelings, attitudes, and motives of people from what they do and say, ability to establish and maintain cooperative relationships, ability to communicate clearly, and ability to influence people.

4. *Administrative skills* include a combination of technical, conceptual, and interpersonal skills; they involve the ability to perform relevant

managerial functions such as setting objectives, planning, organizing, delegating, directing and supervising subordinates, monitoring and evaluating performance, and conducting meetings.

As these definitions reveal, technical skills are primarily concerned with things, conceptual skills with ideas, interpersonal skills with people, and administrative skills with processes. For each skill category, there are diagnostic skills that help a manager determine what is happening and why, and execution skills that help a manager behave in an appropriate and effective manner.

Overview of Contents

This book focuses on the two categories of skills that are most neglected in traditional management texts: interpersonal and administrative skills. Each module in the book involves a different type of skill. The modules explain abstract concepts that are found in basic survey texts but go beyond these texts to present more detailed descriptions and classifications. All but the first two modules include practical guidelines in how to apply the concepts to real management situations. Cases, quizzes, and exercises are included to assess understanding of the basic concepts and help refine diagnostic skills. Role play exercises and simulated management activities provide an opportunity to practice and strengthen skills.

Module 1: Managerial Practices

This module reviews the major categories of managerial behavior relevant to managerial effectiveness. The taxonomy of managerial practices explained in this module helps to bridge the gap between currently popular leadership theories and the practical applications emphasized in this book. The behavior concepts are used throughout this book, and subsequent modules provide guidelines on how to carry out the behaviors in some typical contexts. The module also includes two cases showing how managerial behaviors are related to managerial effectiveness in different situations. The cases demonstrate the importance of selecting an appropriate mix of task- and relationship-oriented behaviors, and the need to adjust behavior to the specific requirements of the manager's immediate situation.

Module 2: Identifying Motives

This module attempts to reduce the confusion in the literature about different types of needs by providing a conceptual framework to aid students in understanding common motive patterns in people. Some insight into motive patterns is important for determining how best to influence people and motivate them. An exercise with short cases provides an opportunity to identify dominant needs from clues such as a person's behavior.

Module 3: Influence Tactics

This module provides concepts to distinguish different types of influence behavior. The taxonomy of influence tactics for exerting power helps to bridge the gap between the discussions of abstract power found in most texts on management and organizational behavior and the skills needed by managers in their day-to-day influence attempts with subordinates, peers, and superiors. Two cases provide an opportunity to apply the concepts by analyzing the amount and types of power available to a manager and the appropriateness of different influence tactics for the manager's immediate situation. Role play exercises for practicing the influence tactics are described in the instructor's manual.

Module 4: Participative Leadership

This module builds on and extends the concepts in Modules 1 and 3 by providing a model for determining when to use different types of participative decision procedures. Students practice diagnostic skills and concept knowledge in an exercise that requires them to analyze decision situations and identify the optimal decision procedure. Students also analyze a case that shows the limitations of some participative procedures and the importance of executing them skillfully.

Module 5: Supportive Communication

This module deals with one of the most important skills for effective management. A major weakness for many managers is the inability to behave in ways that serve to increase their understanding of another person who is attempting to communicate with them. Principles of active listening facilitate understanding and improve a manager's effectiveness in dealing with someone who is anxious, frustrated, or angry. Two cases and a written exercise are included to allow students to refine their understanding of the concepts and guidelines. Additional exercises in the instructor's manual allow students to practice the guidelines in a simulated confrontation.

Module 6: Setting Objectives

Effective managers set objectives to establish priorities for themselves and for subordinates. This planning process is vital for effective time management and efficient utilization of resources and personnel. This module provides guidelines for setting objectives for oneself and for subordinates. An exercise is provided to test and refine understanding of concepts. A case is included to demonstrate some of the complexities and pitfalls in implementing a program of objectives and standards. A role play exercise gives students an opportunity to practice their skills in setting goals for a subordinate.

Module 7: Action Planning

Action planning is the next step after setting objectives and selecting general strategies. This planning is essential for effective implementation of decisions and strategies. The text presents concepts and procedures for carrying out action planning. An action planning exercise provides an opportunity to practice the procedures and obtain feedback. A case demonstrates the coordination problems likely to occur during planning in complex organizations.

Module 8: Monitoring and Reviewing Progress

When plans or decisions are being implemented, it is important to monitor progress. This module describes procedures for monitoring the performance of individual subordinates and evaluating the effectiveness of unit operations. The focus is on procedures for conducting a progress review meeting with a subordinate. A case provides an opportunity for students to test their understanding of the guidelines, and a role play exercise lets students practice the guidelines and get feedback about how they did. Another case shows the relationship between monitoring and strategic planning by top management.

Module 9: Delegation

An important determinant of managerial effectiveness is skill in delegating. This module describes the potential benefits of delegation, reviews reasons why delegation sometimes fails to occur, and discusses the factors that determine whether delegation will be successful or unsuccessful. Guidelines for determining what to delegate and how to do it are presented next. Two cases are provided to help students test and extend their understanding of the guidelines. Finally, a role play exercise allows students to practice the procedures and get feedback to build their skills.

Module 10: Time Management

The hectic pace of work for managers and the constant demands from others for their attention make time management essential for managerial effectiveness. This module describes common problems in time management and helpful remedies to avoid or deal with the problems. A case is provided to allow students to assess their understanding of the concepts and guidelines. An in-basket exercise allows students to apply the procedures to a simulated managerial situation. Students plan daily activities and determine how to handle typical problems and situations confronting a manager.

Module 11: Managing Conflict

Conflict is inevitable in organizations, and it presents managers with serious challenges. This module examines sources of conflict, reviews the options available to a manager for coping with conflict, and discusses the conditions where each response is appropriate. Some of the conflict responses are variations of influence tactics described in Module 3. Procedures for managing conflict between others are reviewed also. Two cases allow students to test their understanding of the causes of conflict and the procedures for third-party interventions. A role play exercise allows students to practice conflict management procedures and get feedback on how they did.

Module 12: Leading Meetings

Meetings occur frequently during the typical day of a manager. Many of the meetings are ones held by the manager to solve problems and make decisions. This module reviews common pitfalls that undermine the effectiveness of decision groups and presents procedures for leading meetings. A case demonstrates some of the pitfalls that occur in decision groups. Three role play exercises allow students to practice the guidelines and experience the difficulties faced by groups in solving complex problems and making important decisions.

Summary

The book enables students to develop their interpersonal and administrative skills. Managers need many different types of skills, and in a small book it is not possible to cover all of them. The modules deal with some skills that are essential for managerial effectiveness and unlikely to be given adequate coverage in regular survey texts. Reading the module text and doing the exercises will not make one an expert in each skill, but most students will experience an increase in both diagnostic and execution skills related to essential managerial functions and responsibilities. Most of the skills can be reinforced by practice outside of the classroom.

References

Bass, B. M. (1981). *The Handbook of Leadership: A Survey of Theory and Research.* New York: Free Press.

Boyatzis, R. E. (1982). *The Competent Manager.* New York: John Wiley.

Cameron, K. S., & Whetten, D. A. (1983). "A Model for Teaching Managment Skills." *Exchange: The Organizational Behavior Teaching Journal,* 8 (2), 21–27.

Finney, M., & Siehl, C. (1985–86). "The Current MBA: Why Are We Failing?" *The Organizational Behavior Teaching Review,* 10 (3), 12–18.

Kaplan, R. E. (1986). *The Warp and the Woof of the General Manager's Job. Technical Report No. 27.* Greensboro, NC: Center for Creative Leadership.

Katz, R. L. (1974). "Skills of an Effective Administrator." *Harvard Business Review,* 51, 90–102.

Kotter, J. P. (1982). *The General Managers.* New York: Free Press.

McCall, M. W., & Segrist, C. A. (1980). *In Pursuit of the Manager's Job: Building on Mintzberg. Technical Report No. 14.* Greensboro: Center for Creative Leadership.

Mandt, E. J. (1982). "The Failure of Business Education—And What to do About It." *Management Review,* 47–52.

Mann, F. C. (1965). "Toward an Understanding of the Leadership Role in Formal Organization." In R. Dubin, G. C. Homans, F. C. Mann, and D. C. Miller (eds.), *Leadership and Productivity.* San Francisco: Chandler.

Mintzberg, H. (1975). "The Manager's Job: Folklore and Fact." *Harvard Business Review,* 53, 49–61.

Porter, L. W., & McKibbin, L. E. (1988). *Future of Management Education and Development: Drift or Thrust into the 21st Century?* New York: McGraw-Hill.

Whetton, D. A., & Cameron, K. S. (1983). "Management Skill Training: A Needed Addition to the Management Curriculum. *Exchange: The Organizational Behavior Teaching Journal,* 8 (2), 10–15.

Managerial Practices

At the completion of this module a student will:

- *Understand a taxonomy of behaviors used by managers to accomplish the work and build effective relationships.*
- *Understand how the managerial practices are distinct yet interwoven in the day-to-day activities of managers.*
- *Understand the purpose of each managerial practice and its importance for effective management.*

- *Text: Managerial Practices*
- *Quiz: Identifying Managerial Practices*
- *Case: Consolidated Products*
- *Case: Foreign Auto Shop*

Managerial Practices

Introduction

During the 1930s and 40s, research on managerial leadership was mostly concerned with traits and skills. Hundreds of studies were conducted to determine what traits and skills are associated with effective management, but the results were inconclusive. In the 1950s, attention turned to managerial behavior. Social scientists began observing managers and collecting descriptions of managerial behavior with interviews and questionnaires in the hope of identifying what effective leaders *do*, rather than what they *are*.

The early research on behavior identified two broad categories: task-oriented behavior and relationship-oriented behavior. A number of studies indicated that both types of behavior are necessary for effective management. However, the research failed to provide much insight into the nature of this behavior. It was not clear what managers actually do to accomplish task objectives or to build effective interpersonal relationships with subordinates and peers. A behavior taxonomy with more specific managerial practices was needed to make further progress in understanding why some managers are more effective than others.

Another discovery made in the 1950s was the fact that aspects of the managerial situation determine what behavior will be effective. The situation presents a manager with certain demands, constraints, and opportunities (Stewart, 1978). The importance of different kinds of behavior varies from one type of manager to another. Even for the same manager, some aspects of behavior that are essential in one situation may be irrelevant or even detrimental in a different situation. A number of situational theories of managerial effectiveness were proposed, but progress was limited by the lack of an adequate behavior taxonomy on which to build the theory (Yukl, 1989).

The situational theories were also limited by the failure to recognize the nature of managerial work. The typical day of a manager is filled with many activities, most of which are of short duration (Kaplan, 1986; Mintzberg, 1973; McCall & Segrist, 1980). There are frequent interruptions, and the activities tend to be fragmented and unsystematic. Most of the activities involve oral communication with subordinates, superiors, managers in other work units, and outsiders such as clients and suppliers. Given this hectic pace of short, diverse activities, it is difficult to identify the practices that managers employ to accomplish the task and build effective relationships. Once again, the lack of an adequate taxonomy for classifying behavior impeded progress in making sense out of the confusing picture of managerial behavior that was provided by observational research.

During the decades of the 1960s and 1970s, many studies were conducted to identify specific managerial practices, and several taxonomies were proposed. A taxonomy based on twelve years of developmental research and designed to integrate the earlier category systems was proposed by Yukl (1989). The eleven managerial practices in this taxonomy (see Table 1–1) include most types of behavior relevant for managerial effectiveness. The categories are generic enough to be applicable to all different kinds of managers, but specific enough to relate to the unique situational demands and constraints confronted by each individual manager. Every category in the new taxonomy has aspects of behavior that are relevant to every type of manager, even though the relative importance of the categories will obviously differ from one type of manager to another. The categories can be used to describe behavior toward peers as well as behavior toward subordinates, making them applicable to matrix managers (e.g., product managers, project managers) as well as to traditional managers with direct authority over

TABLE 1–1 Definitions of the Eleven Managerial Practices

INFORMING: disseminating relevant information about decisions, plans, and activities to people who need it to do their work, answering requests for technical information, and telling people about the organizational unit to promote its reputation

CONSULTING AND DELEGATING: checking with people before making changes that affect them, encouraging suggestions for improvement, inviting participation in decision making, incorporating the ideas and suggestions of others in decisions, and allowing others to have substantial responsibility and discretion in carrying out work activities and making decisions

PLANNING AND ORGANIZING: determining long-term objectives and strategies for adapting to environmental change, determining how to use personnel and allocate resources to accomplish objectives, determining how to improve the efficiency of operations, and determining how to achieve coordination with other parts of the organization

PROBLEM SOLVING AND CRISIS MANAGEMENT: identifying work-related problems, analyzing problems in a timely but systematic manner to identify causes and find solutions, and acting decisively to implement solutions and resolve important problems or crises

CLARIFYING ROLES AND OBJECTIVES: assigning tasks, providing direction in how to do the work, and communicating a clear understanding of job responsibilities, task objectives, deadlines, and performance expectations

MONITORING OPERATIONS AND ENVIRONMENT: gathering information about work activities, checking on the progress and quality of the work, evaluating the performance of individuals and the organizational unit, and scanning the environment to detect threats and opportunities

MOTIVATING: using influence techniques that appeal to emotion, values, or logic to generate enthusiasm for the work, commitment to task objectives, and compliance with requests for cooperation, assistance, support, or resources; also, setting an example of proper behavior

RECOGNIZING AND REWARDING: providing praise, recognition, and rewards for effective performance, significant achievements, and special contributions

SUPPORTING AND MENTORING: acting friendly and considerate, being patient and helpful, showing sympathy and support, and doing things to facilitate someone's skill development and career advancement

MANAGING CONFLICT AND TEAM BUILDING: encouraging and facilitating the constructive resolution of conflict, and encouraging cooperation, teamwork, and identification with the organizational unit

NETWORKING: socializing informally, developing contacts with people who are a source of information and support, and maintaining contacts through periodic interaction, including visits, telephone calls, correspondence, and attendance at meetings and social events subordinates. However, a few categories contain some components that are applicable to subordinates but not to peers (i.e., delegating, mentoring, rewarding).

Explanation of Managerial Practices

Each managerial practice will be explained and its purpose described.

Planning and Organizing

This managerial practice includes decision making about objectives, priorities, strategies, formal structure, allocation of resources, assignment of responsibilities, and scheduling of activities. In other words, planning and organizing means deciding what to do, how to do it, who will do it, and when it will be done. There are many varieties of planning, ranging from the determination of strategic objectives and broad policies for the organizational unit ("strategic planning") to the development of detailed action steps and schedules for implementing a change or policy ("operational planning"). Planning includes:

- The design of the formal structure of the organizational unit ("organizing"),
- The design of individual jobs within the organizational unit ("job design"),
- The allocation of resources among different activities according to their relative importance,
- The development of procedures for avoiding potential problems or disasters ("potential problem analysis"), and the development of procedures for reacting in a quick and effective manner to unavoidable problems and crises ("contingency planning").

The purpose of planning and organizing is to ensure efficiency and effectiveness for the work unit, external coordination with other parts of the organization, and adaptation to the external environment. The importance of this managerial practice for managerial effectiveness has long been recognized in the management literature (Carroll & Gillen, 1987; Drucker, 1975).

Planning is largely a cognitive behavior involving processing of information, analyzing, and deciding. Planning seldom occurs in a single behavior episode; rather it tends to be a prolonged process spanning weeks or months. Most planning is informal and flexible rather than formal and rigid (Kotter, 1982). Because it is a cognitive activity, planning is a form of managerial behavior that is difficult to observe. Nevertheless, there are observable aspects of the behavior such as writing plans and budgets, and meeting with others to develop plans.

Problem Solving

Like planning, problem solving involves processing information, analyzing, and deciding. However, despite the similarities, there are some important differences between the two managerial practices. Whereas the purpose of planning and organizing is to improve work unit efficiency and effectiveness, the primary purpose of problem solving is to maintain orderly, stable operations at the current level of efficiency. Problem solving occurs in response to some immediate disturbance of normal operations, such as an equipment breakdown, a shortage of necessary materials, a customer with a complaint, a mistake in the work, an accident, or an unusual request by higher management. In contrast, planning is more likely to be stimulated by the discovery of an opportunity to be exploited, or by the anticipation of a future problem to be avoided. It is as much a difference in time perspective as in purpose. Planning is a proactive behavior with a long-term perspective, whereas problem solving is a reactive behavior with a short-term perspective. Just as the time perspective varies, so does the typical duration of the decision process. Under the pressure of time, problem solving typically is of shorter duration than planning. Some information seeking, analysis, and consultation with others may be involved in problem solving, but much less than there is with planning. Problem solving is a key behavior in the management of crises, and subordinates usually expect a manager to take decisive action to deal with an emergency or crisis situation quickly, before it becomes worse.

The distinction between problem solving and planning is more a matter of different points on the same continuum than a sharp dichotomy. Nevertheless, the distinction is helpful for understanding managerial effectiveness. Observational research shows that most managers face relentless pressures for dealing with problems and responding to requests for immediate assistance, authorization, or direction (Kaplan, 1986; McCall & Segrist, 1980; Mintzberg, 1973). Responding to these pressures with problem solving contributes to managerial effectiveness, but managers who become too preoccupied with reacting to day-to-day problems have no time left for the reflective planning that would help them to avoid many of the problems or to cope with them better.

These managers are not as effective as managers who do more proactive planning and organizing.

Monitoring Operations and Environment

The behavior in this category involves gathering information about the operations of the manager's work unit, the progress of the work, the performance of subordinates, the success of projects or programs, and the nature of the external environment. Monitoring can take many forms, and some examples include:

- Walking around to observe how the work is going.
- Reading written performance reports or computer printouts.
- Meeting with members of the work unit to review progress.
- Inspecting the work.
- Using a computer terminal to review information about current operations or the status of a particular project.
- Evaluating a project by getting reactions from clients or customers.

Monitoring includes gathering information about the external environment as well as information about internal operations of the work unit (Mintzberg, 1973). The primary purpose of monitoring is to maintain stability of operations and facilitate adjustment to changes in the environment. This process of sensing and adjusting is sometimes referred to in the management literature as "controlling." Other terms used commonly to refer to monitoring behavior include "tracking," "checking," "evaluating," and "assessing."

Monitoring is conceptually distinct from planning and problem solving but is closely related to them. Monitoring provides much of the information needed for planning and problem solving, and this is the reason why it is so important for managerial effectiveness. Monitoring, in turn, is facilitated by the development of detailed action plans and schedules, with checkpoints, intermediate targets, and concrete indicators of performance (Meredith & Mantel, 1985).

Motivating

Motivating behaviors involve the use of influence techniques to generate enthusiasm for the work, commitment to task objectives, and compliance with orders and requests. Motivating includes use of influence tactics in interactions with peers, superiors, and outsiders to obtain necessary resources, cooperation, approvals, and political support. The influence tactics include persuasive appeals based on logic and factual evidence ("rational persuasion"), appeals to a person's values and ideals to inspire enthusiasm and commitment for a task or activity ("inspirational appeals"), and leading by example ("role modeling"). The flavor of motivating is captured best by common action verbs such as encouraging, inspiring, appealing, and persuading.

Motivating behavior involves the use of a manager's "personal power" (e.g., expertise, charisma, charm) as well as "position power" (e.g., authority, incentives, threats). The research literature strongly suggests that effective managers rely more upon personal power to influence subordinates and peers (Podsakoff & Schriesheim, 1985; Yukl, 1989). Motivating behavior also includes the use of visioning speeches and symbolic actions to transmit values and shape the culture of an organization. Symbolic actions can become the subject of stories and legends. For example, the CEO of one company personally destroyed some low quality versions of their product that had been sold previously as "seconds." This widely publicized action supported the new policy that henceforth the company would make and sell only products of the highest quality (Peters & Austin, 1985).

Recognizing and Rewarding

Included in this managerial practice is the giving of tangible or intangible rewards for effective performance, significant achievements and helpful assistance. Tangible rewards for subordinates include such things as a pay increase, promotion, better work schedule, and better assignments. For peers, tangible rewards include shared resources, faster service, and special favors. Intangible rewards include such things as giving praise, expressing personal appreciation, giving public recognition, holding a special ceremony to honor a person's achievements or contributions, and giving awards such as a special pin or certificate. Common action verbs for this behavior include praising, commending, complimenting, and crediting. Recognizing and rewarding is a managerial practice with the dual purpose of influencing behavior and increasing subordinate satisfaction.

Rewarding behavior, which is sometimes called reinforcing, has been the subject of an immense amount of research for several decades in psychology and management. This research clearly demonstrates that managers can influence the behavior and satisfaction of subordinates with recognition and rewards under appropriate conditions (e.g.,

Hamner & Hamner, 1976). Research on effective organizations, such as that by Peters & Waterman (1982), also demonstrates the importance of timely recognition and appropriate rewards.

Recognizing and rewarding differs from motivating with respect to both the purpose and form of the behavior. Recognizing and rewarding are reactive forms of behavior that occur after a person demonstrates competence or desirable behavior, whereas motivating behaviors involve proactive attempts to get the person to do something desired by the manager. The purpose of motivating is clearly task-oriented, even though is is based on personal power, whereas recognizing and rewarding has a dual purpose, and in some cases the objective is more relationship-oriented than task-oriented. For example, recognition and rewards may be used to strengthen a person's job satisfaction and ties to the organization, without any explicit intention to influence the person's immediate task behavior.

Informing

This managerial practice involves the communication of relevant information needed by subordinates, peers, or superiors to perform their jobs. Informing behavior may take many forms, such as:

• Making an explanation in a group meeting.
• Calling someone on the telephone to pass on information.
• Writing memos and reports.
• Sending electronic messages.
• Holding private briefings.
• Putting messages on the bulletin board.
• Distributing a newsletter.
• Relaying written materials to people who would otherwise not receive them.

Informing also includes providing people with information about the organizational unit's activities, capabilities, and achievements in order to foster a favorable image and reputation (e.g., "public relations" activities). Some commonly used action verbs for informing include notifying, alerting, briefing, relaying, reporting, and interpreting.

The primary purpose of informing is to facilitate the work of others who depend upon the manager as a source of important information.

Decision quality and coordination are facilitated by timely distribution of relevant information. Dissemination of some kinds of information has obvious implications for power sharing, and a manager can enhance the benefits of consultation and delegation by providing information necessary for people to participate in making decisions. The importance of informing was noted by Rensis Likert (1967) in his early conception of the manager as a "linking pin," and more recently by Henry Mintzberg (1973) in his conception of the manager as a "nerve center" in the organizational communication network.

Clarifying Roles and Objectives

This category involves the communication of role expectations to subordinates and outsiders who make an important contribution to work unit operations. The purpose of the behavior is to guide and coordinate work activity and make sure people know what to do and how to do it. In contrast to motivating, which seeks to energize behavior, clarifying seeks to orient and guide it. Clarifying can take a wide variety of forms, including giving a simple command, making task assignments, explaining rules and procedures, explaining duties and responsibilities, explaining how to do a task or procedure, communicating priorities, setting standards, setting performance goals, setting deadlines, supervising practice or rehearsal of operations, and meeting with a subordinate or peer to reach agreement on action plans for accomplishing objectives.

Clarifying, like informing, involves communication of information. However, clarifying is an attempt to direct subordinate behavior and enhance knowledge of task procedures, whereas informing seeks only to facilitate subordinate work by providing technical information and information about current developments. This distinction does not imply that the two forms of behavior are unrelated. Sometimes the behaviors occur independently, but in many cases where clarifying is represented in a managerial behavior incident, informing will be represented also. For example, in giving a new assignment to a subordinate, a manager is likely to communicate specific technical information needed by the subordinate to carry out the assignment.

The importance of clarifying for managerial effectiveness is suggested by the fact that many situational theories of leadership have similar hypotheses which say, in approximate terms, that clarifying behavior by the leader will improve subordinate satisfaction and performance in situations where there would otherwise be role ambiguity (e.g., House & Mitchell, 1974). Additional evidence for the relevance of clarifying is provided by the extensive research on goal setting and management by objectives (Locke & Latham, 1984). This research finds that it is important for managers to set clear, specific, and realistic performance goals.

Supporting and Mentoring

Supporting includes a wide range of behaviors by which a manager shows consideration, acceptance, and concern for the needs and feelings of other people. Mentoring is a major subcategory of supporting that is relevant primarily for subordinates. Examples of supporting include:

- Listening carefully to complaints and problems.
- Showing sympathy when someone is upset.
- Making a special effort to help someone with a problem.
- Backing up a subordinate in a conflict with outsiders or superiors.
- Reacting to mistakes in a calm and helpful manner instead of "blowing up."
- Providing helpful career counseling and advice.
- Providing opportunities for a subordinate to learn and demonstrate skills important for advancement to a higher position.

Supporting behaviors are intended to build and maintain effective interpersonal relationships. A manager who is considerate and friendly toward people is more likely to win their friendship and loyalty. The emotional ties that are formed make it easier to gain cooperation and support from persons upon whom the manager must rely to get the work done. A secondary objective of supporting behavior is to increase the job satisfaction of subordinates or co-workers. It is more satisfying to work with people who are friendly, cooperative, and supportive than with people who are cold and impersonal or, worse, hostile and uncooperative. Being a supportive manager in times of stress helps to get a person over the "rough spots" in the job. The positive benefits for the organization are likely to include lower absenteeism and turnover, less alcoholism, and less drug abuse. Supporting behavior has been the subject of extensive research demonstrating that it influences subordinate satisfaction and performance, although not equally across all situations (see Bass, 1982; Yukl, 1989).

Consulting and Delegating

The managerial practice called consulting and delegating involves encouraging the participation of others in making decisions for which the manager is responsible. Different degrees of participation by others are possible, from revising a tentative decision after receiving protests, to consulting with others before making a decision, to asking an individual or group to make the decision within specified guidelines. This last form of participation provides the maximum amount of power sharing for a decision. When used with an individual subordinate, it is usually called "delegation." Delegation was combined with other forms of consulting behavior into a single managerial practice in the new taxonomy, because they are all forms of power sharing and have similar objectives. However, delegating applies mostly to subordinates, whereas consulting is appropriate with both subordinates and peers.

Some specific examples of consulting behavior include:

- Asking for suggestions.
- Encouraging critical evaluation of your proposals.
- Inviting people to attend planning meetings.
- Holding special meetings or hearings to get reactions from people who will be affected by a decision.
- Asking a group to solve a problem with you instead of solving it by yourself.
- Seeking group consensus for a decision.

Consulting and delegating are intended to improve the quality of decisions and acceptance of the decisions by those upon whom the manager depends to get decisions implemented effectively. A secondary purpose is to enrich the jobs of subordinates and make these jobs more interesting and challenging. Like supporting, participative leadership has been the subject of hundreds of studies, and these studies find that it has important implications for managerial effectiveness (see Yukl, 1989). Encouraging subordinate participation is more likely to increase satisfaction than performance, but both may be increased under some conditions

Although consulting-delegating was conceptualized as a distinct category of behavior, it is evident that it usually occurs in combination with other types of managerial behavior. This is especially evident for delegating. Deciding which responsibilities to delegate to whom is planning-organizing. Explaining a subordinate's new responsibilities and scope of authority is clarifying. Asking the subordinate to report on delegated activities is monitoring. Giving a subordinate the information needed to perform delegated responsibilities is informing. Giving encouragement to a subordinate who is anxious about taking on more responsibility is supporting. Resolving disagreements with a subordinate about a delegated responsibility is managing conflict. The multi-dimensional nature of most behavior incidents is nowhere more evident than in incidents involving delegation.

Team Building and Managing Conflict

This managerial practice includes a wide variety of behaviors involving development of teamwork and cooperation. Resolution of conflicts involves external relations with peers, superiors, and outsiders as well as relations within the manager's own work unit. Examples of this managerial practice include:

- Mediating conflicts between others.
- Smoothing over disagreements.
- Encouraging the constructive resolution of conflict.
- Stressing the importance of cooperation.
- Encouraging the sharing of information and ideas.
- Using ceremonies and symbols to develop identification with the organizational unit.
- Facilitating social interaction among work unit members (e.g., parties, luncheons, picnics).

The common purpose of these behaviors is to maintain effective working relationships with subordinates, peers, superiors, and outsiders. A secondary purpose is to build a cohesive work unit with strong member identification.

The importance of cooperation, identification with the work unit, and constructive resolution of conflict are central themes in the literature on organizations. This concern is reflected in the research on group cohesiveness and teamwork, in the organization development research on team building, in the organization design research on "integrators" (Lawrence & Lorsch, 1967), in the conflict management literature (Brown, 1983), and in the recent literature on effective Japanese and American management.

Networking

This category includes a wide variety of behaviors intended to develop and maintain contacts with people who are important sources of information and assistance, both within and outside of the organization. Some types of behavior in this category are used to maintain relationships with subordinates, particularly "socializing" and informal discussions of subjects not related to the work, such as sports, hobbies, and family. However, most networking behavior involves peers and outsiders such as clients, customers, suppliers, vendors, and subcontractors. Examples include attending social and ceremonial events, participating in recreational and leisure activities (e.g., handball or golf), joining professional associations or social clubs, meeting or having lunch with customers or clients, and visiting the facilities of other managers in the same organization or in different organizations. Networking also includes behaviors intended to establish an exchange relationship with other managers, such as offering assistance, doing favors that will be appreciated, and providing helpful information. Many examples of networking involve other managerial practices at the same time, such as informing, consulting, supporting, recognizing, and monitoring.

Research shows that it is important for general managers to develop an extensive network of contacts with persons in other parts of the organization and with important outsiders (Kanter, 1983; Kaplan, 1984; Kotter, 1982). In research on managerial excellence, Peters and Waterman (1982) found that it is important for managers to keep closely attuned to the needs and concerns of customers and clients.

Summary

Some of the eleven managerial practices, such as planning, problem solving, clarifying, and monitoring, are concerned primarily with attaining task objectives; others, such as supporting, team building, conflict management, and networking, are concerned with maintaining interpersonal relationships. Nevertheless, each type of managerial practice can be enacted in specific ways that reflect a concern for both task and relationships. For example, a manager can provide clarification of job responsibilities in a manner that is polite and helpful rather than arrogant and bossy, thereby showing concern for relationships as well the task. Planning and problem solving may be done only with task objectives in mind, or they may be done in a way that also considers the needs and preferences of subordinates. Informing may include only information needed to do the task, or it may include information desired by subordinates but not necessary for the task. Monitoring can be an annoying form of close supervision, or it can be an unobtrusive form of reviewing progress and checking outcomes. Managing conflict can be done in a way that seeks to attain task objectives as well as to maintain harmonious relationships. Networking can be guided by a need to develop information sources and alliances necessary to accomplish task objectives, as well as by a desire to socialize and build friendships. Recognizing can be done in a way that reinforces effective task behavior while also improving relationships. Consulting can be done in a manner intended to improve both the quality of task decisions and decision acceptance by people who must implement them. Supporting and mentoring need not be concerned only with the needs and feelings of subordinates; they may be done in a way that also seeks to increase the capacity of subordinates to accomplish the work. Effective managers demonstrate this dual set of concerns for task and relationships (Blake & Mouton, 1982). They have the ability to select appropriate forms of behavior for the situation and to execute these behaviors in a skillful manner. Each of the modules in this book deals with aspects of these skills relevant to effective management.

References

Bass, B. M. (1982). *The Handbook of Leadership: Revised and Expanded Edition*. New York: Free Press.

Blake, R. R., & Mouton, J. S. (1982). "Management by Grid Principles or Situationalism: Which?" *Group and Organization Studies, 7,* 207–210.

Brown, L. D. (1983). *Managing Conflict at Organizational Interfaces*. Reading, MA: Addison-Wesley.

Carroll, S. J. Jr., & Gillen, D. J. (1987). "Are the Classical Management Functions Useful in Describing Managerial Work?" *Academy of Management Review, 12,* 38–51.

Drucker, P. F. (1974). *Management: Tasks, Responsibilities, Practices*. New York: Harper & Row.

Hamner, W. C., & Hamner, E. P. (1976). "Behavior Modification on the Bottom Line." *Organizational Dynamics, 4* (4), 2–21.

House, R. J., & Mitchell, T. R. (1974). "Path-goal Theory of Leadership." *Contemporary Business, 3* (Fall), 81–98.

Kanter, R. M. (1983). *The Change Masters*. New York: Simon & Schuster.

Kaplan, R. M. (1984). "Trade Routes: The Manager's Network of Relationships." *Organizational Dynamics,* Spring, 37–52.

Kaplan, R. E. (1986). *The Warp and Woof of the General Manager's Job. Technical Report #27*. Greensboro, NC: Center for Creative Leadership.

Kotter, J. P. (1982). *The General Managers*. New York: Free Press.

Lawrence, P. R. & Lorsch, J. W. (1967). "New Management Job: The Integrator." *Harvard Business Review*, 45 (November–December), 142–151.

Likert, R. (1967). *The Human Organization: Its Management and Value*. New York: McGraw-Hill.

Locke, E. A., & Latham, G. P. (1984). *Goal Setting: A Motivational Technique That Works*. Englewood Cliffs, NJ: Prentice Hall.

McCall, M. W., & Segrist, C. A. (1980). *In Pursuit of the Manager's Job: Building on Mintzberg. Technical Report #14*. Greensboro, NC: Center For Creative Leadership.

Meredith, J. R., & Mantel, S. J. Jr. (1985). *Project Management: A Managerial Approach*. New York: John Wiley.

Mintzberg, H. (1973). *The Nature of Managerial Work*. New York: Harper & Row.

Peters, T. J., & Austin, N. (1985). *A Passion for Excellence: The Leadership Difference*. New York: Random House.

Peters, T. J., & Waterman, R. H. Jr. (1982). *In Search of Excellence: Lessons from America's Best-Run Companies*. New York: Harper & Row.

Podsakoff, P. M., & Schriesheim, C. A. (1986). "Field Studies of French and Raven's Bases of Power: Critique, Reanalysis, and Suggestions for Future Research." *Psychological Bulletin*, 97, 387–411.

Stewart, R. (1976). *Contrasts in Management*. Maidenhead, Berkshire, England: McGraw-Hill UK.

Yukl, G. A. (1989). *Leadership in Organizations, Second Edition*. Englewood Cliffs, NJ: Prentice Hall.

QUIZ ON IDENTIFYING MANAGERIAL PRACTICES

Instructions

The purpose of this short quiz is to test your understanding of Yukl's 11 Managerial Practices. The exercise consists of 22 randomly ordered behavior descriptions. The first eleven items are examples of effective behavior, and the second eleven items are examples of ineffective behavior. Your task is to identify the the type of managerial practice depicted by each behavior example. If an example involves more than one managerial practice, select the one you think is best represented by the example. On the line next to each item, write the code of the managerial practice it best depicts. The codes are shown in Table 1–2.

TABLE 1–2 Codes for Managerial Practices

PLN	PLANNING AND ORGANIZING
PS	PROBLEM SOLVING
MON	MONITORING
MOT	MOTIVATING
REC	RECOGNIZING AND REWARDING
INFO	INFORMING
CLR	CLARIFYING
SUP	SUPPORTING AND MENTORING
CON	CONSULTING AND DELEGATING
CM	TEAM BUILDING AND MANAGING CONFLICT
NET	NETWORKING

Examples of Effective Behavior:

_____ 1. Passes on relevant information obtained in conversations with other people.

_____ 2. Walks around to observe how the work is going.

_____ 3. Asks others for their ideas and suggestions before making an important decision.

_____ 4. Reminds members of the work unit or team that they depend on each other and must cooperate to attain their mutual objectives.

_____ 5. Determines in advance what resources are needed to carry out a task or project.

_____ 6. Describes a new task or project in an enthusiastic way that makes it seem important and worthy of a person's best efforts.

_____ 7. Establishes performance goals for important aspects of the work.

_____ 8. Takes the time to listen to someone with a personal problem or complaint.

_____ 9. Acts decisively in dealing with a work-related crisis.

_____ 10. Explains why he/she thinks a person's performance was exceptional.

_____ 11. Calls a manager in another work unit to offer assistance on a problem the manager is having.

Examples of Ineffective Behavior:

_____ 12. Asks for suggestions, then makes an arbitrary decision that ignores the suggestions.

_____ 13. Jumps to conclusions about the cause of a problem on the basis of insufficient information.

_____ 14. Gives contradictory directions when assigning a task.

_____ 15. Waits until the last minute to tell people about an important meeting they should attend.

_____ 16. Fails to follow up to verify that a requested action was carried out.

_____ 17. Says things to foster distrust and hostility between two members of the work unit or team.

_____ 18. Sets a poor example by leaving early when there is important work to finish.

_____ 19. Looks for something to criticize rather than complimenting a person for a successfully completing a difficult assignment.

_____ **20.** Finds excuses for not attending ceremonial events held by the organization.

_____ **21.** Blows up and insults a subordinate in front of other people.

_____ **22.** Refuses to revise a plan that is not working well.

Case: Consolidated Products

Ben Morelli was a plant manager for Consolidated Products for fifteen years, and he was very well liked by the employees there. They were grateful for the fitness center he built for employees, and they enjoyed the social activities sponsored by the plant several times a year, including company picnics and holiday parties. He knew most of the workers by name, and he spent part of each day walking around the plant to visit with them and ask about their families or hobbies.

Ben believed that it was important to treat employees properly so they would have a sense of loyalty to the company. He tried to avoid any layoffs when production demand was slack, figuring that skilled machine operators are difficult to replace, and the company could not afford to lose them. The workers knew that if they had a special problem, Ben would try to help them. For example, when someone was injured but wanted to continue working, Ben found another job in the plant that the person could do with a disability. Ben believed that if you treat people right, they will do a good job for you without close supervision or prodding. Ben applied the same principle to his supervisors, and he mostly left them alone to run their departments as they saw fit. He did not set objectives and standards for the plant, and he never asked the supervisors to develop plans for improving productivity and product quality.

Under Ben, the plant had the lowest turnover among the company's five plants, but the second worst record for costs and production levels. When the company was acquired by another firm, Ben was asked to take early retirement, and Phil Jones was brought in to replace him.

Phil had a growing reputation as a manager who could get things done, and he quickly began making changes. Costs were cut by trimming a number of activities such as the fitness center at the plant, company picnics and parties, and the human relations training programs for supervisors. Phil believed that human relations training was a waste of time. His attitude was if workers don't want to do the work, get rid of them and find somebody else who does.

Supervisors were instructed to establish high performance standards for their departments and insist that people achieve them. A computer monitoring system was introduced so that the output of each worker could be checked closely against the standards. Supervisors were told to give one warning to any worker who had substandard performance, then if performance did not improve within two weeks, to fire the person. Phil believed that workers don't respect a supervisor who is weak and passive. When Phil observed a worker wasting time or making a mistake, he would chew out the person right on the spot to set an example. Phil also checked closely on the performance of his supervisors. Weekly meetings were held with each supervisor to review department performance, and Phil insisted that supervisors check with him first before taking action on any important matters.

As another cost-cutting move, Phil reduced the frequency of equipment maintenance, which required machines to be idled when they could be productive. Since the machines had a good record of reliable operation, Phil believed that the current maintenance schedule was excessive and was cutting into production. Finally, when business was slow for one of the product lines, Phil laid off workers rather than finding something else for them to do.

By the end of Phil's first year as plant manager, production costs were reduced by 20% and production output was up by 10%. However, three of his seven supervisors left to take other jobs, and turnover was also high among the machine operators. Some of the turnover was due to dismissals, but competent machine operators were also quitting, and it was becoming increasingly difficult to find replacements for them. Finally, there was increasing talk among the workers of unionizing.

1. Describe and compare the managerial behavior of Ben and Phil, using the general task-oriented and relationship-oriented categories, and the specific behavior categories from Yukl's taxonomy.

2. Compare the two managers in terms of their influence on employee attitudes, short-term performance, and longer-term plant performance.

3. If you were selected to be the manager of this plant, what would you do to achieve high employee satisfaction and performance?

Case: Foreign Auto,* Part 1

Alan had been running his foreign auto repair shop for six years. It was initially a gas station with repair work as a sideline. The business eventually moved from the gas station to a larger auto shop, and the number of mechanics increased from one to eight.

Gil and Hans are the oldest mechanics, and they are the easiest to supervise. All Alan has to do is to assign them the work (mostly high-precision, specialist jobs) and consult with them about how to plan a schedule. Gil is forty-eight years old, many of those years having been spent working in a Mercedes-Benz dealership. He works very fast, very efficiently, and as far as Alan can tell, has never made a mistake. Hans is forty years old. He was raised and did his apprenticeship in Austria. Though not quite as fast as Gil, Hans seems more adaptable to a variety of jobs.

Three younger workers do the jobs that call for lower-level skills, under Alan's more careful guidance. These are Kirk, LaMont, and Joanie. Kirk is thirty years old and has a degree in Industrial Arts. He couldn't get a job in his speciality without moving to another city, and he seems to have resigned himself to auto repair work. He likes mechanical things. LaMont is twenty-four years old. He is a "sports car nut" and is getting to be quite expert at operating the electronic diagnostic machines. Joanie is twenty-three years old. She does general mechanical work and does it well.

There are two more specialists in Alan's crew—Bart and Herbie. Bart is twenty-seven years old, and he is a motorcycle salesman in addition to doing the repair work on motorcycles. Herbie is only twenty-three years old, but he is a whiz kid at troubleshooting.

Alan spends much of his time working alongside of his mechanics to repair and paint cars. He does not spend much time actually directing their work. He plans the work schedules, assigns jobs to mechanics, then gets involved only if they need technical advice. He almost never tells someone to do something. Instead, he sort of suggests things. This style of leadership suits his easy-going personality. Alan's fairness and openness have earned him the mechanics' continuing respect and trust. His decisions are accepted, largely because he encourages his mechanics to participate in making them. The mechanics know that Alan is sincere in asking for their opinions—he isn't just doing it as a manipulative strategy to minimize their opposition to decisions that have already been made.

* Adapted from W. J. Wasmuth and L. Greenhalgh, *Effective Supervision.* Englewood Cliffs, NJ: Prentice Hall, Copyright © 1979.

1. Describe the leadership situation in terms of behavioral requirements imposed by the nature of the task, subordinates, and environment.

2. Describe Alan's typical leadership style and determine if it is appropriate for his leadership situation.

Foreign Auto Shop, Part 2

Alan looked anxiously out of his office window. The sky was very dark over the nearby hills, and the storm seemed to be advancing rapidly toward the valley where his auto repair shop was located.

Just to be on the safe side, Alan went out and rolled up the windows of the customers' cars in the parking lot. He noticed the creek was already running high, the result of melting snow during the warm spring days.

Before he could get back into the shop, a sudden downpour of huge drops of rain soaked his clothing. His mechanics laughingly teased him for "not having enough sense to come in out of the rain."

After fifteen minutes of the pelting rain, however, Alan realized that this was no ordinary rainstorm. The creek had already risen to almost the height of its banks, and Alan figured it wouldn't be long before the muddy water would flood the parking lot and come swirling around the shop doors.

He leaped into action. First he told three of his mechanics to drop everything and start moving cars. The cars that were parked next to the creek needed to be driven, pushed, or towed up to the high ground across the road.

Next, Alan told the others to put tools away and help move all the many boxes of parts and supplies off the floor and into the storage racks in the storeroom and the office.

Nobody seemed to be moving, however, despite Alan's yelling for action. If anything, the mechanics seemed to be amused. Kirk strolled over to Alan with a tolerant smile on his face.

"Come on, Alan," he said. "There's no sweat. The water's never been more'n an inch deep in the parking lot. We've never had any inside."

"Listen, Kirk, and listen good!" Alan interrupted him, looking him right in the eye. "You and the rest of the crew are going to do what I say. And you're going to do it now! We can talk later about whether it was a good idea."

This time, the mechanics dropped everything and began preparing for a flash flood. Alan barked instructions as he helped them move everything that could be damaged by water.

All of the boxes were off of the floor before the first trickle of water came under the door. By the time the water was ankle-deep, all the cars inside the shop had been jacked up and were sitting on cement blocks.

At its peak, the water was ten inches deep in the shop, but by this time, the rain had stopped and the sun was already shining. The water level started to recede slowly, but didn't drop below shop-floor level until after 9 P.M.

At 10 P.M. the mechanics voluntarily returned to the shop to help with the cleanup, which was not completed until 3 A.M. Alan personally thanked each one and gave them all the next morning off.

The next afternoon, Alan gave an informal "speech" during the coffee break.

He gave the mechanics all the credit for avoiding thousands of dollars of property damage. He even went to the trouble of pointing out particular contributions each of them had made. For instance, he thanked LaMont for his quick thinking in throwing the master switch before the water reached the electric outlets. He thanked Kirk for the idea of jacking up all the disabled cars inside the shop. And so on until everyone's contribution, no matter how, minor, had been recognized.

At 5 o'clock, everyone left but Gil, the oldest mechanic. He decided to stay and chat with Alan.

"You really surprised us yesterday!" Gil told Alan. "We could hardly believe it was you."

"Whaddaya mean?" Alan asked, pretending to be offended.

"You sounded like my old drill sergeant!" Gil chuckled. "Usually, you're so mild-mannered we forget you're the boss!"

"Maybe I'm a little too mild-mannered," Alan retorted. "When I told you guys to 'jump' you all laughed at me."

Questions for Students

1. Describe Alan's leadership style during the flood.

2. Was this leadership behavior appropriate for the leadership situation? Explain your answer.

3. Identify effective behaviors exhibited by Alan after the flood subsided.

Identifying Motives

After completing this module a student will:

- *Understand the six primary social needs.*
- *Understand clues that help identify strong needs.*
- *Understand the implications of different motive patterns for job performance by managers.*

- *Text: Needs and Motivation*
- *Needs Quiz*
- *Motive Identification Exercise*

Needs and Motivation

Motivation is usually defined as the process by which behavior is energized and directed. Motivation cannot be observed directly. It is a hypothetical process that is inferred by observing people's behavior, asking people what they want, and inquiring why they act as they do. Inferring motives from behavior is difficult because behavior can serve more than a single motive. Use of self-reports is risky because people may not be able to identify their own motives, particularly if motives are operating on an unconscious level. Even when a person is aware of his or her own motives, these may not be reported if the researcher's questions are threatening or embarrassing. Thus, the various ways for learning about motivation are quite limited.

Our understanding of human motivation has been aided by the concept of needs. Some physiological needs, such as hunger and thirst, are similar for everyone, but social needs are strongly influenced by one's early experiences and vary more from person to person. Because of the difficulty of measuring motivation, psychologists do not agree on the identity and importance of social needs. However, the six needs discussed in this module appear meaningful and useful for understanding behavior in organizations. Forms of gratification for each need are summarized in Table 2–1.

TABLE 2–1 Forms of Gratification for the Six Needs

Need for Achievement

- Doing better than competitors
- Attaining or surpassing a difficult goal
- Solving a complex problem
- Carrying out a challenging assignment successfully
- Developing a better way to do something

Need for Power

- Influencing people to change their attitudes or behavior
- Controlling people and activities
- Being in a position of authority over others
- Gaining control over information and resources
- Defeating an opponent or enemy

Need for Affiliation

- Being liked by many people
- Being accepted as part of a group or team
- Working with people who are friendly and cooperative
- Maintaining harmonious relationships and avoiding conflicts
- Participating in pleasant social activities

Need for Independence

- Assuming responsibility for your own life and how you live it
- Being free from control by authority figures
- Reducing dependence on others for resources and support
- Working without close supervision or elaborate restrictions
- Being your own boss

Need for Esteem

- Being respected by people whose opinion you value
- Receiving praise and recognition from co-workers and superiors
- Having high status and visibility in an organization or community
- Being treated like a celebrity or VIP
- Collecting appropriate status symbols

Need for Security

- Having a secure job
- Being protected against loss of income or economic disaster
- Having protection against illness and disability
- Being protected against physical harm or hazardous conditions
- Avoiding tasks or decisions with a risk of failure and blame

Need for Achievement

A person with a high need for achievement obtains satisfaction from accomplishing a difficult task successfully, attaining a standard of excellence, or developing a better way of doing something. Such people prefer tasks in which success depends on their own efforts and ability rather than on chance factors beyond their control or on a group effort. They prefer jobs in which they can exercise individual initiative in solving problems. They desire frequent, concrete feedback about their performance, so they can enjoy the experience of making progress and attaining challenging objectives. Although they enjoy competition with other people, they are just as attracted by an opportunity to set new records or accomplish something never done before.

A strong need for achievement is distinct from the need for esteem because its gratification depends on objective feedback about successful performance, not on recognition of success by other people. A person with a strong need for achievement will enjoy challenging activities, regardless of whether others recognize his or her accomplishments as worthwhile. Such a person will continue to be motivated by new challenges, even after he or she already has all the esteem he or she desires.

Need for Esteem

People typically have a desire to be respected and appreciated. However, this need is not as great in people who judge themselves primarily in terms of their own inner standards, such as moral values or religious convictions, as it is in people who judge their self-worth primarily by what others think of them. The need for esteem is satisfied through various forms of recognition from other people, such as praise, awards, applause, honors, testimonials, titles, and status symbols. People with a strong need for esteem seek out recognition for their talents and accomplishments. Sometimes the need for esteem can be satisfied only by gaining the respect of persons whose opinions are valued, such as professional colleagues, co-workers, and peers.

Need for esteem is sometimes referred to as an "ego need." People with a strong need for esteem are likely to be upset if they are not given appropriate status symbols for their position in the organization, or appropriate recognition for their accomplishments. They are sensitive to cues indicating possible disrespect or criticism. In extreme cases, even disagreeing with the person may be interpreted as a sign of disrespect.

People with strong ego needs may seek to satisfy them by gaining fame, social position, membership in prestigious groups, and pursuit of high status occupations. Public speaking, acting, and performing in front of a live audience provide other avenues for satisfaction of esteem needs, if the audiences show appreciation.

Need for Power

A person with a high need for power finds great satisfaction in influencing people and arousing strong emotions in them, such as fear, awe, pleasure, anger, and surprise. A strong need for power can be satisfied in a variety of ways, including some that are vicarious, such as watching movies with explicit violence and sex. The most direct form of gratification of a need for power is the exercise of influence over the attitudes and behavior of other people. People with a strong need for power enjoy winning an argument, defeating an opponent, eliminating a rival or enemy, and directing the activities of a group. They usually seek out positions of authority (e.g., a manager, administrator, public official, police officer, lawyer, military officer) in which they can exercise influence and direct the activities of others. They are likely to be very sensitive to power politics in an organization and may attempt to increase their own power by building alliances and gaining control over budgets, resources, information, and projects.

People with a weak need for power are likely to avoid positions requiring them to influence others. They are not likely to be assertive, and they may sincerely believe that it is improper to tell others what to do.

Need for Affiliation

All people have some desire for companionship and friendly interpersonal relationships in which affection and nurturance are given and received. However, the strength of this need varies greatly from person to person. People with a strong need for affiliation are especially concerned about being liked and accepted. They are very sensitive to cues indicating rejection or hostility from others. They find enjoyment in social interactions with friends, such as parties, reunions, or recreational activities. They like to work with other people as part of a team as long as the co-workers are friendly and cooperative.

People with a strong need for affiliation are unwilling to let the work interfere with harmonious relationships. They are more concerned with "getting along" than with "getting ahead." They seek to avoid conflicts or smooth them over rather than to confront genuine differences. If a person with a strong affiliation need is in a position of authority, he or she is likely to avoid making unpopular demands on subordinates, permit exceptions to rules, and dispense rewards in a way designed to win and keep friends.

A person with a very low need for affiliation tends to be a loner or a recluse. Such a person avoids social activities and feels uncomfortable when required to attend social functions.

Need for Dependence-Independence

Dependence is a natural condition in early childhood, but as people grow older, they become increasingly independent and assume more responsibility for running their own lives. Nevertheless, people differ in the extent to which they prefer to become independent. People also differ in the way they have learned to react to authority figures during their childhood.

People with a strong need for independence want to have a lot of freedom and autonomy in their lives. They become very upset when an authority figure attempts to impose restraints or restrictions on their behavior, and they tend to distrust powerful authority figures. On the job, people with a strong need for independence prefer to be left alone to do their work without close supervision or meddling by superiors or peers. They may resent being dependent on others for provision of resources and support. They prefer to become entrepreneurs who manage their own businesses, rather than becoming employees of someone else.

People with a strong need for dependence never develop a strong desire to "leave the nest." They feel most comfortable when there is a parent figure to tell them what to do and to provide coaching and close supervision. Attitudes toward authority figures are determined by culture as well as by early family experiences. Some cultures place a strong emphasis on obedience to parents and authority figures, whereas others value individual freedom, rugged individualism, and a skeptical attitude toward authority figures.

Need for Security

Everyone desires to avoid physical harm and economic disaster, but some people worry about it much more than others. People with a strong need for security are likely to worry frequently about such things as illness, accidents, crime, natural disasters, wars, and economic depression. They are especially likely to be concerned about job security and loss of income. They are likely to seek out a secure job with little chance of layoffs or dismissal. Somebody with a strong need for security places special importance on job features such as tenure protection, long-term employment contracts, guaranteed salary increments, health insurance, disability insurance, and a strong pension plan.

People with a strong need for security tend to avoid jobs and assignments for which there is a high risk of visible failure. In a job situation where a person can be dismissed for incompetence, people with strong needs for security will take great care to "cover their asses." They will avoid making risky decisions for which they could be held accountable, and will rigidly observe rules and regulations rather than exercising initiative in solving problems.

People with a very low need for security are likely to ignore risks and threats to their safety, health, or finances. They tend to have little concern for their own safety and may believe that they are immune to serious accidents or economic disaster. When combined with a strong need for achievement or power, people with low need for security may seek out dangerous but exciting activities such as racing cars, rock-climbing, combat, theft, or gambling on speculative business ventures.

Relationship Among The Needs

The six key needs are distinct from each other, but they are not entirely independent. Certain combinations of needs tend to occur more often than others. For example, people with a strong need for esteem are more likely to have a strong need for power, since power provides opportunities to gain esteem. People with a strong need for achievement are unlikely to have a strong need for security, since some degree of risk-taking is necessary to achieve difficult objectives. People with a strong need for independence are less likely to have a strong need for affiliation, since freedom of action is constrained by strong social obligations and group norms.

The manner in which a need is expressed depends on the person's overall pattern of needs. The various needs are integrated with each other and with the person's values and beliefs. In order to understand a person's behavior, it is necessary to consider the total pattern of needs. To give some examples, a person with strong needs for both power and achievement is likely to use influence to build the organization, accomplish its goals, and empower subordinates. In contrast, someone with strong needs for both power and esteem is likely to use influence to promote his or her own prestige and status, and will try to dominate subordinates and keep them weak and dependent. Someone with a strong need for both power and security is likely to be a paranoid manager who worries about eliminating enemies and crushing rivals. Someone with strong needs for achievement and independence is likely to establish his or her own business organization and make all the important decisions. Of course, not everybody is able to have all these needs satisfied. The extent to which gratification is possible depends on other factors such as available opportunities and the person's skills and abilities.

Identifying Motive Patterns

There are a variety of types of information that can be used to infer somebody's motive pattern. First is the observed behavior of the person during interactions with peers, subordinates, superiors, clients, and other outsiders. Some information about the person's behavior comes from second-hand sources rather than from direct observation. Aspects of behavior that are most informative involve styles of decision-making, use of influence, intensity of work effort, reaction to criticism, and handling of conflicts and crises. Clues can be found in what gets the person upset, what the person is enthusiastic about, what the person pays most attention to, and what seems to make the person especially happy. Decisions that people make involving choices between satisfying two different needs are especially useful for identifying motive patterns. For example, managers sometimes have to choose between maintaining their popularity or accomplishing the task; between achieving excellence in the work or protecting their own job security; and between promoting their own reputation or allowing subordinates an opportunity to show what they can do. Decisions involving career choices between different types of jobs are also very informative, although they do not occur as frequently. Examples are choices between working alone in a job with a lot of autonomy or being part of a team; between a job with authority over people or a non-supervisory job with opportunity for individual achievement; and between a job in a different location with more prestige or a job in the same location where a person can maintain friendships and be close to family.

In addition to behavior, clues about motive patterns can be inferred from a person's expressed values, attitudes, beliefs, and career objectives. Clues are sometimes available in information about a person's childhood experiences and cultural, ethnic or religious background. Other clues are provided by information about the person's family or social life, including hobbies, interests, activities, and memberships in social clubs and professional organizations. Finally, there are usually some clues in aspects of an individual's own physical environment, such as the pictures, awards, charts, signs, and slogans displayed in his or her office, the arrangement of furniture in the office, the way he or she dresses, the type of car he or she drives, and where he or she lives. Inferences about motives are never easy to make, but one can have more confidence in them if there is a pattern of consistent evidence gathered over a period of time from several different types of clues.

References

Alderfer, C. P. (1972). *Existence, Relatedness, and Growth: Human Needs in Organizational Settings*. New York: Free Press.

Allport, G. W., Vernon, P. E., & Lindzey, G. (1960). *A Study of Values*. Boston: Houghton-Mifflin.

Boyatzis, R. E. (1982). *The Competent Manager*. New York: John Wiley.

Landy, F. J., & Becker, W. W. (1987). "Motivation Theory Reconsidered." In L. L. Cummings and B. M. Staw (eds.), *Research in Organizational Behavior, Vol. 9*. Greenwich, CT: JAI Press, pp. 24–35.

Maslow, A. (1954). *Motivation and Personality*. New York: Harper & Row.

McClelland, D. C. (1985). *Human Motivation*. Glenview, IL: Scott-Foresman.

McClelland, D. C. (1975). *Power: The Inner Experience*. New York: Irvington.

Miner, J. B. (1977). *Motivation to Manage: A Ten-Year Update on the Studies in Management Education Research*. Atlanta: Organizational Measurement Systems Press.

Pervin, L. (1985). "Personality." In M. Rosenzweig and L. W. Porter (eds.), *Annual Reviews of Psychology, Vol. 36*. Palo Alto, CA: Annual Reviews.

Stahl, M. J. (1983). "Achievement, Power and Managerial Motivation: Selecting Managerial Talent With the Job Choice Exercise." *Personnel Psychology*, 36, 775-789.

Steers, R. M., & Braunstein, D. N. (1976). "A Behaviorally-Based Measure of Manifest Needs in Work Settings." *Journal of Vocational Behavior*, 9, 251–266.

Steers, R. M., & Porter, L. W. (1987). *Motivation and Work Behavior, 4th. Edition*. New York: McGraw-Hill.

Weiner, B. (1972). *Theories of Motivation*. Chicago: Rand McNally.

Weiss, H. M., & Adler, S. (1984). "Personality and Organizational Behavior." In B. M. Staw and L. L. Cummings (eds.), *Research in Organizational Behavior*, Vol. 6, pp. 1–50.

Winter, D. G. (1973). *The Power Motive*. New York: Free Press.

NEEDS QUIZ

Instructions

This exercise consists of a short quiz to assess your understanding of the six needs and how they are reflected in a person's attitudes and behavior. Your instructor will tell you when to do the quiz and will provide instructions on how to score it.

For each type of need, find the three descriptions that best indicate the need is a strong one. Put the letter code for each description you select on the lines provided next to the need.

Achievement ＿＿ ＿＿ ＿＿   Independence ＿＿ ＿＿ ＿＿

Power   ＿＿ ＿＿ ＿＿   Esteem   ＿＿ ＿＿ ＿＿

Affiliation   ＿＿ ＿＿ ＿＿   Security   ＿＿ ＿＿ ＿＿

Descriptions:

A. Enjoys being a celebrity.

B. Resents authority figures.

C. Worries about making mistakes.

D. Prefers tasks that are very challenging.

E. Desires recognition for contributions.

F. Likes to manipulate people.

G. Tries to please everybody.

H. Worries about losing his or her job.

I. Likes to solve problems that test his or her skill.

J. Gets lonely when traveling alone.

K. Likes to work at his or her own pace without inteference.

L. Wants to be in charge and run things.

M. Collects status symbols.

N. Wants more authority over subordinates.

O. Prefers participating in team tasks rather than individual tasks.

P. Enjoys planning how to improve things.

Q. Worries about being disabled by illness.

R. Would like to start his or her own company.

MOTIVE IDENTIFICATION EXERCISE

Instructions

The object of this exercise is to provide an opportunity to practice analyzing managerial motivation. Motivation is described in terms of six needs: achievement, power, affiliation, esteem, security, and independence-dependence. The exercise consists of four short cases, each describing a different manager. For each case, consider information about the manager's behavior, expressed values and beliefs, cultural background, childhood experiences, and physical environment at work and at home. Use this information to make inferences about the manager's dominant needs. Dominant needs are any especially strong ones, although in the case of need for independence-dependence, either extreme can be a dominant need. For each case, make a check mark next to the two or three dominant needs for the manager, using the form provided for that purpose on the next page.

Form for Motive Identification Exercise

Arnold Green

_____ Achievement   _____ Affiliation

_____ Esteem   _____ Power

_____ Dependence-Independence _____   _____ Security

Notes:

Charley Adams

_____ Achievement   _____ Affiliation

_____ Esteem   _____ Power

_____ Dependence-Independence _____   _____ Security

Notes:

Bill Stuart

_____ Achievement   _____ Affiliation

_____ Esteem   _____ Power

_____ Dependence-Independence _____   _____ Security

Notes:

Ray Johnson

_____ Achievement   _____ Affiliation

_____ Esteem   _____ Power

_____ Dependence-Independence _____   _____ Security

Notes:

Case 1: Arnold Green

Arnold Green was recently appointed head analyst in the finance department, and he has ten junior analysts reporting to him. His appointment was based on an outstanding record for accuracy during his eight years as a junior analyst. In those days, Arnold carefully checked and rechecked each of his reports before submitting them. In his current position, Arnold has continued this obsession for avoiding errors. He insists that all rules and procedures be followed exactly, and he frequently gets out his calculator and checks the work of subordinates.

Arnold was concerned about accepting the promotion to head analyst, because his job security would become dependent upon how well subordinates do their jobs. He accepted the position only because his boss, George Smith, kept encouraging him to do so. Arnold greatly admires George, who was himself the head analyst before being made department head. Arnold feels comfortable working for George, who seems almost like a second father to him. He is completely loyal to George and accepts his orders without question. Arnold relies heavily on George for advice. He always checks with George before starting any new project, and he asks George to look at the draft of a report before having the final draft typed. When George is not around and there is a crisis requiring immediate action, Arnold becomes panicked. He seldom exercises any initiative because he is afraid of making a mistake and losing his job.

When Arnold took over as head analyst, he felt very awkward about exercising authority over the junior analysts, who had been his co-workers. He is a timid person who finds it difficult to be assertive. He is likely to back down if a subordinate objects strongly to something he says. Arnold has doubts that he is cut out to be a manager, and he sometimes finds himself wishing that he were back in his former position as a junior analyst.

Arnold comes from a rural background. He grew up on a farm, and his family was very religious with strict rules and stern discipline. Arnold's office is unusually neat and orderly. Everything has its place, and his desk and files are carefully organized. He has detailed charts on the wall to keep track of the progress of each project assigned to his group.

Arnold worries about the course of events in the country. He is concerned about the possibility of a serious recession. He believes the country is experiencing a crisis of leadership and longs for a strong, capable President who can "set things right" and deal with the nation's problems.

Case 2: Charley Adams

Charley Adams is an operations manager with 12 subordinates reporting to him. He is a very easy-going person who loves to swap jokes and tell stories. Charley believes that it is important to maintain good relations with people, and he stresses the importance of cooperation and teamwork. He is uncomfortable when a conflict develops, and he tries to smooth it over quickly or find an acceptable compromise.

Before becoming a manager, Charley was always willing to take on extra assignments for his boss, and to provide helpful advice to less experienced co-workers in his department. Charley is proud of his reputation as a "good team player" and a "loyal company man." It is very important to Charley to be respected and appreciated by people in the organization. Perhaps that is why he is inclined to talk about his accomplishments, even though they are not particularly outstanding. In his office, a letter of commendation from his boss is framed and displayed on the wall, next to a picture of the company president shaking hands with Charley at the annual picnic. Charley gets very upset when someone criticizes his performance or questions his expertise.

On his desk, Charley has several pictures of his family. Charley comes from a cultural background emphasizing the importance of close family ties. He holds frequent Sunday dinners at which the entire Adams clan gathers for an afternoon of swimming, baseball, eating, and singing. Charley is proud of his children and happy that they have chosen to live in the same city where he can often see them and his grandchildren. Charley is active in social clubs and enjoys making speeches and acting as master of ceremonies. On Saturdays, he likes to play golf with friends, including some of the other managers in the company.

Charley is not very competitive. He wants his department to have a good performance record, but he has no ambition to become the best department in the company. Charley is reluctant to jeopardize relations with subordinates by pushing them to improve their performance beyond current levels, which he believes are adequate. When Charley gives out performance bonuses to subordinates, he usually tries to give something to everyone, rather than using the bonus to reward only superior performance.

In Charley's opinion, the problems of the nation are due primarily to constant conflict and distrust among the many factions, regions, and special interest groups. If people could learn to stop fighting and unite in pursuit of common goals, we could overcome most of our problems.

Case 3: Bill Stuart

Bill Stuart is the head of an engineering group in Research and Development. He was promoted to that position because he was the best design engineer in the company and was ambitious to further his career by going into management. At the time, Bill had little understanding of what the job would be like, but he saw it as both an opportunity and a challenge.

Bill was an only child, and he grew up as somewhat of a loner. He had few close friends and did not join any social groups. Bill still feels awkward around people he doesn't know well, and he dislikes social functions such as cocktail parties and company picnics. As a design engineer, he preferred assignments that allowed him to work alone rather than on team projects.

Bill had a mean and domineering father, and he has had difficulty getting along with authority figures ever since his childhood. He has had some heated arguments with superiors in previous jobs which caused him to resign. His present boss is easier to tolerate, because Bill is left alone to run his engineering group in his own way. Nevertheless, there is still some friction due to Bill's resistance to corporate policies that he regards as too restrictive. Bill has aspirations to start his own little engineering firm some day after he gains more administrative experience and develops more contacts. He is sure that he would find great satisfaction in being his own boss and building a new firm into a successful operation.

Bill believes in the old saying, "If you want something done right, do it yourself." He saves the most difficult design projects for himself, and he gets so wrapped up in doing these projects that his administrative duties suffer. He doesn't delegate enough responsibility to subordinates or spend enough time training and developing them. Two of his best design engineers left the company to work for a competitor after they became discouraged at the lack of opportunity and challenge.

Bill likes challenging individual sports such as skiing, mountain-climbing, and jogging long distances. However, he usually has little time left for recreation or his family because he spends so much time at the office and on work that he brings home.

Bill believes that many of the country's problems are attributable to the inefficiency and stifling effects of big government. He thinks that high taxes and excessive regulation of business have inhibited innovation and limited growth. Bill believes the welfare system is promoting laziness and dependence instead of encouraging people to use their energy and ability.

Case 4: Ray Johnson

Ray Johnson is a divisional vice president. He grew up in a poor ethnic neighborhood where he learned to be tough in order to survive. His greatest ambition was to rise above his humble origins and become rich and respectable. He has worked hard to get where he is, but the work itself has never interested him very much. For Ray, good performance has been a way to get ahead rather than something he enjoys for its own sake. If there had been an easier road to success, he would have taken it.

Ray lives in a large house with a big swimming pool in the best part of town. He wears expensive clothes and drives a big, prestigious car. Ray belongs to the best country club, where he enjoys playing tennis and handball. Ray likes to throw big parties at his home in the summer. He is married, but fancies himself as quite a playboy and has had many affairs, including some with female subordinates.

Despite his affluence and prominent position in the company, Ray is not relaxed. He worries about losing what he has worked so hard to get. Ray is concerned that some factions in the company are "out to get him." He views the organization as a political jungle, and he is quick to defend himself against any threats to his reputation, authority, or position. He uses spies and informers to find out what his opponents are doing, and he tries to undermine, isolate, or discredit anybody who criticizes or opposes him. Ray can be quite ruthless with his enemies, and he finds great pleasure in outmaneuvering them.

Ray tries to keep his subordinates weak so that they are dependent on him and cannot easily challenge his authority or judgment. He monopolizes important information, he makes all the important decisions in his division, and he insists that subordinates check with him before taking any action that is not routine. He tries to take complete credit for the successes of his division, and he covers up any serious problems or finds a scapegoat to blame them on. Ray's manipulative, autocratic management style has caused a lot of resentment among subordinates. The only subordinates who support him strongly are those whose own prospects depend on his continued power.

In Ray's opinion, the major problem with this nation is the lack of strong leaders. He would like to see the election of a President who would suppress domestic troublemakers and get tough with foreign enemies. Ray is opposed to any reduction in our military strength and would like to see an expansion in our military presence in trouble spots around the world.

Module 3

Influence Tactics

LEARNING OBJECTIVES

After completing this module a student will:

- *Understand the relationship between power and influence behavior.*
- *Understand the major tactics of face-to-face influence.*
- *Understand the advantages and disadvantages of each influence tactic.*
- *Understand the conditions determining when each influence tactic is appropriate.*
- *Understand which tactics are compatible with each other.*

CONTENTS OF MODULE

- *Text: Power and Influence Tactics*
- *Case: Sports Store*
- *Case: Westgate Hospital*

Power and Influence Tactics

Influence is the essence of managing. Influence is necessary to sell your ideas, to gain acceptance of your policies or plans, and to motivate others to implement your decisions. Much has been written about the best way to influence and motivate subordinates, but less is known about upward influence on superiors and lateral influence on peers over whom a manager has no direct authority. This module will examine sources of influence and the influence tactics used most commonly to influence subordinates, peers, and superiors.

A Model of Power and Influence

Figure 3–1 shows a model that depicts the relationship between power and managerial effectiveness (Yukl, 1989; Yukl & Taber, 1983). The model differs from traditional views about power, in that the emphasis is on influence behavior rather than power. The mere possession of power is not enough to insure that a manager will successfully exercise influence over other people. Power is exercised through influence behavior involving a variety of different influence tactics. A manager's influence behavior directly affects outcomes such as the attitudes and behavior of peers; this is shown in Figure 3–1 by an arrow from "influence behavior" to "outcomes." The success of an influence attempt de-

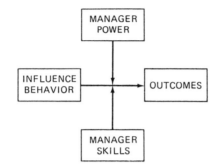

FIGURE 3–1 A Model of Power and Influence

pends in part on the manager's power and influence skills, but power and skills are not important unless the manager makes an influence attempt. That is why "power" and "skills" in Figure 3–1 do not have arrows directly to "outcomes." In the jargon of behavioral science, they are "moderator variables": they modify the relationship between influence behavior and outcomes. Next, each element of the model will be explained in more detail.

Outcomes of Influence Attempts

Success of an influence attempt is a matter of degree, but it is helpful to differentiate among three levels of success: "commitment," "compliance," and "resistance" (Yukl, 1989):

- **Commitment:** Most successful; the person is enthusiastic about carrying out the request and makes a maximum effort.
- **Compliance:** Partially successful; the person is apathetic about carrying out the request and makes only a minimal effort.
- **Resistance:** Unsuccessful; the person is opposed to carrying out the request and tries to avoid doing it.

An influence attempt is most successful if it results in commitment. Commitment means that the target person internally agrees with the action or decision he or she is asked to carry out. Commitment results in a maximum effort, and the person is likely to exercise initiative in trying to find a way to do the task effectively.

An influence attempt is partially successful if it results in compliance. With compliance, the target person will carry out the requested action but is apathetic about it and will make only a minimal effort. Of course, there are some cases where compliance is all that is required. For example, compliance is usually sufficient for a very simple, routine task.

An influence attempt is unsuccessful if it results in resistance. Resistance is a condition wherein the target person is opposed to the requested action and will try to avoid doing it. The person may refuse to carry out the request, may seek to have it nullified by higher authorities, or may delay acting in the hope that the manager making the request is not serious about it; in the worst case, the person will make a pretense of complying but will try to sabotage the task.

Power

Power is the potential of one person (the "agent") to exert influence on another person (the "target"), and it stems from some type of dependency of the target person on the agent. There are several different sources of power (French & Raven, 1959; Kotter, 1985; Podsakoff & Schriesheim, 1985). Power comes in part from attributes of the agent ("personal power") and in part from attributes of the situation ("position power").

Attributes of the manager include task-relevant expertise ("expert power"), and various aspects of temperament, personality, appearance, and reputation that cause others to like a person and identify with him or her ("referent power"). The latter category may include such diverse qualities as charm, humor, cheerfulness, thoughtfulness, courtesy, charisma, physical attractiveness, and fame.

Attributes of the manager's position that contribute to the manager's power include legitimate authority to make task assignments or direct the behavior of others ("legitimate power"), control over rewards ("reward power"), control over punishments ("coercive power"), access to information, and control over the distribution of information.

Power determines whether influence attempts will be successful. For example, an attempt to influence someone by offering rewards will fail if a manager has no control over rewards valued by the person.

Influence Skills

Influence skills include diagnostic skills and execution skills. Diagnostic skills (for example, empathy, insight, social sensitivity) help the manager to select an appropriate influence tactic. It is important for a manager to analyze the situation and understand the motives and values of the people to be influenced. Also important is the effective execution of whatever influence tactics are selected as appropriate to the situation. Execution skills include persuasiveness, decisiveness, bargaining ability, and acting ability.

Skills and power jointly moderate the effects of an influence attempt. For example, persuasive skill and task expertise are both important moderators of influence attempts that involve appeals to reason. Logical arguments are sometimes successful in influencing others even when a manager is not perceived to be an expert, but success is more likely when the manager is perceived to have superior task expertise. In the same way, a manager who is perceived to be an expert is sometimes able to influence others even when his or her arguments are weak and flawed, but success is more likely when the manager has the skills necessary to present persuasive, logical arguments that make full use of his or her expertise.

Influence Behavior

Influence behavior is easier to understand if we identify different forms of the behavior, sometimes called "influence tactics." A few exploratory studies have attempted to identify categories of influence

TABLE 3–1 Definitions of Influence Tactics

Legitimating Tactic: Verifying that a request is within your scope of authority or is otherwise consistent with organizational policies, practices, and professional role expectations

Rational Persuasion: Use of logical arguments and factual evidence to persuade a person that a proposal or request is viable and likely to result in the attainment of task objectives

Exchange Tactic: A request or proposal that includes an explicit or implicit promise to reward the person who carries it out

Personal Appeals and Ingratiation Tactics: Asking a person to do something out of loyalty or friendship, and doing things to make the person feel more positive toward you before making a request

Inspirational Appeal: An emotional request that arouses enthusiasm and commitment by appealing to a person's central values and ideals, or by increasing the person's self-esteem and confidence

Consultation: Efforts to involve a person in the planning of specific details and action steps of a policy, strategy, or decision

Pressure Tactic: A request with an explicit or implicit threat that failure to comply will result in unpleasant consequences for the person

Coalition Tactic: Enlisting the support of other people to directly influence the target person, or to allow you to tell the target person that others support your proposal or request behavior (Kipnis, Schmidt & Wilkinson, 1980; Schilit & Locke, 1982; Yukl & Falbe, 1990). Findings from this research can be summarized in a taxonomy with eight distinct influence tactics. The taxonomy includes most forms of influence behavior used by managers to influence peers and superiors as well as subordinates. The influence tactics are defined in Table 3–1. Each form of influence is appropriate in some situations but not in others. In any particular situation, some influence tactics are more effective than others. Managers typically use some combination of influence tactics, with the particular mix depending upon the situation and the individual manager's preferences.

Explanation of Influence Tactics

Each type of influence tactic will be explained briefly, and the conditions favoring its use will be described.

Legitimating Tactics

A common form of influence in organizations is a request based on legitimate power ("legitimate request"). The manager asks someone to do something that he or she has a right to request. In the case of subordinates, the right to ask is based on the manager's direct authority. In other cases, as with peers, the right to ask is based on organizational policies, standard procedures, and traditional practices. Some research has found that influence attempts based on legitimate power are more successful if the request is reasonable and clearly relevant for the effective performance of the manager's job. A request of this type is usually honored, unless it causes great inconvenience or jeopardizes the target person's own job performance. However, the response to a legitimate request may be one of slow, minimal compliance rather than enthusiastic, prompt commitment. In order to elicit prompt commitment and extra effort, it is usually necessary for a manager to supplement a legitimate request with some other form of influence.

If the agent believes a request is legitimate but the target does not, the result is likely to be resistance rather than compliance. Usually, the legitimacy of a request is less clear for peers than it is for subordinates, unless there are well established standard procedures. It is important for a manager to be aware of the possibility that unusual requests will not be immediately perceived by the other person as legitimate. When authority is ambiguous or legitimacy in doubt, a manager may use a "legitimating tactic" at the same time as the initial request, or soon afterward.

Legitimating tactics are forms of behavior intended to establish the legitimacy of a request. Examples include:

- Providing evidence of prior precedent.
- Showing consistency with organizational policies that are involved in the type of request being made.
- Showing consistency with the duties and responsibilities of the person's position or with professional role expectations.
- Indicating that the request has been endorsed by higher management or by the person's boss (also a coalition tactic).

Rational Persuasion

When a manager has substantial expert power, it may be possible to get compliance with a request merely on the basis of the manager's greater knowledge. In this case, the target person accepts on faith the advice or directions provided by the manager. An example is the advice given by a physician to a patient. In most cases, however, a manager does not have such a high level of expert power. Instead of relying on automatic compliance, the manager must use his or her expertise to present logical arguments, backed by factual evidence that a proposed policy, strategy, action plan, or procedural change is the best way to attain some objective or accomplish some task.

Rational persuasion is most appropriate when the target person shares the same task objectives as the manager but does not recognize the proposal is the best way to attain the objectives. Rational persuasion is also feasible when the target's objectives are different but still compatible with those of the manager. However, in a situation where the manager and target person have incompatible objectives, rational persuasion is unlikely to be successful for obtaining commitment or even compliance. Thus, it is usually advisable to discuss the target person's objectives before using this influence tactic.

A manager's technical knowledge is a major source of facts and evidence needed to build a persuasive case. However, in addition to facts and evidence, a persuasive case usually includes some opinions or inferences that the manager asks others to accept at face value because there is insufficient evidence to verify them. Therefore, influence derived from rational persuasion depends on the extent to which others recognize the manager as credible and trustworthy. A manager should build credibility by keeping informed about technical matters and relevant developments, and by avoiding rash, careless, or deceptive statements. If a manager is caught distorting facts or lying to deceive people, credibility will be lost and it may be impossible to regain it. Finally, a manager needs considerable skill in persuasive speaking to present a case effectively and with the maximum influence.

Inspirational Appeal

This tactic involves an emotional appeal, in contrast to the appeal to logic used in rational persuasion. An inspirational appeal attempts to enlist the target person's underlying values and ideals as the basis for motivating him or her to carry out a request. For example, soldiers are asked to volunteer for a dangerous mission as an expression of their patriotism, or a group of employees is asked to work extra hours on a special project because it may save many lives. The manager does not offer any tangible rewards to people, only the prospect that they will feel good as a result of "doing something that is noble and just," "making an important contribution," "performing an exceptional feat," or "serving God and country."

The complexity of an inspirational appeal depends in part on the size of the task to be undertaken, the amount of effort and risk involved, and the extent to which people are asked to deviate from established, traditional ways of doing things. An inspirational appeal may be as simple as a brief explanation of the reasons why a new task or project is important to the organization. A more complex form of inspirational appeal is a major speech presenting a common vision that embodies the hopes and ideals of the group and articulates a plan of action to make the vision a reality. In order to formulate an appropriate appeal, the manager must have insight into the values, hopes, and fears of the person or group to be influenced. The effectiveness of an inspirational appeal also depends on the manager's communication skills, such as his or her ability to use vivid imagery and metaphors, to manipulate symbols, to coin appealing slogans, and to employ tone and gestures to generate enthusiasm and excitement.

Inspirational appeals attempt to arouse emotions as the mechanism for motivating commitment to a strategy, project, or mission. However, in some cases, it is necessary not only to arouse a desire to undertake the proposed activity, but also to build confidence that the effort will be successful. A "pep talk" to build confidence is important if the individual or group lacks self confidence, or if the task is very difficult or dangerous.

Inspirational appeals have long been popular with political leaders, but it is only in recent years that the relevance of this form of influence for managers has come to be recognized. Recent studies of effective organizations and "transformational leaders" find that one secret of their success is greater use of inspirational appeals to develop commitment and loyalty among members of the organization (Bass, 1985; Bennis & Nanus, 1985; Tichy & Devanna, 1986).

Consultation

Consultation is an influence process in which the motivation of a person to implement a decision is increased by allowing the person to participate in making the decision. The process illustrates the apparent paradox, that you can gain more influence by giving up some influence. This is possible because influence between two people is not a fixed sum. Consultation increases the total influence in the relationship. However, for consultation to be effective as an influence technique, the resulting decision must be consistent with the manager's task objectives. It is only feasible for a manager to give others considerable influence over a decision if their objectives are compatible with those of the manager.

Consultation can take a variety of forms. It may occur with a single individual or with a group. It may occur in the context of a formal group meeting, or as a casual conversation during a brief encounter with someone. It may involve participation in various stages of the decision, from diagnosis of the problem, to identification of possible solutions, to selection of a preferred solution, to the planning of specific actions to implement the decision. In one common variation of consultation, the manager presents a proposed policy, plan, or procedure to a person who will be involved in implementing it to see if the person has any doubts or concerns. In the discussion, which is really a form of negotiation and joint problem solving, the manager tries to find ways to modify the details of the decision to deal with the person's major concerns. In another common variation of consultation, the manager presents a general strategy or objective to the other person rather than a detailed proposal, and asks the person to suggest specific action steps for implementing it. The suggested action steps are discussed until there is agreement by both parties.

There is a large body of research on the effects of participation on decision acceptance, but the reasons for the effects are still not very well understood (Anthony, 1978; Strauss, 1963). One explanation is that participation provides a better understanding of the decision and the reasons for it. Another explanation is that participation gives people a feeling of ownership of a decision and makes them feel responsible for making it successful. Another explanation is that anxiety and resistance to change are reduced when people have an opportunity to express their reservations and incorporate safeguards into the decision. Whatever the reasons, the evidence suggests that greater involvement in the decision-making process results in stronger commitment to implement the decision effectively (Vroom & Jago, 1988).

Exchange Tactics

This form of influence involves the explicit or implicit offer of rewards for doing what the manager requests. Use of an incentive is especially appropriate when the person is indifferent or reluctant about complying with a request. In effect, the manager offers to make it worthwhile to comply by promising to provide something that is desired by the target person.

The use of exchange tactics is a way of attempting to enact one's reward power. The essential condition for use of this type of influence tactic is that the manager has control over rewards that are attractive to the person. The first step is to determine which of the rewards controlled by the manager are desired by the person. It is futile to offer an incentive that is not attractive to someone. If the manager does not know what the person wants, some exploratory discussion may be necessary to identify an appropriate incentive.

The reward offered by the manager may take many forms:

• Recommending a pay increase or promotion.
• Sharing scarce resources.
• Helping the person do another task.
• Providing information.
• Providing political support on some issue or proposal.
• Putting in a good word to help advance the person's career.

The promise may be implicit rather than explicit. That is, the manager may offer to return the favor in some unspecified way at a future time. If it is not obvious what rewards the manager controls, it may be appropriate for the manager to clarify some of the things he or she can do for the person.

It is important for the manager to maintain credibility about promised rewards. Credibility will be undermined if the manager promises more than he or she can deliver, forgets to deliver on a promise, or fails to return a favor that is owed. It is advisable to use incen-

tives sparingly, since there is a direct cost in terms of expended resources. Another disadvantage of using incentives is the tendency for
others to perceive the relationship purely in exchange terms rather
than in terms of friendship or professional cooperation. If incentives are
offered too freely, people come to expect to be rewarded every time the
manager asks them to do something.

Personal Appeals and Ingratiation Tactics

A personal appeal involves asking someone to do a favor based on
friendship or loyalty to the manager. The reward received for complying with the request is not something tangible, as in the case of exchange tactics, but rather the internal satisfaction of doing something
that will be appreciated by a manager whom the person likes or admires. In order to use this influence tactic, a manager must have considerable referent power. In other words, the person to be influenced
must like the manager or feel a sense of personal loyalty to the manager. If considerable effort will be required to comply with a request,
the person should understand that the request is indeed important to
the manager. If a request is not perceived to be important to the manager, it may be ignored or carried out with only a minimal effort.
Whenever appropriate, the manager should explain why the request is
important to him or her, and say that he or she is counting on the
person to help out in a difficult situation or in a time of great need.
The stronger the friendship or loyalty, the more a manager can ask
of a person. However, personal appeals are somewhat like checking
accounts; the more you draw upon them without making deposits, the
less the remaining balance for future drafts. If a manager asks for more
than is appropriate given the intensity of the relationship, the request
will probably be rejected. Likewise, if a manager asks for personal
favors too often without reciprocating, the person may conclude that he
or she is being exploited and re-evaluate the relationship. Only in cases
of intense love or devotion is it possible to continue making request
after request without undermining a relationship. Managers seldom
enjoy this degree of devotion from subordinates or peers. Thus, personal
appeals should be used sparingly, and the manager should make an
effort to maintain strong relationships by acting considerate, loyal, and
supportive whenever possible.
Even when there is no substantial bond of friendship or loyalty, a
personal appeal may be made if the other person feels a sense of obligation to return past favors. Reciprocity is strongly valued in most cultures, and it is usually a sufficient basis for influencing compliance, as

long as the request is commensurate with the person's perception of his or her obligation. In other words, a person who owes you a small favor cannot be asked to provide a very large favor to "balance the books." A personal appeal based on prior obligation sometimes includes a reminder of the debt ("you owe me one"). This type of personal appeal is similar in some respects to an exchange tactic.

The referent power on which personal appeals are based can be given a boost by the use of ingratiation tactics. Ingratiation involves behavior that makes someone feel better about you. Examples include giving compliments, doing a favor for someone, telling someone that he or she is the most qualified person for a task, and acting especially friendly and polite before making a request. Ingratiation tactics can be manipulative if they are not sincere. However, when sincere, they are a way to strengthen a friendship and provide a stronger basis for using personal appeals. It is possible to regard ingratiating tactics and personal appeals as distinct categories of influence behavior, but they are lumped together here because they both involve positive regard as a basis for influencing someone.

Pressure Tactics

Pressure tactics include coercion, intimidation, and "pushy" behavior such as repeated demands for compliance. Coercion involves the threat of undesirable consequences for non-compliance. The threatened punishment may take many different forms:

- Complaints to the person's boss.
- Efforts to get the person dismissed.
- Efforts to block the person's promotion.
- Opposition to some project or proposal that is important to the person.
- Efforts to undermine the person's reputation in the organization.
- Withholding information, resources, or assistance that the person is dependent upon.

The threat may be very explicit, or it may only be a hint that the person will be sorry if he or she fails to cooperate with the manager. Sometimes, when a request has been ignored, an angry complaint to the person is sufficient to invoke the possibility of unpleasant consequences and induce the person to do what is requested, particularly if the person is just lazy or apathetic rather than strongly opposed to the action.

The likelihood of compliance is greatest when the other person perceives the manager's threat to be credible. Sometimes it is necessary for a manager to establish credibility by showing that he or she actually has the power to cause unpleasant consequences for the person and is willing to use this power. Credibility will be undermined by rash threats that are not carried out despite non-compliance. Even when a threat is perceived to be credible, it may be unsuccessful in motivating compliance because the person refuses to be intimidated, or because the person believes that he or she can avoid complying without being caught. Pressure tactics sometimes have serious side effects. Threats and intimidation are likely to undermine working relationships, and may lead either to avoidance or to counter-aggression against the manager. For this reason, effective managers prefer not to use pressure tactics except as a last resort, after other influence tactics have failed.

Coalition Tactics

All of the influence tactics discusssed so far are direct ones carried out by a single agent. Sometimes it is not possible for a single person to influence someone by acting alone. Coalition tactics may then be used. These are indirect influence attempts which involve getting the support of other people. Coalitions may be formed with peers, subordinates, superiors, or outsiders such as clients and suppliers. These other people may be active or passive partners in the influence attempt.

Coalition partners are active if they make direct influence attempts of their own on your behalf. For example, you may ask others to approach the target person on their own and lobby for your proposals. A coalition with someone in a position of higher authority than the target person is sometimes called an "upward appeal" or "upward bypassing." For example, you may ask the boss of a lateral peer to back up your request to the peer to do something (this is also a legitimating tactic).

Passive coalition partners do not make any direct attempt to influence others on your behalf. But they agree to let you inform the target person of their support for your proposals. Sometimes it is enough just to tell a reluctant target person that your proposal has widespread support by others whom the person likes or respects.

Coalition tactics can be used with any of the direct influence tactics, but little is known about the most effective combinations. For example, we do not know if it is better for coalition partners to use the same influence tactics or different ones.

Combining Influence Tactics

It is often feasible for a manager to use more than one direct influence tactic at the same time. Some combinations work better than others, because not all tactics are compatible with each other. It is common to supplement a legitimate request with a legitimating tactic. A legitimate request may be supplemented also with rational persuasion or an exchange tactic. Rational persuasion is usually compatible with a personal appeal, an inspirational appeal, or an exchange tactic. A personal appeal should not be combined with an exchange tactic. Offering a tangible reward to do something undermines the feeling of satisfaction from doing a favor out of friendship or loyalty.

There is also a potential conflict between exchange tactics and inspirational appeals. An appeal to underlying values may be weakened if tangible rewards are overemphasized at the same time. However, a skillful manager can present a vision that appeals to the target person's ideals and values, while at the same time offering the prospect of tangible benefits if the strategy or project is successful.

As noted earlier, consultation often involves the use of rational persuasion during the course of mutual problem solving. Other influence tactics may also be combined with consultation. For example, if the discussion indicates that the person has serious concerns that cannot be dealt with by modifying the decision, then it may be necessary to introduce an incentive in order to persuade the person to accept the inconvenience or risks inherent in the plan. An inspirational appeal may be used to bolster the person's confidence that he or she will be able to do his or her part successfully and make a significant contribution to the overall project.

Most pressure tactics are incompatible with personal appeals, because they weaken feelings of friendship and loyalty. Coercion is incompatible with consultation, because it undermines the trust and respect required for mutual problem solving. Coercion may be combined with a legitimate request, but it should be delayed until it is obvious that compliance will not otherwise occur. There is some research that finds coercion to be more effective when combined with the offer of rewards rather than used alone. The use of this combination makes it less likely for the person to perceive the request as merely a case of intimidation.

As noted earlier, in addition to combining direct tactics, a manager may also combine direct tactics with indirect ones involving the assistance of coalition partners. For example, the manager may use consultation with a group that includes some supporters who will speak out in favor of his or her proposals.

In summary, combining different tactics increases the potential for influencing a person as long as the tactics are compatible. However, successfully combining different forms of influence tactics requires considerable insight and skill on the part of the manager.

References

Anthony, W. P. (1978). *Participative Management.* Reading, MA: Addison-Wesley.

Bass, B. M. (1985). *Leadership and Performance Beyond Expectations.* New York: Free Press.

Bennis, W. G., & Nanus, B. (1985). *Leaders: The Strategies for Taking Charge.* New York: Harper & Row.

Cohen, A. R., & Bradford, D. L. (1989). "Influence Without Authority: The Use of Alliances, Reciprocity, and Exchange to Accomplish Work." *Organizational Dynamics,* 17, 5–17.

French, J., & Raven, B. H. (1959). "The Bases of Social Power." In D. Cartwright (ed.), *Studies of Social Power.* Ann Arbor, MI: Institute For Social Research.

Kipnis, D., Schmidt, S. M., & Wilkinson, I. (1980). "Intra-Organizational Influence Tactics: Explorations in Getting One's Way." *Journal of Applied Psychology,* 65, 440–452.

Kotter, J. P. (1985). *Power and Influence: Beyond Formal Authority.* New York: Free Press.

Kouzes, J. M., & Posner, B. Z. (1987). *The Leadership Challenge: How to Get Extraordinary Things Done in Organizations.* San Francisco: Jossey-Bass.

Pfeffer, J. (1981). *Power in Organizations.* Marshfield, MA: Pittman.

Podsakoff, P. M., & Schriesheim, C. A. (1985). "Field Studies of French and Raven's Bases of Power: Critique, Reanalysis, and Suggestions for Future Research. *Psychological Bulletin,* 97, 387-411.

Porter, L. W., Allen, R. W., & Angle, H. L. (1981). The Politics of Upward Influence in Organizations. In L. L. Cummings & B. M. Staw (eds.), *Research in Organizational Behavior,* Vol. 3. 109–149. Greenwich, CT: JAI Press.

Sayles, L. R. (1979). *What Effective Managers Really Do and How They Do It.* New York: McGraw-Hill.

Schilit, W. K., & Locke, E. A. (1982). "A Study of Upward Influence in Organizations." *Administrative Science Quarterly,* 27, 304–316.

Strauss, G. (1963). "Some Notes on Power Equalization." In H. J. Leavitt (ed.), *The Social Science of Organizations: Four Perspectives.* Englewood Cliffs, NJ: Prentice Hall.

Stevenson, W. B., Pearce, J. L., & Porter, L. (1985). "The Concept of Coalition in Organization Theory and Research." *Academy of Management Review,* 10, 256–268.

Tichy, N. M., & Devanna, M. A. (1986). *The Transformational Leader.* New York: John Wiley.

Vroom, V. H., & Jago, A. G. (1988). *The New Leadership: Managing Participation in Organizations.* Englewood Cliffs, NJ: Prentice Hall.

Yukl, G. (1989). *Leadership in Organizations.* Englewood Cliffs, NJ: Prentice Hall.

Yukl, G. & Falbe, C. (1990). "Influence Tactics and Objectives in Upward, Downward, and Lateral Influence Attempts." *Journal of Applied Psychology.*

Yukl, G. & Taber, T. (1983). "The Effective Use of Managerial Power." *Personnel,* March-April, 37-44.

Case: Sporting Goods Store

Bill Thompson is the new manager of a retail sporting goods store that is part of a national chain. Bill, who is 23 years old, has been working for the company since he finished college three years ago. Before his promotion, he was the assistant manager for two years at another store in the chain. Last week, he was briefly introduced to the daytime employees by his boss, the regional manager. The profit performance of his new store is below average for its location, and Bill is looking forward to the challenge of improving profits. When he was an assistant manager, he was given mostly minor administrative duties and paperwork, so this will be his first opportunity to show he can be an effective manager.

The base salaries of the fifteen employees who work in Bill's store are set by the regional office, but appraisal ratings by the store manager influence the size of an employee's annual merit raise. These recommendations must be justified to the regional manager, especially if they are not consistent with individual and department sales. Bill can suspend or fire employees with the approval of his boss, but in practice it is difficult to do so unless there is a strong case. The basic store layout and most prices are set by the headquarters office. However, store performance can be affected to a limited extent by the store manager. One way is to keep cost of staff low by making sure they are working efficiently and not taking excessive sick days. Another way is to insure that employees are providing a high level of customer service so that customers will return to make other purchases rather than going to a different store next time. Customer service depends on knowing the products well, being polite, providing prompt service, and making sure that inventories of popular goods are maintained so that customers can find what they want. Pay is low for this type of retail selling job, turnover is high, and it takes a few months for a new employee to learn the merchandise well enough to be helpful to customers. Thus, it is also desirable to keep effective employees satisfied enough to stay with the company.

Although it is only his first week on the job, Bill believes that he has already discovered some of the problems at this store. The ski department is potentially the highest profit department in the store, but its sales are only about average for the stores in this region. He noticed that service in the ski department appears to be very slow. There has been a line of customers waiting to be served on several occasions, and he has overheard some grumbling about how long it takes to get served. One customer said he was leaving to go to another store that didn't make him "wait all day to have the privilege of spending hundreds of dollars on ski equipment." Upon close examination, Bill observed that Sally Jorgenson, the department manager, spends a lot of time socializing with her three sales people and with customers, including friends who drop in to visit and talk about ski conditions, resorts, fashions, equipment, racing, and so forth. On a couple of occasions, Bill saw customers waiting while she was talking to friends. Bill, who doesn't ski, cannot understand what they find so interesting to talk about or, for that matter, why anybody in their right mind would want to spend a small fortune and risk permanent injury to hurtle down a mountain in blizzard conditions, and then stand in long lines and ride up a freezing chairlift just to do it all over again.

Questions for Students

1. How much of each type of power does Bill have now (e.g., none, a limited amount, a lot)? Explain your answer in the space provided.

    a. *Legitimate Power*

    b. *Reward Power*

    c. *Coercive Power*

    d. *Expert Power*

    e. *Referent Power*

2. How useful are each of the following influence tactics in this situation?
   Explain your answer in the space provided.

   a. *Legitimating Tactics*

   b. *Pressure Tactics*

   c. *Exchange Tactics*

   d. *Rational Persuasion*

   e. *Inspirational Appeals*

f. Personal Appeals and Ingratiation

g. Coalitions

h. Consultation

3. Which combination of tactics is likely to be most effective?

4. Briefly describe what Bill should do and what he should say to Sally in order to use each of the following influence tactics.

a. Rational Persuasion

b. Consultation

c. Inspirational Appeal

Case: Westgate Hospital*

Manuel Martinez was the administrator of Westgate Community Hospital. The controller, Sam Westin, directed the financial affairs of the hospital and reported to Martinez. Westin's general attitude was that of a tight-fisted guardian of the dollar. He was rigid, not wanting to approve any action that was a departure from routine or at variance with policy. Martinez was the type who desired to take action, regardless of the restrictions of past practice or policy. The differing attitudes of the two men had led to conflicts in the past. On two occasions, Martinez had warned that he would fire Westin if he did not follow orders. Westin held his ground and usually won his arguments, contending that his approach was proper accounting practice and therefore not subject to challenge by Martinez.

One afternoon Martinez approached Westin with another request:

Martinez: Sam, here's a merit wage increase that I just put through for Clara Nesbit. She's the best floor supervisor we have, and she deserves the increase. I promised this on her next paycheck, so be sure to put it through at once.

He gave the merit increase form to Westin, who looked at it and frowned.

Westin: Manuel, you know I can't put this through. It's contrary to policy. She's already making the top rate for her classification.

Martinez: That does not make any difference. Put it through. I'm the boss here, and I say do it.

Westin: I can't do it. The pay ceilings for each job classification are specified in the compensation policy approved by the board of directors.

Martinez: It's the job of the administrator to run this hospital and keep it profitable. The compensation policies provide general guidelines, but I'm not bound by them.

Westin: Policy is policy and I'm not going to violate it.

A shouting match developed and diverted the attention of the entire office.

Martinez: Who's the boss here, Sam?

Westin: You are.

Martinez: Then put through this raise!

Westin: No!

Martinez: Sam, I've had enough. You are fired!

---

* Adapted from Keith Davis and John W. Newstrom, *Human Behavior at Work: Organizational Behavior.* McGraw-Hill, Copyright © 1989.

Westin: You can't fire me for that!

Martinez: I just did. You are through!

Martinez did not retract his action. Westin was removed from the payroll and left the hospital that afternoon.

Questions for Students

1. What influence tactics did Martinez use with Westin?

2. Why did these influence tactics fail?

3. Cite other examples of ineffective behavior by Martinez.

4. What actions could Martinez have taken that may have been more success-ful in influencing Westin?

Module 4

Participative Leadership

LEARNING OBJECTIVES

After completing this module a student will:

- *Understand the advantages and disadvantages of the three primary decision procedures.*
- *Understand how to identify relevant aspects of the decision situation.*
- *Understand a model for selecting the most appropriate decision procedure.*

CONTENTS OF MODULE

- *Text: Selecting An Appropriate Decision Procedure*
- *Decision Case Exercise*
- *Case: Alvis Corporation*

Selecting An Appropriate Decision Procedure

Making decisions is one of the most important activities carried out by managers. Before making a decision, a manager must determine whether to involve other people in the decision process. There are a variety of decision procedures from which to choose, and each procedure differs in the extent to which subordinates or other people such as peers are allowed to influence the decision. Involving subordinates in making a leader's decisions has important implications for the successful implementation of a decision and the satisfaction of subordinates (Anthony, 1978; Bass, 1981; Yukl, 1981).

Decision procedures can be classified into three primary types that are easy to distinguish from each other. The three primary procedures are ones that most managers and behavioral scientists agree are meaningful. Once you go beyond these three categories, behavioral scientists begin to disagree about the number of procedures and their appropriate definitions (Heller & Yukl, 1969; Tannenbaum & Schmidt, 1958; Vroom & Yetton, 1973; Vroom & Jago, 1988). The three types of decision procedure are defined as follows:

Autocratic Decision: The leader makes a decision alone without asking subordinates (or group members) for their ideas and suggestions.

Then the leader tells them what was decided, and if necessary, explains the decision or tries to "sell" it.

Consultation: The leader explains the decision problem to subordinates (or group members) and asks them for their ideas and suggestions. The leader may consult with subordinates individually or together as a group. Then the leader makes the final decision after careful consideration of their input.

Group Decision: The leader meets with subordinates (or group members) to discuss the decision problem and reach a decision that is acceptable to everyone or at least to a majority of group members. The leader runs the meeting but has no more influence over the final decision than any other group member.

The success of a decision depends primarily on three things: decision quality, decision acceptance, and the amount of time needed to make the decision (Maier, 1963; Vroom & Jago, 1988). Each of these criteria will be considered separately, then a model combining them will be presented.

Decision Quality

A decision is successful if it accomplishes a manager's objectives. Success depends jointly on decision quality and decision acceptance. The quality of a decision is high when the selected alternative is the best one among those available. "Best" means that the selected alternative will solve the decision maker's problem and will result in desirable outcomes at minimal cost if implemented properly. For example, an efficient work procedure is selected rather than some less efficient ones, or a critical assignment is given to the most qualified person rather than to someone less qualified.

Decision quality is not always an important issue. For some decisions, all of the obvious alternatives are equally desirable. For example, a manager may need to choose among three brands of supplies, all of which are comparable. In some cases, the decision itself is a trivial one without serious consequences for the organization. For example, which brand of coffee to use in the work unit's coffee maker is a trivial decision for the organization, even though members of the work unit may have strong preferences in the choice. When decision quality is not important, selection of a decision procedure need not consider implications for quality.

For the majority of a manager's decisions, quality is likely to be important. No single decision procedure is always superior for making decisions where quality is important. The implications of the three primary decision procedures for decision quality depend on aspects of the situation, especially the distribution of relevant information and the extent to which it is possible to bring this information to bear on the solution of the decision problem.

Participative decision procedures such as consultation and group decision making will increase decision quality if the people who participate in making the decision possess relevant information and problem-solving skills lacked by the leader, and if they share the leader's objectives. On the other hand, if the leader already has the information and expertise necessary to solve a problem or identify the best alternative, then participative procedures will not improve decision quality. On the contrary, a group decision may risk a decrease in quality if the group members have much less expertise than the leader. The leader is likely to lack relevant information possessed by subordinates (or group members) if the decision has the following attributes: the cause of the problem is not obvious, there is no best solution, any solution is likely to have undesirable side effects, and tradeoffs among benefits must be considered because more of one benefit implies less of another.

Consultation and group decision making are equally effective for improving decision quality when the leader has the skills necessary to use these decision procedures in an appropriate manner. For example, the leader must be able to keep the discussion on track, facilitate efficient problem solving, and avoid process problems such as hasty decisions where the group fails to consider important information. Participative procedures will not result in improved decision quality unless subordinates share the leader's objectives and are willing to cooperate in making a good decision. When subordinates have objectives that are incompatible with those of the leader, consultation usually results in better quality decisions than group decision making. With the latter procedure, the leader gives up control over the final choice to the group members, who may select an alternative that is not consistent with the leader's objectives. For example, if asked to determine their own pay increases, subordinates may give themselves larger increases than the leader would consider appropriate.

Decision Acceptance

The second requirement for a successful decision is the extent to which the persons who must implement the decision believe in it and are motivated to make it work regardless of the obstacles. If a manager depends on other people to implement a decision, their acceptance of the decision will largely determine whether it is implemented effectively. Regardless of how good a decision is in terms of decision quality, apathy or resistance by the people who must implement it may cause it to fail.

Whether decision acceptance is important depends on the situation. Decision acceptance by subordinates (or group members) is not important if the leader implements the decision himself and it does not seriously threaten the self-interest of subordinates. Sometimes, when decision acceptance is important, it can be achieved with an autocratic decision. One example is when the leader selects the alternative that is favored by subordinates, due either to luck or to a good understanding of subordinate preferences and attitudes. Another example is the case where subordinates share the leader's objective, and the leader has the skills to persuade them that his or her decision is the best way to attain the objective. A third example is the situation where subordinates will accept the decision out of loyalty to the leader, or because they believe that he or she has the expertise to determine what is best.

In situations where decision acceptance is unlikely with an autocratic decision, a participative decision procedure is one way to increase decision acceptance by subordinates (or group members). Group decision making usually increases decision acceptance more than consultation does. There are several reasons why participative procedures may increase decision acceptance. When people have substantial influence over a decision, they tend to identify with it and come to assume ownership of the decision. By participating in making a decision, people gain a better understanding of the reasons for the decision. Knowing that there are good reasons why a particular alternative was selected and others rejected increases decision acceptance. Moreover, if people have the opportunity to express reservations about possible adverse consequences of various alternatives, it is more likely that the final decision will deal with their concerns, thereby reducing the likelihood of resistance to change. Finally, when people make a group decision with a choice process they consider legitimate, the group is likely to apply social pressure on any reluctant members to do their part in implementing the decision. In order to achieve greater decision acceptance with participative procedures, the leader must have the skills to involve each member of the group without appearing manipulative. Skilled leaders avoid common group process problems such as interpersonal conflicts that result in polarized positions or domineering members who inhibit other members from expressing ideas and opinions.

Decision Time

The third requirement for a successful decision is the amount of time required to make it. Decision time is most important when there is a crisis situation that will get much worse if not dealt with quickly. However, even when there is not an immediate crisis, delays may entail direct costs and lost opportunities. Furthermore, the time devoted to making a decision involves an overhead cost in terms of managerial time and salaries. This cost escalates rapidly when many people spend hours in meetings to make a decision. Time is one of a manager's most valuable and scarce resources, so it is desirable to reach a decision as quickly as possible without jeopardizing decision quality and acceptance.

The three primary decision procedures differ in the amount of time they require. Autocratic decisions are usually the quickest, because little or no discussion occurs with subordinates (or group members). Even when it is necessary for the leader to meet with subordinates to explain and "sell" the decision, less time is needed for an autocratic decision than for consultation, which also requires a post-decision announcement to people who will implement the decision and people who will be affected by it. Group decisions require the most time, especially when the group is large or there is substantial conflict to be resolved. The amount of time needed to make a decision increases if the leader desires to reach a consensus decision with everybody in agreement rather than a majority decision.

The Decision Model

It is desirable for a manager to consider the likely implications for decision quality, acceptance, and time before selecting a decision procedure. Behavioral scientists have developed normative decision models to aid managers in determining which decision procedure is optimal. The best known model is the one developed by Vroom and Yetton (1973). Their model incorporates some earlier conceptual contributions made by Maier (1963), Tannenbaum and Schmidt (1958), and Heller and Yukl (1969). The Vroom-Yetton model has been revised recently by Vroom and Jago (1988). The model presented here is similar in its logic and assumptions to the earlier ones, but is much less complicated and has some other advantages. Rather than a set of feasible procedures for each situation, as in the Vroom-Yetton model, the current model prescribes the single best procedure for each situation.

It is important to recognize that prescriptive models are based on assumptions about the relative priorities of different criteria contributing to decision success, such as decision quality, acceptance, and time.

Changes in priorities result in changes in the prescriptions. The decision model presented here gives highest priority to protecting decision quality, second priority to insuring decision acceptance, and lowest priority to saving decision time. The model incorporates three criteria of decision success (decision quality, acceptance, time) and five aspects of the situation (importance of quality, leader information, importance of acceptance, likelihood of an autocratic decision being accepted, congruence between leader and subordinate objectives). The five aspects of the situation combine to create seven distinct decision situations. The following rules determine the optimal decision procedure for each decision situation:

- Do not make an autocratic decision when decision quality is important and subordinates (or group members) have relevant knowledge not possessed by the leader (cells 5, 6, 7).

- Do not make an autocratic decision when acceptance by subordinates is important and is not assured with this procedure (cells 2, 4, 6, 7).

- Do not make a group decision when decision quality is important and the objectives of subordinates (or group members) are not compatible with the leader's objectives (cell 7).

- Do not use consultation or group decision making when neither decision quality nor acceptance will be improved (cells 1, 3).

- Use consultation rather than group decision making when decision quality is important and the leader has the information needed to make a good decision, but acceptance is important and not assured with an autocratic decision (cell 4).

- Use a group decision rather than consultation when decision quality is not at risk but acceptance is important and not assured with an autocratic decision (cells 2, 6).

- Use consultation rather than group decision making when quality is important and subordinates (or group members) have relevant knowledge not possessed by the leader, but acceptance is not important or is assured (cell 5).

The Decision Style Matrix shown in Figure 4–1 provides a graphic depiction of the model and is much easier to use than the decision rules. Each distinct decision situation is represented by a different cell in the Decision Style Matrix. The numbers in parentheses after each decision rule listed above indicate the cells affected by that rule and show the basis for identifying the optimal procedure for each cell. To use the matrix, a manager must determine which cell best describes the deci-

Decision Quality	Subordinate Acceptance of the Decision	
	Not Important or Assured with an Autocratic Decision	*Important and Not Assured with an Autocratic Decision*
Quality not important (decision is trivial or there are many obvious good solutions)	#1 AUTOCRATIC DECISION	#2 GROUP DECISION
Quality is important; leader has all of the essential information to find best solution	#3 AUTOCRATIC DECISION	#4 CONSULTATION
Quality is important; leader lacks essential information that the subordinates possess	#5 CONSULTATION	#6: GROUP DECISION If subordinate goals consistent with the leader's goals
		#7: CONSULTATION If subordinate goals inconsistent with the leader's goals

FIGURE 4–1 Decision Style Matrix

sion situation in question, then look in the cell to learn the optimal procedure for that situation.

It is important to point out that successful use of the model depends on a manager's ability to classify a decision situation accurately. Errors in judgment about the situation may result in selection of the wrong decision procedure. If a manager is unsure about some aspects of the situation, it is best to use consultation, which provides a good compromise choice. Skill in assessing the situation increases with practice in using the model.

Guidelines for Diagnosing Situation

The following guidelines facilitate diagnosis of a decision situation.

1. Decision quality is likely to be important if:
   - The decision has important consequences for the organization or group.
   - Some of the alternative choices are much better than others.

2. Decision quality is *not* assured with an autocratic decision if:
   - Subordinates (or group members) have relevant information and ideas needed by the leader to solve the problem.
   - The decision problem is complex, and the best way to resolve the problem is not clear from the data or from prior experience with similar problems.
3. Decision acceptance is likely to be important if:
   - The leader must depend on subordinates (or group members) to implement the decision.
   - Successful implementation requires a high degree of effort and initiative by subordinates (or group members).
   - Failure to gain acceptance would have unfavorable consequences for relations with subordinates (or group members).
4. Decision acceptance is *not* assured with an autocratic decision if:
   - The leader does not have enough personal power and influence over subordinates (or group members) to ensure their loyalty and support.
   - Subordinates (or group members) are likely to resist any decision that is not consistent with their strong preferences in the matter, and the leader does not know what these preferences are.
   - Subordinates (or group members) expect to participate in making the decision and may resist even a decision consistent with their preferences if excluded from the decision process.
5. Subordinate (or group member) goals are *not* likely to be compatible with the leader's goals if:
   - They prefer an alternative that is outside of the leader's range of acceptable choices.
   - They are known to be hostile or unsympathetic with regard to the leader's objectives.
   - There is an obvious conflict of interest or difference in priorities between leader and subordinates (or group members).

References

Anthony, W. P. (1978). *Participative Management*. Reading, MA: Addison-Wesley.

Bass, B. M. (1981). *Handbook of Leadership: Survey of Theory and Research*. New York: Free Press.

Heller, F., & Yukl, G. (1969). "Participation, Managerial Decision Making, and Situational Variables." *Organizational Behavior and Human Performance, 4,* 227–241.

Kanter, R. M. (1979). "Power Failure in Management Circuits." *Harvard Business Review, 57,* 65–75.

Maier, N. R. F. (1963). *Problem Solving Discussions and Conferences.* New York: McGraw-Hill.

Tannenbaum, R., & Schmidt, W. H. (1958). "How to Choose a Leadership Pattern." *Harvard Business Review, 36,* March–April, 95–101.

Vroom, V. H., & Jago, A. G. (1988). *The New Leadership: Managing Participation in Organizations.* Englewood Cliffs, NJ: Prentice Hall.

Vroom, V. H., & Yetton P. W. (1973). *Leadership and Decision Making.* Pittsburgh: University of Pittsburgh Press.

Yukl, G. A. (1981). *Leadership in Organizations.* Englewood Cliffs, NJ: Prentice Hall.

DECISION CASE EXERCISE

Instructions

The purpose of this exercise is to provide students with an opportunity to practice analyzing a decision situation and selecting an appropriate procedure for involving others in the decision. Read each decision case carefully and use the questions following each case to guide your analysis of the situation. After you finish the situational analysis, use the simplified decision model to determine which of the following decision procedures would be most appropriate in that situation.

Autocratic Decision: The leader makes the decision alone without asking subordinates (or group members) for their ideas, suggestions, or preferences.

Consultation: The leader explains the decision problem to subordinates (or group members), asks them for their ideas and suggestions, then makes the decision after careful consideration of their input.

Group Decision: The leader meets with subordinates (or group members) to discuss the problem and reach a joint decision; the leader runs the meeting but has no more influence over the final decision than any other group member.

Case 1

Assume that you are a production manager and one of your responsibilities is to order the materials used by your subordinates in production jobs. Extensive stockpiling of materials is not feasible, and having idle workers due to lack of materials is costly. Based on past records, you have been able to determine with considerable accuracy which materials subordinates will need a few weeks in advance. The purchase orders are executed by the Purchasing Office, not by your subordinates. How would you make material procurement decisions?

Is decision quality important? _____ Yes _____ No

Does the leader have the information to make a high-quality decision alone, without subordinate participation?

_____ Yes _____ No

Is decision acceptance important? _____ Yes _____ No

Is acceptance assured with an autocratic decision?

_____ Yes _____ No

Do subordinates share the leader's task objectives?

_____ Yes _____ No

Cell in Model: _____

Best Procedure:

_____ Autocratic Decision

_____ Consultation

_____ Group Decision

Notes:

Case 2

Assume that you are the vice president for production in a small manufacturing company. Your plant is working close to capacity to fill current orders. Now you have just been offered a contract to manufacture components for a new customer. If the customer is pleased with the way you handle this order, additional orders are likely and the new customer could become one of your company's largest clients. You are confident that your production supervisors can handle the job, but it would impose a heavy burden on them in terms of rescheduling production, hiring extra workers, and working extra hours. How would you decide whether to accept the new contract?

Is decision quality important? _____ Yes _____ No

Does the leader have the information to make a high-quality decision alone, without subordinate participation?

_____ Yes _____ No

Is decision acceptance important? _____ Yes _____ No

Is acceptance assured with an autocratic decision?

_____ Yes _____ No

Do subordinates share the leader's task objectives?

_____ Yes _____ No

Cell in Model: _____

Best Procedure:

_____ Autocratic Decision

_____ Consultation

_____ Group Decision

Notes:

Case 3

Assume that you are an office manager with eight subordinates, each of whom have identical jobs. It is time to set up a vacation schedule for the summer. All of the workers are highly competent, but you can spare only one of them at a time to go on vacation. Each worker gets two weeks of vacation time, but the two weeks do not need to be taken together. Several of the workers have mentioned that they would like to take their vacations in July. Your subordinates are eager for the vacation schedule to be determined so that they can plan their vacations. How would you make this scheduling decision?

Is decision quality important? _____ Yes _____ No

Does the leader have the information to make a high-quality decision alone, without subordinate participation?

_____ Yes _____ No

Is decision acceptance important? _____ Yes _____ No

Is acceptance assured with an autocratic decision?

_____ Yes _____ No

Do subordinates share the leader's task objectives?

_____ Yes _____ No

Cell in Model: _____

Best Procedure:

_____ Autocratic Decision

_____ Consultation

_____ Group Decision

Notes:

Case 4

Assume that you have been appointed the chairperson of a committee formed to coordinate the interdependent activities of several departments in the company. Coordination problems have interfered with the flow of work, causing bottlenecks, delays, and wasted effort. The coordination problems are complex, and solving them requires knowledge of ongoing events in the different departments. Even though you are the designated chairperson, you have no formal authority over the other members, who are not your subordinates. You depend on committee members to return to their respective departments and implement the decisions made by the committee. You are glad that most members appear to be sincerely interested in improving coordination among departments.

Is decision quality important? _____ Yes _____ No

Does the leader have the information to make a high-quality decision alone, without subordinate participation?

_____ Yes _____ No

Is decision acceptance important? _____ Yes _____ No

Is acceptance assured with an autocratic decision?

_____ Yes _____ No

Do subordinates share the leader's task objectives?

_____ Yes _____ No

Cell in Model: _____

Best Procedure:

_____ Autocratic Decision

_____ Consultation

_____ Group Decision

Notes:

Case 5

Assume that you are a store manager in a large chain of retail stores. The manager of another store in town has been caught short-handed, and your boss, the regional manager, has asked you to loan the other store two of your employees for a few days. You know the qualifications of your employees, and there are several who could do the work in the other store. In fact, it would be the same kind of work they are doing now. The work schedule in your store could be adjusted to allow any two of these employees to be away for a few days. It is now evening, and the two employees to be selected must be notified before they report to work tomorrow. How would you decide which two employees to send?

Is decision quality important? _____ Yes _____ No

Does the leader have the information to make a high-quality decision alone, without subordinate participation?

_____ Yes _____ No

Is decision acceptance important? _____ Yes _____ No

Is acceptance assured with an autocratic decision?

_____ Yes _____ No

Do subordinates share the leader's task objectives?

_____ Yes _____ No

Cell in Model: _____

Best Procedure:

_____ Autocratic Decision

_____ Consultation

_____ Group Decision

Notes:

Case 6

Assume that you are the manager of a production facility with five operating departments. The department managers are your immediate subordinates. The budget expenses for your facility have just been reduced, without any reduction in workload. Now you have to decide how much to cut each department's budget. None of the department managers wants to suffer a budget cut, and each believes that his department's activities should have the highest priority. You find it difficult to evaluate how budget cuts would affect each department's capacity to do its work. This evaluation requires more detailed information about the current operations of each department. How would you decide where to make the budget cuts?

Is decision quality important? _____Yes _____No

Does the leader have the information to make a high-quality decision alone, without subordinate participation?

_____Yes _____No

Is decision acceptance important? _____Yes _____No

Is acceptance assured with an autocratic decision?

_____Yes _____No

Do subordinates share the leader's task objectives?

_____Yes _____No

Cell in Model:_____

Best Procedure:

_____Autocratic Decision

_____Consultation

_____Group Decision

Notes:

Case: Alvis Corporation

Kevin McCarthy was the manager of a production department in Alvis Corporation, a non-union firm that manufactures office equipment. After taking a management course that stressed the benefits of participative management, Kevin believed that these benefits could be realized in his department if his workers were allowed to participate in making some decisions on matters that affected them. He selected two decisions for his experiment in participative management.

The first decision involved vacation schedules. Each summer the workers get two weeks vacation, but no more than two workers can go on vacation at the same time. In prior years, Kevin had made this decision himself. He would first ask the workers to indicate their preferred dates, then he considered how the work would be affected if different people were out at the same time. It was important to make sure that vacations were planned in a way to ensure adequate staffing for all the essential operations performed by the department. When more than two workers wanted the same time period, and they had similar skills, he usually gave preference to the workers with the highest productivity.

The second decision involved production standards. Sales had been increasing steadily over the past few years, and the company had recently installed some new equipment to increase productivity. The new equipment would allow Kevin's department to produce more with the same number of workers. The company had a pay-incentive system in which workers received a piece rate for each unit produced above a standard amount. Separate standards existed for each type of product, based on an industrial engineering study conducted a few years earlier. Top management now wanted to readjust the production standards to reflect the fact that the new equipment made it possible for the workers to earn more without working any harder. The savings from higher productivity were needed to pay for the new equipment.

Kevin called a meeting of his 18 workers an hour before the end of the work day. He explained that he wanted them to discuss the two issues and make recommendations. Kevin figured that the workers might be inhibited about participating in the discussion if he were present, so he left them alone to discuss the issues. Besides, Kevin had an appointment to meet with the quality control manager. Quality problems had increased after the new equipment was installed, and the industrial engineers were studying the problem in an attempt to determine why quality had gotten worse rather than better.

When Kevin returned to his department just at quitting time, he was very surprised to learn that the workers recommended keeping the standards the same. He had assumed they knew the pay incentives were no longer fair and that they would set a higher standard. The spokesman for the group explained that their base pay had not kept up with inflation, and the higher incentive pay merely restored their real income to prior levels.

On the vacation issue, the group was deadlocked. Several of the workers wanted to take their vacations during the same two-week period and could not agree on who should go. Some workers argued that they should have priority because they had more seniority, while others argued that priority should be based on productivity, as in the past. Since it was quitting time, the group concluded that Kevin would have to resolve the dispute himself. After all, wasn't that what he was being paid for?

1. Were the two decisions suitable ones for a group decision? Explain your answer in terms of the decision styles model.

2. What mistakes did Kevin make in the way he used a group decision-making procedure for the two decisions?

3. What issues of implementation and timing are involved in making these decisions in an effective manner? Describe how Kevin should have handled each decision.

4. Evaluate how appropriate these decisions were for introducing participation into Kevin's department.

MODULE 5

Supportive Communication

LEARNING OBJECTIVES

After completing this module a student will:

- *Understand common barriers to effective communication.*
- *Understand determinants of effective interpersonal communication.*
- *Understand procedures for active listening and supportive communication.*

Supportive Communication

In the past few decades, the technology for communicating messages from one place to another has advanced greatly, but there has been much less progress in improving interpersonal communication. Communication breakdowns commonly occur in organizations, and they result in a variety of undesirable outcomes, including errors, disagreements, hurt feelings, and hostility. Communication between two people is especially difficult with sensitive, emotional issues, and in relationships that have been strained in the past.

Even under the most ideal conditions, the limitations of language make interpersonal communication difficult. In order to comprehend a message, the recipient must be able to understand the language and to interpret the meaning in the way intended by the communicator. However, the language used in a message seldom means the same thing to the recipient as to the communicator. Meanings are in people rather than in words or symbols. A particular word or symbol may have many meanings, and the meaning to the recipient may not be the same as the intended meaning of the communicator. For example, a sales manager told a shipping supervisor to "rush" an order to an important customer. The sales manager wanted the order shipped by air freight so that it would arrive the next day. The shipping supervisor interpreted "rush" to mean sending a special truck, which cost more and took several days.

Another example is an executive who asked not to be interrupted in a meeting. The executive's secretary refused to send in a message about an impending crisis, and by the time the executive finally received the message, it was too late to prevent the crisis. The executive failed to make it clear that interruptions were okay for some special types of messages.

Use of words or symbols that are unfamiliar to the recipient is likely to impede comprehension. An example is provided by the anecdote about a plumber who discovered that hydrochloric acid opened clogged drains and wrote to a government bureau to inquire if it was a good thing to use. The reply by a bureaucrat was as follows: "The efficacy of hydrochloric acid is indisputable, but the corrosive residue is incompatible with metallic permanence." The plumber was not very well educated and interpreted the message to mean that it was all right to use the acid. After he wrote to the bureau to thank them for their assurance, the bureaucrat sent another message with easier language: "Don't use hydrochloric acid, it eats the hell out of pipes!" Technical terminology and jargon usually facilitate communication with people in the same field of specialization who understand the precise and limited meaning of the words or symbols, but jargon reduces communication to people who are not trained in that field of specialization. It is a common problem for people used to talking with someone in their own specialization to forget and use jargon with people who don't understand the technical meanings.

Sometimes a message contains words or symbols that unintentionally evoke memories and emotions in the recipient and bias the interpretation of the message in ways not anticipated by the communicator. The surplus meaning of the words or symbols changes the intended meaning of the message in ways that may not be desirable. For example, in the early years of commercial aviation, passengers would be told: "We're flying through a storm . . . fasten your safety belts; it will be less dangerous." These instructions caused some passengers to fear that the plane was in danger of crashing. So the language was eventually changed to elicit more pleasant and secure associations. Today passengers are told: "We're flying through some turbulence now; please fasten your seat belts; you will be more comfortable" (Haney, 1973, p. 443).

Communication skills are among the most important determinants of managerial effectiveness. Among the various communication skills, one of the most important is skill in listening. Communication books and chapters usually focus on ways to compose and transmit messages more effectively. Ways to improve listening skills usually receive less attention. Listening means more than just hearing what is said; it means understanding what the person was trying to communicate. This module will emphasize listening skills.

Barriers to Interpersonal Communication

Barriers to interpersonal communication cause the listener to misinterpret what the speaker said, and in some cases, inhibit the speaker from saying more. In addition to language problems, communication barriers include listener tendencies toward over-interpretation, evaluation, and projection. Arrogance on the part of either the speaker or the listener is another barrier. These communication barriers will be examined in more detail.

Over-interpretation

When listening to someone, it is a natural tendency to interpret the meaning and intent of the speaker. However, many times the message is too incomplete and ambiguous to make an accurate interpretation. Many people are prone to jump to conclusions about what the speaker means, and they make little effort to validate their initial impressions. This type of over-interpretation is especially likely when the listener has a strong desire for approval or agreement from the speaker. For example, wanting to believe that a female co-worker is attracted romantically to him, a manager misinterprets willingness to work late on a special project as an invitation to make sexual advances. Over-interpretation is also likely when the speaker is believed to be hostile and untrustworthy. For example, convinced that another manager is opposed to his proposal for a new strategy, a manager misinterprets a suggestion for improving the proposal as a criticism.

With active listening, all impressions and interpretations are treated as tentative until they are verified. Various techniques for validation are used, including asking probing questions, restating comments, and testing interpretations.

Evaluative Tendencies

A common tendency when listening to a message is to make an evaluative response. Making an evaluation means deciding that the message is right or wrong, or that the speaker is good or bad, competent or incompetent. Evaluative responses are especially likely when the communicator says something to arouse anxiety in the listener or make the listener feel uncomfortable. For example, the person may threaten the self-esteem of the listener or question his or her beliefs. Evaluative responses make it more difficult to understand what the person is trying to say. If the evaluation is negative, there is a tendency to dismiss the message as biased or inaccurate. The listener is likely to concentrate on formulating a reply rather than trying to understand what the speaker is saying. When this happens, much of what the speaker says may not be heard at all.

When a negative evaluation is communicated back to the speaker, it is likely to arouse defensiveness and anger. For example, consider the following responses:

"You are wrong about that."

"That was not a very smart thing to do."

"That is a stupid suggestion."

In each case, the response implies that the speaker or the message is without merit. After such a response, relations are likely to deteriorate even more. In the escalating process of verbal attacks and counterattacks, little understanding is likely to occur.

With active listening, covert judgmental responses are avoided, and the listener is careful not to communicate a rejection of the message. The initial objective is to understand the speaker's attitudes and emotions. Any disagreements are handled tactfully, by exploring the basis for the person's assertions or conclusions, rather than by challenging the other person's intelligence or honesty.

Projection and Stereotypes

Empathy means understanding how someone else feels and perceives things. A common tendency is to assume that others feel and perceive things the same way as you do. This tendency to project one's own attitudes and feelings onto others makes it difficult to have empathy for people who do not see things the same way you do. It is common for someone to say, "I know how you feel." However, much of the time we do not know how someone else feels.

Sometimes projection involves attributing your own motives and intentions to another person. For example, a person who exploits others may see them as trying to exploit him or her. A person who is ambitious may incorrectly perceive others to be equally ambitious and eager to get ahead in the organization.

Projection makes empathy difficult when the other person has very different values and personality traits. For example, a person who values material things and assumes that other people hold the same values finds it difficult to understand someone who values spiritual things instead. A person who enjoys competitive activities finds it difficult to understand someone who abhors them. A person with strong self-confidence finds it difficult to understand someone who is very insecure.

Stereotypes are beliefs that a particular category of people all share the same traits and attitudes. National origin, race, sex, age, and religion are commonly stereotyped categories. Like projection, stereotyping impedes communication because the person with the stereotype already believes that he or she understands the speaker. The speaker's comments will be interpreted in the context of these preconceptions, and any aspect of the message that is incongruent with them will tend to be ignored or reinterpreted so that the stereotype can be maintained.

People with effective listening skills make no assumptions about someone's attitudes and perceptions. Instead, they are willing to suspend their biases and preconceptions and make an active effort to discover the other person's values and perceptions. Empathy is sought rather than assumed.

Arrogance and Superiority

People who are arrogant and conceited have difficulty understanding others. They are intolerant of other points of view. Since they assume most people have nothing of value to offer, they fail to listen carefully or to probe to understand the meaning of a message. Such people are so wrapped up in themselves, they are insensitive to the needs and feelings of others. They frequently interrupt or cut off other people and try to dominate the conversation. When giving advice to people, they act superior, thereby decreasing the likelihood that the advice will be accepted. When giving directions or instructions, they tend to be bossy and impatient, thereby increasing the likelihood of resistance. Some examples of arrogant comments are:

"I doubt that you could understand."

"You keep missing the point."

"This is so simple that even you can understand."

Effective communicators view other people as worthy of respect and consideration. They are polite and diplomatic rather than arrogant and conceited when giving instructions or directions. Suggestions are made in a tentative way, rather than with implications that the person is inferior and needs help. When another person is speaking, an effective communicator pays full attention and shows interest in what the other person has to say.

Techniques for Active Listening

Counselors, therapists, and communication scholars have identified a variety of techniques to facilitate active listening. The techniques are designed to put the speaker at ease, to show interest, to express acceptance and respect, to overcome the speaker's inhibitions about revealing what is on his or her mind, and to check if the message has been interpreted accurately. Each technique will be described briefly.

1. Maintain attention.

An obvious indicator of how much you value someone's comments is the amount of attention you pay to the person when he or she is speaking. Attention is indicated by a number of verbal and non-verbal cues, including:

• Maintaining a fairly high degree of eye contact rather than looking around, reading, or writing (except for taking notes on what was said).
• Maintaining an alert posture rather than slouching.
• Avoiding distractions such as shuffling papers, clicking a pen, or rocking the chair back and forth.
• Use of facial expressions and comments to show understanding.

Examples of facial expressions and comments include nodding your head, and saying something like, "Yes, I see what you mean," or "Uh-huh." Such responses show attention and encourage a speaker to continue with a message. However, they do not test your comprehension. It is possible to say "I see" when you actually do not understand what the speaker is trying to say.

2. Use restatement.

Restating or paraphrasing what you believe the speaker has just said offers several benefits. First, it shows the person that you have been listening carefully. Second, it lets you test your understanding.

Rather than assuming comprehension, you have an opportunity to test it. Some examples of restatement lead-ins include the following:

"In other words, you believe that . . ."
"So your position is . . ."
"You are saying . . . , is that correct?"
"Let me see if I understand. You propose to . . ."

This technique can be overused, however. It is most appropriate in situations of apparent conflict or disagreement. For a very simple, uncomplicated message, it is not necessary to test comprehension except perhaps at the end. Summarizing the major points of a fairly long message is a way to test whether you have missed anything important.

3. Show empathy.

People are hesitant to communicate some types of messages, such as the admission of an error, feelings of affection, criticism of someone, or a description of an embarrassing incident, fear of rejection or ridicule. Implying that a person's feelings are unreasonable or improper, or that you disapprove of the person, will inhibit further communication. Some examples of evaluative statements that are likely to have this effect are the following:

"You don't really mean that."
"It is ridiculous to get so upset over this."
"How could you say such a thing?"

The active listener recognizes that it is sometimes necessary to encourage a reluctant speaker to continue beyond an initial, ambiguous reference to a highly emotional experience or an embarrassing subject. One form of encouragement is to show empathy for the person's feelings. If the person has expressed his or her feelings, it is sometimes useful to reflect these feelings, a tactic similar to restating the content of a message. Two examples are:

"So you were angry that the proposal was not even considered."
"So you don't feel that you are getting an opportunity to show what you can do?"

Sometimes, when the speaker has not expressed feelings explicitly, they can only be inferred. Helping to bring feelings out into the open may reduce inhibition in the speaker to continue expressing them in more detail. For example:

"You must have been really upset by that."
"I would have been really embarrassed if that happened to me."

Testing your interpretation of someone's feelings is not without risk, since it may reveal so little empathy that the speaker gives up trying to communicate. People prone to projection will have difficulty inferring feelings in someone who is very different from them. Finally, showing empathy for someone who is emotionally upset may be jeopardized if the listener appears to be completely aloof and indifferent. It is not necessary to mirror a person's emotional state exactly (e.g., extreme anger or fear), but part of showing empathy is to reflect in your speech and manner that you really care about what is happening to the other person.

4. Use probes to draw the person out.

Showing empathy is only one of several tactics for drawing a person out and overcoming inhibitions. Another tactic is the use of silence together with non-verbal indications of interest and attention. Sometimes direct probes such as the following are necessary to encourage somebody to say more:

"What happened next?"
"How did you feel about that?"
"Can you describe a specific incident when that happened?"
"What specific things do you find annoying?"

Probes and questions should be used in a non-threatening manner, and there should be no hint of evaluation or rejection in the tone of voice or wording. Some negative examples are as follows:

"How could you do that to me?"
"Do you have any proof to back up your wild accusations?"

5. Encourage suggestions.

In situations where the person has a problem, it is usually better to have the person try to solve it rather than offering advice. A person may be very sensitive about advice from others, especially if it implies that the person is not as smart or capable. A number of lead-ins can be used to encourage a person to suggest ways to deal with a problem. They are useful also in the situation where you want to get ideas and suggestions from someone who is very shy or insecure.

"What would you recommend?"
"How would you do that?"
"What are the alternatives?"
"What could I do to help?"

In order to encourage suggestions and criticisms from people who are inhibited, it is essential to downplay evaluative responses. Compliment someone for good ideas and insights. Try to find positive aspects of a suggestion before mentioning negative aspects. Express concerns tactfully to avoid threatening the self-esteem of the person. Some negative examples include the following:

"You aren't serious about that?"
"What a ridiculus idea!"
"That has been tried before and it doesn't work."

When you have some concerns about a suggestion made by someone, it is usually possible to express concerns in the form of a question. Also, it is helpful to use the term "we" to emphasize a shared effort. For example:

"What risks would there be for us in that project?"
"Your suggestion is a promising approach for reducing delays, but I am concerned about the cost. Is there any way we could do it without exceeding our budget?"

6. Synchronize interaction.

Communication between two people is more effective if the interaction is managed so that disruptive elements are minimized. Disruption of smooth communication is caused by lack of synchronization between the comments made by the two parties (Wiemann, 1977). Synchronization is reduced when:

- Both people try to talk simultaneously.
- One party keeps interrupting the other.
- One person shifts topics in the middle of a conversation when it is clearly inappropriate.
- One person makes comments that completely disregard what the other person has said previously.

In each case, someone does something that shows lack of respect for the other person. Synchronization is also disrupted by lengthy pauses that occur before or during a person's comments, slowing progress and making the interchange awkward. Effective communicators develop a good sense for the appropriate time to enter a conversation, and the appropriate time to allow the other person to speak. Since different people have different speaking patterns, success requires sensitivity and the flexibility to adjust your own speaking patterns to be compatible with those of another person (Chapple & Sayles, 1961).

Summary

Communication skills are essential for effective management. Even under the best of conditions, accurate communication between two people is difficult to achieve. Communication is impeded when the speaker or listener acts arrogant or superior, when listeners are prone to over-interpretation, projection, and stereotyping, and when listeners are inclined to make evaluative responses. The various techniques for active listening and supportive communication are helpful, but they must be adapted to the needs of the situation and the natural style of the person. The techniques can become manipulative, and they can be overdone to the point where they become barriers rather than facilitators of communication between people. Each technique is based on the belief that showing respect to and acceptance of the other person facilitates communication processes and improves understanding. These attitudes should guide the selection of appropriate techniques for active listening.

References

Athos, A., & Gabarro, J. (1978). *Interpersonal Behavior.* Englewood Cliffs, NJ: Prentice Hall.

Chappel, E., & Sayles, L. (1961). *The Measure of Management.* New York: MacMillan.

Haney, W. V. (1973). *Communication and Organizational Behavior*. Homewood, IL: Irwin.

Murphy, K. J. (1987). *Effective Listening*. New York: Bantam.

Rogers, C., & Farson, R. (1976). *Active Listening*. Chicago: Industrial Relations Center.

Weimann, J. M. (1977). "Explication and Test of a Model of Communicative Competence." *Human Communication Research*, 3, 195–213.

Whetton, D. A., & Cameron, K. S. (1984). *Developing Management Skills*. Glenview, IL: Scott Foresman.

Case: Rejected Plans*

Ellen: How did your meeting go with Peterson yesterday?

Bob: Well, uh, it went . . . aaa . . . it was no big deal.

Ellen: It looks as if you're pretty upset about it.

Bob: Yeah, I am. It was a totally frustrating experience. I, uh, well, let's just say I would like to forget the whole thing.

Ellen: Things must not have gone as well as you had hoped they would.

Bob: I'll say! That guy was impossible. I thought the plans I submitted were very clear and complete. Then he rejected the entire package.

Ellen: You mean he didn't accept any of them?

Bob: You got it.

Ellen: Bob, you do such good work, it's hard for me to figure out why your plans were rejected by Peterson. What did he say about them?

Bob: He said they were unrealistic and too difficult to implement.

Ellen: Really?

Bob: Yeah, and when he said that, I felt he was attacking me personally. But on the other hand, I was also angry because I thought my plans were very good, and I paid close attention to every detail in those plans.

Ellen: I'm certain that you did.

Bob: It just really ticks me off.

Ellen: I'll bet it does. I would be upset, too.

Bob: Peterson must have something against me.

Ellen: After all the effort you put into those plans, you still couldn't figure out whether Peterson was rejecting you or your plans, right?

Bob: Yeah. Right. How could you tell?

Ellen: I can understand the confusion and uncertainty that were caused when you felt Peterson's actions were unreasonable.

Bob: I just don't understand why he did what he did.

Ellen: Sure. If he said your plans were unrealistic, what does that mean? I mean, how can you deal with a rationale like that? It's just too general . . . meaningless, even. Did he mention anything specific? Did you ask him to point out some problems or explain the reasons for his rejection more clearly?

Bob: Good point, but, uh, you know . . . I was so disappointed at the rejection that I was kinda like in outer space. You know what I mean?

Ellen: Yeah. It's an incapacitating experience. You have so much invested personally that you try to divest as fast as you can and forget about it.

Bob: That's it alright. I just wanted to get out of there before I said something I would be sorry for.

Ellen: Yet, in the back of your mind, you probably figured that Peterson wouldn't risk the company's future just because he didn't like you personally. But then, well . . . the plans were good! It's hard to deal with that contradiction on the spot, isn't it!

---

* Adapted from D. A. Whetten and K. S. Cameron, *Developing Management Skills.* Glenview, IL: Scott Foresman and Company, Copyright © 1984.

Bob: Exactly. I knew I should have pushed him for more information, but I just stood there like a dummy. But what can you do about it now? It's spilled milk.

Ellen: I don't think it's a total loss, Bob. I mean, from what you've told me— what he said and what you said—I don't think a conclusion can be reached. Maybe he doesn't understand the plans, or maybe it was just his off day. Who knows, it could be a lot of things. What would you think about pinning Peterson down by asking for his objections, point by point? Do you think it would help to talk to him again?

Bob: Well, I would sure know a lot more than I know now. As it is, I wouldn't know where to begin revising or modifying the plans. And you're right, I really don't know what Peterson thinks about me or my work. Sometimes I just react and interpret with little or no evidence.

Ellen: Maybe, uh . . . maybe another meeting would be a good thing then.

Bob: Well, I guess I should get off my duff and schedule a meeting with him for next week. I am curious to find out what the problem is with the plans, or with me . . . Thanks, Ellen for helping me work through this thing.

Questions for Students

1. What were the communication barriers in the conversation between Bob and Peterson?

2. Describe examples of effective behavior by Ellen.

Case: Allied Industries*

Marvin was the supervisor of the Customer Accounts Department at Allied Industries. An important customer had complained to the industrial sales manager about the "bad service" he had been getting from Marvin's department. Marvin assured the industrial sales manager that he would figure out what the problem was, take steps to make sure it wouldn't happen again, and also calm down the angry customer.

Marvin knew that Sylvia usually handled that particular account, so after pausing for a moment to collect his thoughts, he called Sylvia in to see what she knew about the situation.

Sylvia immediately became angry. "I've had it!" she exclaimed. "That guy has stretched my patience for the last time! He doesn't listen to a word I try to tell him! I don't even know why we do business with that creep! The guy is a chiseler from the word go. He's probably got cash-flow problems and is making excuses so he can delay payment until he can scrounge up another loan from somewhere."

"Hey, come on, Sylvia! You lost me! First off, how on earth did you find out he's got financial problems?"

Sylvia thought for a moment, then replied, "Well, I don't know . . . It seems a pretty good bet to assume he does, though. Otherwise, why would he be trying to bully us into giving him discounts he's not entitled to?"

"Well, look, Sylvia," Marvin replied, "I don't think it's really fair to make assumptions like that."

"OK, OK," conceded Sylvia. "But the guy really is impossible to deal with. I suppose you want me to call him and beg him to forgive me. I could also tell him to disregard the invoices and pay whatever amount pleases him!"

"What I want you to do," said Marvin, ignoring Sylvia's sarcasm, "is to help me figure out what this complaint is all about so we can take some action to get Industrial Sales off our backs. Can we do that?"

"OK," Sylvia agreed, "let me get the records."

Having let off a little steam, Sylvia was able to bring Marvin up to date in her dealings with the customer quickly and efficiently. Only two invoices were in dispute. The customer was not entitled to a discount on the first because it involved special sale items not subject to a discount. The second was a replacement order for goods for which a discount had already been given. Marvin noted that nothing was written on these invoices to explain why the discounts were not allowed. When the customer had called about the invoices, Sylvia said he was very abusive, and she in turn had not gone out of her way to be polite and cooperative.

As Marvin picked up the phone to call the customer, Sylvia started to leave.

"Come on, stick around." Marvin said good-naturedly. "I might need some moral support."

* Adapted from W. J. Wasmuth and L. Greenhalgh, *Effective Supervision, Developing Skills Through Critical Incidents.* Englewood Cliffs, NJ: Prentice Hall, Copyright © 1979.

Sylvia was glad she did, because when Marvin got his first earful of abuse from the customer, a broad "I told you so" grin spread across her face.

"Every damn invoice I get from your department is screwed up," the customer was saying. "I'm tired of spending all my time straightening out other people's mistakes. I haven't dealt with one competent clerk in your department. I don't have this problem with other suppliers, and frankly, I can't think of a good reason why I keep doing business with your company. It's nothing but damn aggravation!"

"Let me be sure I understand what you're saying," Marvin said calmly, now that the customer had paused in his tirade. "You're saying that all the clerks in this department appear to be incompetent. Do I understand you correctly, sir?"

"Well, not all of them. I didn't mean all of them," replied the customer in a slightly less angry tone of voice. "But enough so that I have to spend a lot of time trying to straighten your people out. I'm a very busy man and I've got better things to do . . ."

"Look, sir, could you please clarify something for me?" Marvin interrupted politely. "I was under the impression from talking to the clerk in charge of your account that there are problems with only two of the thirty invoices you've received so far this quarter."

"Well, yes," the customer conceded, somewhat reluctantly. "But what the hell! Those were very important invoices."

"Yes, of course," Marvin agreed, "and I know you're a busy man, so let's you and I clear up these two discount questions that have been bothering you so you can go on to something more important."

As Marvin gave a polite, logical account of the two invoices, he paused frequently and asked whether what he was saying was making sense. At the end of his explanation, the customer seemed satisfied and obviously less angry, especially after Marvin thanked him for bringing to his attention the fact that explanations of special discount situations were not being written on the invoices.

As soon as Marvin hung up the telephone, his secretary brought in a message. His wife had called to report that his son had once again put a baseball through the picture window.

"Dammit," Marvin growled. "Every time I leave the house, I come home and all the windows are broken!"

Sylvia laughed and went back to her desk. She wondered how well Marvin would "practice what he had been preaching" about good communication when he got home.

Questions for Students:

1. What was the cause of the communication breakdown between the customer and Sylvia?

2. Give some examples of effective communication behavior by Marvin when he was dealing with Sylvia.

3. Give some examples of effective behavior by Marvin in dealing with the customer.

EXERCISES IN SUPPORTIVE COMMUNICATION

Instructions

The following exercises are designed to help students apply the concepts and guidelines from the module on supportive communication and to assess their skill in active listening. Read each exercise and answer the questions in the space provided. Additional instructions will be provided by your instructor.

Exercise 1

Assume that you are an office manager in a large insurance company. You have 12 subordinates who process claims. One of your subordinates, Joe McDonald, has been in his current job for only a few weeks and he is having problems learning how to operate the computer. You are meeting with him to discuss this problem. Joe says, "I just can't seem to learn how to use the software program correctly. I tried to get somebody to explain it to me, but the other people in the office are not very helpful. They don't pay any attention to me and seem very annoyed when I ask questions."

Some possible responses to Joe are listed below. In the space beneath each response, explain why it is appropriate or inappropriate for understanding Joe's problem. Use the concepts and guidelines from the module on supportive communication.

1. "The computer is complicated, and it takes a while to learn how to use the new software. Hang in there and keep trying."

2. "You are not trying hard enough. You should spend more time studying the manuals and practicing entries."

3. "I will show you how to use the software. You work on the computer for a while and I will watch to see what you are doing wrong."

4. "I will tell one of the other workers to help you."

5. "Why do you think the other employees won't help you?"

6. "You feel that the other employees in the office don't pay any attention to you?"

Exercise 2

Another subordinate—Jane Jarvis—seems very upset, and you ask her what is wrong. She replies that her car broke down on the highway, and she had to walk a mile in the rain to a gas station to get help. As she was walking along the highway, she twisted her ankle and ruined her expensive new shoes in the mud. She got to work late and is behind on an important claims report due today. Her ankle is sore and she is having a hard time concentrating on the report.

Some possible responses to Jane are listed below. In the space beneath each response, explain why it is appropriate or inappropriate. Use the concepts and guidelines from the module on supportive communication.

1. "It's been a rough day for you, Jane, but that claims report still has to be completed today."

2. "You think that's bad. Let me tell you what happened to me yesterday."

3. "Jane, we need to talk about the schedule for testing the new software."

4. "You can't let these things get you down. Try to forget about it and concentrate on your work."

5. "You must be really upset."

6. "Is there something I can do to help you with the report?"

MODULE 6

Setting Objectives

After completing this module a student will:

- *Understand the different types of goals and the reasons for setting goals.*
- *Understand the appropriate way to write goal statements.*
- *Understand the appropriate level of difficulty at which to set goals.*
- *Understand the appropriate measures to use in setting goals.*
- *Understand the procedures to use in conducting a goal-setting meeting with a subordinate.*

CONTENTS OF MODULE

- *Text: Setting Appropriate Goals*
- *Goal Setting Exercise*
- *Case: Potholes*
- *Goal Setting Role Play*

Setting Appropriate Goals

A goal, or objective, is an explicit intention to achieve a specified result, or outcome. Formal programs for setting objectives, sometimes called "management by objectives" or "management by results" are widely used in large companies in the United States (Schuster & Kendall, 1974). Research finds that specific, challenging goals serve a variety of useful purposes (Locke & Latham, 1984; Morrissey 1977; Raia, 1974). Among the various approaches for clarifying responsibilities and motivating effort, goal setting has the strongest evidence of success (Locke & Latham, 1988; Locke, Shaw, Saari, & Latham, 1981; Tubbs, 1986).

Advantages of Goals

Goals serve a guidance function by directing effort toward performance of important duties and responsibilities. They provide a motivating function by encouraging a person to strive toward completing a task or raising the level of performance. Challenging goals not only increase work effort, they also encourage a person to find more efficient ways to do the work. Goals facilitate evaluation of employee performance by providing a benchmark against which to compare performance. Finally, when goals are set mutually between a manager and a subordinate, or between a manager and a peer, each party knows what the other expects, and misunderstandings are less likely to occur.

Types of Goals

It is useful to distinguish between two major types of goals according to their purpose: performance goals and personal development goals. Performance goals are related to key results or outcomes expected for work activity and are set in terms of outcome measures. Some writers differentiate subvarieties of performance goals. A "maintenance goal" may be set when the existing level of performance is already exceptional, or when it is satisfactory and no improvement is possible due to factors beyond the person's control. A "problem-solving goal" may be set when a current or anticipated problem threatens to reduce performance to an unsatisfactory level, with serious consequences for the work unit. An "innovation goal" may be set when opportunities exist to raise performance, or when higher management wants to start a new project or activity.

Personal development goals are intended to increase the job knowledge and skills of an employee. They are appropriate when anticipated changes in the job, or an expected transfer or promotion, will require the employee to learn new skills. They are appropriate also when additional challenge and growth are necessary to satisfy an employee's desire for personal development and career advancement.

Since every work situation is different, it is not possible to say in advance how many goals of each type are appropriate. The goals set at any given time should reflect the needs of the work situation and the personal development needs of the employee. In general, the total number of goals set for any given performance period (e.g., next quarter, next year) should range from 5 to 9. The true complexity of most jobs will not be captured with fewer than five goals, even if none of them are personal development goals, but more than nine goals is likely to cause excessive confusion about role expectations and frustration in trying to balance competing objectives.

Characteristics of Effective Goal Statements

The effectiveness of a goal depends upon a number of characteristics, and all of these characteristics must be present for a goal to be effective.

Clear and Specific

A goal should be specified in clear, concise language. Statements usually include an action verb and a specific outcome. The outcome may be a quantitative measure or the completion of an activity. Examples of specific, result-oriented goal statements include the following:

"Increase monthly sales to 500 units."
"Complete the training of three new employees by January 1."

Statements like "do your best" and "make a substantial improvement" are vague and should not be used. A goal statement should include only one outcome. Unnecessary detail, such as justification for the goal or the action plan to attain it, should not be included in the goal statement.

Measurable and Verifiable

If possible, a goal should be stated in terms of a quantitative measure of results. It is best to use a measure that is objective and reliable. The goal can be stated in relative terms (for example, "improve production by 10 percent"), but it is less confusing to use abolute terms (for example, "an average daily output of 200 units"). If an accurate measure is not available and cannot be developed, then the next best thing is an activity for which successful completion can be verified. For example, it is usually possible to verify that a goal to implement a policy, train an employee, attend a workshop, or complete a report has been completed in a satisfactory manner. Note that some subjectivity may be necessary in making a judgment about "satisfactory" completion, but the indicators to be used and the criteria for determining what is satisfactory should be specified in advance (such as a report by a reliable third party that a task is finished, or passing scores obtained by a trainee on an achievement test).

Time Bounded

A goal statement should include a target date or deadline for accomplishment. The date should be specific (for example, "June 1, 1990") not vague (such as "by spring," or "as soon as possible"). A specific deadline, like a specific result, reduces the chance of misunderstandings about what is expected.

Challenging but Realistic

A goal should be difficult enough to be <u>perceived as a challenge.</u> This does not necessarily mean that it should require an improvement in performance. If performance is already at an exceptional level, it may be challenging just to maintain this level, especially if conditions are worsening. The goal should be challenging but not so difficult that it appears impossible or unrealistic. In determining whether a goal is realistic, it is useful to consider prior performance by the same person, performance by people in comparable positions, available resources, likely conditions that will affect performance, and the amount of time until the deadline. A goal is probably too easy if it calls for little or no improvement in performance when conditions are becoming more favorable, or if the targeted level of performance is well below that of most other employees in comparable positions. A goal is probably too difficult if it calls for a large improvement in performance when conditions are worsening, or if the targeted level of performance is well above that of people in comparable positions.

Relevant

Goals should be set for <u>results related to primary responsibilities.</u> When trivial goals are set, they interfere with attainment of more important goals by competing for attention, time, and energy. Goals should not be stated in terms of an activity that is only a means to a desired result. For example, a goal involving product quality should be stated in terms of reducing quality defects, not in terms of increasing the frequency of inspections. Inspection is merely one of several possible action steps that may help to reduce defects, and it is possible that more inspections would merely increase costs without improving quality. With respect to personal development goals, they should have relevance to the organization as well as to the employee. For example, it is not enough to set a goal for the employee to attend a workshop; the subject of the workshop should be relevant to the employee's current position in the organization, or to a higher position for which the employee is being prepared.

Cost Effective

The results of attaining the goal <u>should justify the expected costs</u> in resources and work hours. There is usually a tradeoff between goal difficulty and cost. The harder a goal is, the more effort and resources are needed to attain it, and the greater is the cost.

Selection of Measures

In setting goals for a particular results area, such as quality of performance or relations with subordinates, there are usually a variety of outcome measures that can be used. No measure is perfect, but some are better than others. It is useful to consider several aspects of outcome measures.

Controllable versus Uncontrollable Outcomes

Some performance outcomes are more controllable by an employee than others, and controllable outcomes are more appropriate for goal setting. For example, if the manager of a profit center (such as a product manager or a manager of a product division) has more potential to influence profit margin than sales volume, then the former is a more appropriate measure of performance. On the other hand, for a sales department that has no control over available products, product costs, or marketing costs, sales volume may be a more appropriate measure than profits generated by the sales. It is more difficult to measure performance by someone who is part of a team than performance by someone who works alone. To evaluate someone who is part of a team, measures based on the person's contribution to the team are more appropriate than measures of overall team performance.

Multiple versus Composite Measures

Sometimes there is no single indicator that accurately represents a results area. When there are multiple outcomes for a results area, it is necessary to choose between setting a separate goal for each outcome or setting a single goal in terms of a composite outcome measure. When a composite measure is used, the relative importance of each component must be determined in order to assign differential weights to the component outcomes. For example, if a sales representative has several products with different profit margins, and the goal is to be set in terms of overall sales, then some type of differential weighting may be necessary to encourage the person to emphasize sales of more profitable products. In this case, the easiest solution is to use total profits generated by sales rather than sales volume. Likewise, if dissatisfied customers can return a product, then sales may need to be adjusted to reflect the cost of returns, both in terms of lost sales and overhead costs. The goal should encourage the employee to be concerned about satisfying the customer's needs, rather than merely pushing products that are easy to sell, or using high-pressure sales methods, without concern for customer satisfaction. In this case, the composite goal could be set in terms of adjusted profits. However, the more adjustments are made to a composite measure, the more difficult it becomes to interpret reasons for particular results. For example, if adjusted profits decline, it could be due to lower sales or to higher returns, or both.

The more difficult it is to form a composite measure and interpret it, the more reason there is to set goals in terms of individual outcome measures. However, when a separate goal is set for outcomes representing the same results area, it is still necessary to determine the relative priorities of each goal in order to evaluate overall performance in this results area. For example, if quality of the product is measured in terms of inspection reports and customer complaints, it is necessary to decide whether these two outcomes will be weighted equally or whether one will be given priority. The weighting of each outcome determines how much attention and effort is devoted to it in relation to the others.

One-time versus Repeated Measures

It is usually necessary to decide the frequency of measurement for outcomes and the time interval in which to aggregate the data. The accuracy of a measure is greater if it is obtained repeatedly over a period of time rather than only once. Multiple measures averaged over time provide a more accurate indicator of performance because random fluctuations are smoothed out. A longer time interval is especially appropriate for events that rarely occur such as accidents and turnover. However, it is not always easy to determine the appropriate time period for which to aggregate measures. For example, if sales are measured on a daily basis, they could be reported in terms of daily sales, weekly sales, monthly sales, or quarterly sales. A short time period provides information about the trend of performance and how rapidly it is improving or declining. Short measurement periods also provide more opportunity to monitor improvement if there are performance deficiencies. However, reliability is usually lower for short time periods; furthermore, it may be more expensive to collect data frequently, and the measurement process may intrude upon the work.

The most appropriate time interval for measuring results will vary from one type of job to another, and from one results area to another. Usually some compromise is appropriate to balance the tradeoffs. Sometimes it is not feasible to obtain a measure more than once a year due to the extreme difficulty and/or cost of obtaining it. Such a measure may still be appropriate as a basis for setting a goal if there is reason to believe it is fairly accurate (for example, an annual survey of employees or clients).

Subjective versus Objective Measures

A final choice involves the use of objective or subjective measures. Each approach has limitations.

It is difficult to obtain objective outcome measures that are not seriously contaminated by extraneous factors. For example, sales volume or profits for a regional manager may be partly dependent upon how favorable the region is compared to those of other regional managers. An objective sales criterion gives an unfair advantage to a manager in a favorable region, and the performance of the managers cannot be compared to evaluate goal difficulty unless some type of handicapping adjustment is made to compensate for these extraneous factors. A similar problem of contamination exists for production measures for two machine operators, one with a new, highly efficient machine and one with an old, inefficient machine. Here again, to compare managers in terms of objective measures of production output requires some type of adjustment for machine differences. One remedy is to compare a person only to his or her prior performance in the same situation. Here, goals can be set in terms of improvement over prior performance. However, conditions may change over time. For example, one machine operator may have a machine that is breaking down more often as it gets older, causing performance to decline through no fault of the employee. Thus, as conditions change, adjustments are again necessary to reduce contamination of the criterion by extraneous variables.

Subjective outcome measures consist of performance ratings or behavior ratings. Somebody, such as the boss of an employee, rates the employee's performance on each results area, or rates how often the employee displays effective behaviors. Subjective ratings are usually biased by typical human errors such as incorrect assumptions and attributions. Subjective ratings of behavior are more likely to be accurate if the rater has ample opportunity to observe the person's behavior and keep notes or a diary. Subjective ratings of results areas such as performance quality and effectiveness are more likely to be accurate if the rater has information about objective indicators of these results and knowledge about extraneous factors to take into account. One approach to reduce error is to have multiple raters for the same employee. Averaging the ratings from different raters often provides a more accurate measure. However, sometimes there is only a single rater with enough information to make an accurate rating and, here, averaging across multiple raters is unlikely to improve accuracy.

Setting Goals for Subordinates

Managers need to be skilled not only in setting goals for themselves, but also in managing the process of goal setting for subordinates. It is desirable to hold goal-setting meetings at least once a year with each subordinate. The meeting should be scheduled early in the new business year to provide clear direction for the work to be done. The purpose of the meeting is to clarify expectations for a subordinate and to facilitate coordination of plans for the work unit. Goal-setting meetings usually involve considerable planning and negotiating between manager and subordinate. Ample time should be set aside for the meeting (one or two hours), and it should be held at a time when interruptions are unlikely to occur.

How to Prepare for a Goal-setting Meeting

When scheduling the goal-setting meeting, the manager should inform the subordinate how to prepare for it. The manager should ask the subordinate to prepare a list of responsibilities, a summary of information about prior performance, proposed goals for key results areas, and proposed action plans for attaining each goal. The manager needs to determine whether the action plans should be detailed or sketchy. If feasible, the subordinate's information and proposals should be submitted prior to the meeting to help the manager prepare for it. However, in some cases, with very trusted and competent subordinates, it is okay to have the subordinate present the information and proposals at the goal-setting meeting. For his or her part, the manager should supply the subordinate with any relevant information needed to prepare goals and plans.

Just before the meeting, the manager should review information about the subordinate's performance, goals, and plans. The manager should also use available information about earlier performance, performance by others in comparable positions, and information about changing conditions and trends to evaluate whether each goal is challenging and realistic, and the action plans are feasible. It is common for the manager to develop some counter-proposals when a subordinate's goals appear too easy or too difficult. At this time, the manager should also determine the relative priority of the different goals. The priority of a goal will be higher if it is necessary for the attainment of the manager's own goals, if it involves a key results area with important implications for the orgnization, and if it is important for the subordinate's career. Proposals from different subordinates should be examined for compatibility with each other and with the goals and plans of the manager. Personal development goals for the subordinate should be considered at this time also, not just performance goals. In addition, the manager may have some goals or activities mandated by higher management to communicate to the subordinate.

Guidelines for Conducting Goal-setting Meetings

1. Review the purpose of the meeting with the subordinate and show enthusiasm that it will be mutually beneficial.

2. Briefly review the relative priorities for different results areas in the subordinate's job, and identify the highest priority results area.

3. Ask the subordinate to review his or her proposed goal and action plan for this results area.

4. Discuss whether the goal is challenging and realistic in light of prior performance, performance by comparable units or employees, and information about factors likely to affect performance.

5. Discuss the subordinate's proposed action plan and identify any aspects in need of revision, including aspects that would create coordination problems across subordinates and with other units in the organization.

6. Reach agreement on an action plan and the necessary resources and assistance to be provided by the manager.

7. Go on to the next most important results area and repeat the process (steps 3 through 6).

8. When all goals have been discussed separately, consider their collective feasibility and make any adjustments required to eliminate inconsistencies, to coordinate related activities, and to allocate resources appropriately, according to priorities.

9. Summarize all agreements and record them in writing, using an appropriate form, and give a copy to the subordinate.

10. Set the date for the first progress review meeting.

If the subordinate proposes a goal that appears too easy, or the deadline appears too distant, as part of steps 4 through 6 the manager should:

- Ask the subordinate to identify obstacles preventing better performance or a shorter deadline.
- Invite the subordinate to suggest ways to overcome these obstacles. If appropriate, suggest possibilities overlooked by the subordinate.
- If appropriate, offer additional resources or extra assistance to aid the subordinate in attaining a more difficult goal or a shorter deadline.
- After considering the obstacles and resource requirements to overcome them, re-evaluate whether the goal is indeed too easy (the difficulties may have been underestimated).

Procedure if the Goal Appears Unrealistic

Sometimes the subordinate proposes a goal or deadline that appears to be unrealistic. In this event, as part of steps 4 through 6 the manager should:

- Show appreciation for the subordinate's desire to achieve difficult goals but reiterate the importance of setting realistic goals.
- Probe for reasons why the subordinate expects the action plan to succeed, especially if it is untested or has failed previously. Look for biased forecasts and unjustified assumptions about likely outcomes of actions.
- Probe for factual information and assumptions used in making time estimates for key action steps to see if these are over-optimistic.
- Probe for unrealistic assumptions about the availability of supplies, funding, equipment, facilities, support services, and personnel, including cooperation from people in other work units and outsiders.
- After considering this information, if it becomes obvious that the goal is unrealistic, or that it could be attained only at an excessive cost, mutually set a more realistic goal.

Coordinating across Levels and Units

It is important for managers to coordinate the goals of different subordinates with their own goals and with the goals of people in other units with interrelated tasks. Managers also need to coordinate their goals with those of higher management. Coordination can be achieved only through a process of successive mutual adjustments among levels and between units. This process is difficult and complex, and there is no easy way to do it. Sometimes it is necessary to hold meetings with several people to develop coordinated plans and schedules. In the special case of teams, it may be more feasible just to set group goals rather than individual goals. When setting goals for subordinates who are themselves managers, some flexibility should be allowed for subordinates to negotiate with their own subordinates. In general, managers should recognize the need for initial flexibility in their goals and plans until coordination problems are resolved. For jobs with complex interrelationships and unpredictable environments, coordination problems are never resolved entirely, and initial goals and plans may need to be revised frequently during the course of the year.

Viewed in this light, the task of mutual goal setting and action planning appears formidable, but it can be very beneficial if managers do not lose sight of the purpose. Goal setting is a management tool, not an end in itself, and procedures must be adapted to the manager's needs and the realities of the situation.

References

Giegold, W. C. (1978). *Management by Objectives: A Self-instructional Process. Volume 2: Objective Setting and The MBO Process.* New York: McGraw-Hall.

Latham, G. P., & Yukl, G. (1975). "A Review of Research on The Application of Goal Setting in Organizations." *Academy of Management Journal,* 18, 824–845.

Locke, E. A., & Latham, G. P. (1984). *Goal Setting: A Motivational Technique That Works.* Englewood Cliffs, NJ: Prentice Hall.

Locke, E. A., Shaw, K. N., Saari, L. M., & Latham, G. P. (1981). "Goal Setting and Task Performance." *Psychological Bulletin,* 90, 125–152.

McConkie, M. L. (1979). "A Clarification of the Goal Setting and Appraisal Processes in MBO." *Academy of Management Review,* 29–40.

Mento, A. J., Steele, R. P., & Karren, R. J. (1987). "A Meta-analytic Study of the Effects of Goal Setting on Task Performance: 1966–1984." *Organizational Behavior and Human Decision Processes,* 39, 52–83.

Morrissey, G. L. (1977). *Management by Objectives and Results for Business and Industry.* Reading, MA: Addison-Wesley.

Raia, A. P. (1974). *Managing by Objectives.* Glenview, IL: Scott-Foresman.

Schuster, F., & Kendall, A. F. (1974). "Management by Objectives, Where We Stand—A Survey of The Fortune 500." *Human Resource Management,* Spring, 8–11.

Tubbs, M. E. (1986). "Goal Setting: A Meta-analytic Examination of the Empirical Evidence." *Journal of Applied Psychology,* 71, 474–483.

Weihrich, H. (1985). *Management Excellence: Productivity Through MBO*. New York: McGraw-Hall.

GOAL SETTING EXERCISE

The purpose of this exercise is to provide an opportunity to determine if you understand how to write goal statements, set goals that are challenging but realistic, and select appropriate measures of results. The exercise has three parts: (1) writing goal statements; (2) setting goal levels; and (3) selecting indicators.

Part 1: Goal Statements

Instructions

Read each goal statement, determine what is wrong with it, and write a better one.

Goal 1: Complete the required training of new employees as soon as possible.

Goal 2: Reduce the error rate in the department to an acceptable level by the end of the year.

Goal 4: Eliminate all customer complaints by summer.

Goal 3: Reduce unit cost on the new product to $80 by implementing new work procedures immediately.

Part 2: Goal Difficulty

Instructions

For each goal, consider the background information and determine whether the goal is easy (E), challenging (C), or unrealistic (U). Put the appropriate letter code on the line provided next to the goal to indicate your evaluation of goal difficulty. Note that deadlines are worded in a way to indicate how much time is available to implement the goal.

_____ 1. Goal: Reduce average daily error rate to 5% by the end of next quarter.

The error rate for the department was 7% during the last quarter and 8% the quarter before last. The error rate last quarter for three similar departments was 5%, 4%, and 6%, respectively.

Notes:

_____ 2. Goal: Attain a production level of 75 units/day for next two quarters.

The production output for a manufacturing plant was 70 units/day for the quarter just ended. Production for the three previous quarters was 80, 75, and 85 units/day. The company is in a stable industry without major changes in products or technology.

Notes:

_____ 3. Goal: Increase the number of safety inspections by 25% next year.

The budget does not allow for any increase in inspection personnel for next year. The inspectors in the department are currently making around 10 percent more safety inspections than last year or the year before.

Notes:

_____ **4.** Goal: Attain a productivity index score of 75 for the next year.

For the year just ended, a composite productivity index for the data processing department was 60 on a scale of zero to one hundred. The new computer system to be installed next month is expected to increase productivity by around 25%.

Notes:

_____ **5.** Goal: Reduce absenteeism in the department to 5% by the end of the next quarter.

The rate of absenteeism for the department last year was 10%. The average rate of absenteeism was 6% and 5% for two other operating departments in the company with similar employees and type of work.

Notes:

_____ **6.** Goal: Reduce unit cost to $85 by the end of the coming year.

Unit cost for output in a production department was $100 for the year just ended. In the previous three years it was $95, $90, and $92. Unit cost for another production department in the company that makes the same product and has comparable employees was $80 last year.

Notes:

Part 3: Selecting Relevant Indicators

Instructions

For each results area, determine which three indicators are likely to provide the most relevant and accurate measure of a manager's performance. Place a check on the line next to your three choices. Under the 3 rejected choices write a brief explanation why they are not as relevant or accurate.

1. Maintain efficient operation of a service center (such as equipment repair, consulting services, information gathering services, etc.).

   _____ a. Monthly operating cost of the service program.

   _____ b. Number of clients per month given service.

   _____ c. Average cost per client of service provided.

   _____ d. Operating costs as a percentage of budgeted costs.

   _____ e. Average man-hours/client required to provide service.

   _____ f. Monthly cost of salaries for service personnel.

2. Design and conduct effective and efficient training programs (personnel department or training center).

   _____ a. Number of training hours conducted per month.

   _____ b. Number of employees trained to required levels of proficiency.

   _____ c. Average cost per trainee of training provided.

   _____ d. Ratings by trainees at end of training on how much they learned.

   _____ e. Ratings by trainees at end of training on how much they enjoyed it.

   _____ f. Improvement in knowledge determined by comparing scores on a test given before and after training.

3. Maintain effective interpersonal relations with subordinates.

_____ a. Turnover among subordinates.

_____ b. Ratings of a manager's interpersonal skills made by subordinates.

_____ c. Number of subordinate grievances and complaints about the manager.

_____ d. Subordinate productivity.

_____ e. Ratings by subordinates of satisfaction with the manager.

_____ f. Monthly quality index for subordinate performance.

4. Process applicant requests for social services and notify applicants promptly (government agency or welfare office, or volunteer social service organization).

_____ a. Average response time from receipt of application to response.

_____ b. Number of applicant complaints about delays.

_____ c. Average number of visits to center required before decision is made.

_____ d. Number of applications processed each month.

_____ e. Average employee man-hours required to process an application.

_____ f. Percentage of applications processed within a specified number of days.

Case: Potholes and More Potholes

In snow belt regions, rapid weather changes at certain times of the year cause potholes to form in the roads. The potholes make driving unpleasant and can cause damage to vehicles. The administrator of the Metropolis Highway Department believed that road crews assigned to fill potholes were not working fast enough. He decided to initiate a goal-setting program to improve the performance of the road crews. After conducting some time studies to determine how long it should take to fill a pothole, the administrator set a standard at 20% above the current average number of potholes filled per day. The same standard was used for all of the crews. Road crews were instructed to record the location of each pothole they filled on a work sheet. Supervisors spot-checked on a random basis to make sure the records were accurate, and they reviewed performance at weekly intervals to determine if each crew achieved the standard. Weekly performance data were posted on a bulletin board so that the crews could compare their performance. In order to encourage a sense of friendly competition and further motivate the workers, the best crew was identified each week and given a special award.

At first, the program seemed to be working out well. The number of potholes filled each week increased. However, complaints from drivers about pothole damage to their cars did not decrease. In checking the records, it was discovered that some of the worst potholes were ones that had been filled just recently. Further investigation revealed that many of the crews were not following all of the recommended procedures for doing the work. In order to fill the holes more quickly, crews were skipping some of the steps needed to ensure that the repairs would last more than a few weeks.

Questions for Students

1. Evaluate the goal-setting program and identify mistakes made by the administrator.

2. What could have been done to make the program more successful?

GOAL SETTING ROLE PLAY

Instructions

The purpose of this role play is to give students an opportunity to experience what it is like to conduct a goal-setting meeting with a subordinate. The role play also provides an opportunity to practice and strengthen skills, including listening skills, conflict management skills, and planning skills, that determine whether a goal-setting meeting will be effective.

For this role play it will be necessary to form three-person groups and determine for each group who will play the role of the boss, who will play the role of subordinate, and who will be the observer. Do not look at the materials or instructions for any other role than the one you have been selected to play.

If you have been selected to be the boss or subordinate, take about 10 minutes to read your role and plan what you will say. Students selected to be observers should study the instructions for observers and the form for taking notes on how well the meeting was handled. These notes will be the basis for feedback to the students who play the role of the boss.

In the role play, the quantity goal should be discussed and agreement reached before going on to discuss the quality goal.

Role for Boss

You are the vice president of a product division in a large multi-national manufacturing company. You manage several facilities that produce paint and other types of protective coatings. Your subordinate in this role play is the manager of a plant that makes paint. It is now January 15, and you are holding a meeting to jointly determine the performance goals for the subordinate. Goals are typically set for several aspects of plant performance, but this role play will concentrate on only two: quantity of output (measured in terms of gallons per day), and quality (percentage of defective batches). Both are high-priority goals, but quantity is slightly more important than quality.

Production for last year was 15,000 gallons per day. This level of output was the highest of the division's four paint plants. The plant is currently producing at capacity, but you believe that output can be increased if two additional mixing tanks are installed. You have discussed this subject with your subordinate in an earlier meeting and have agreed to purchase the new mixing tanks. The tanks have been ordered already, and they are scheduled to be installed and operational by March 1. Installation will be done by the maintenance department's product division, which reports directly to you. The specifications for the new equipment suggest that it would increase production by at least 3,000 gallons per day. Thus, you consider a goal of 18,000 gallons per day by March 15 to be realistic. You are willing to consider some additional expenditures to increase output as long as they do not exceed budget limitations. For example, if needed, you are willing to replace worn parts on some of the older equipment, or to hire one or two additional workers to operate the new equipment.

The percentage of defective batches of paint last year was 7% for your subordinate's plant. The average for the other three paint plants last year was 4% (the rate was 5% for one plant, 4% for the second, and 3% for the third). You would like to see the defective batch rate for your subordinate's plant reduced to 4% by the end of December. You expect the plant manager to make some concrete proposals, but you are concerned that he/she may be too optimistic about the potential for improving quality. Getting down to the division average is a challenging goal, and to do more in one year may be unrealistic. However, you are open-minded and willing to consider the subordinate's plans as long as they are not too expensive. Since some of the problems involve worker errors, one promising strategy that you learned in a management development workshop is to get the workers committed to the quality goals and provide them with daily feedback about quality so they can monitor their own progress. You may want to recommend that your subordinate add this to his/her list of action strategies.

In conducting this goal-setting meeting, use the guidelines presented in the text for the goal-setting module. Use the Goal Planning Record form to record agreements about goals, key action strategies, and resources or support to be provided to the subordinate. Normally, a copy of the completed form would be provided to the subordinate after the goal-setting meeting.

Goal Planning Record

Subordinate:

Date of meeting:

Goal #1 and deadline:

Priority:
Action Strategy:

Notes:

Goal #2 and deadline:

Priority:
Action Strategy:

Notes:

Role for Subordinate

You are the plant manager of a facility that makes paint. Your boss manages a product division in a large multi-national manufacturing company. The division has several facilities that produce paint and other types of protective coatings. It is now January 15, and you are meeting with your boss to jointly determine the performance goals for your plant. Goals are set for several aspects of plant performance, but this role play will involve only two goals: quantity of output (measured in terms of gallons per day), and quality (percentage of defective batches). Both are high-priority goals, but you are not sure which goal is more important to your boss.

Production by your plant for last year was 15,000 gallons per day. This level of output was the highest of the division's four paint plants. You have done everything you can think of to increase production, and the plant is now operating at capacity. Your boss has agreed to purchase two new mixing tanks to increase output even more, and they are scheduled to be installed and operational by March 1. However, you have doubts that the new tanks will be operational by that date. The tanks would be installed by the maintenance department which is already overloaded with work at some of the other plants. Since the manager of the maintenance department reports to your boss, you hope that your boss will intercede to ensure quick service on the installation of the new mixing tanks.

Another potential problem involves the personnel needed to operate the new equipment. You estimate that two new employees will be needed, and that it will take at least six weeks to hire and train them if all goes well. However, it is difficult to find qualified people in the current tight labor market. If it takes longer than six weeks to hire and train the workers, the March 1 target date for making the new tanks operational will not be met.

Another concern is whether production on the existing equipment can be maintained at the current high level. Operating at capacity reduces the amount of time available for preventative maintenance on the equipment. Equipment breakdowns have been increasing in recent months, and breakdowns result in lower output. You are especially concerned that the valves on the filling machines are worn and will need to be replaced soon. Replacing the valves will be an expensive job, but you don't see any alternative to avoid frequent breakdowns. Considering all of the potential problems, you plan to propose a goal of 16,000 gallons per day to be achieved by April 15.

For the quality goal, you plan to propose that defective batches will be reduced from the current rate of 7% to 2% by the end of December. You have three strategies for achieving this goal. The first is the replacement of the valves on the mixing machines, which are sometimes a source of defective batches. The second strategy is to double the frequency of batch sampling to detect any quality problems faster. The third strategy is to provide additional instruction to plant personnel in adjusting equipment settings properly for different types of paint. The latter two strategies would not be expensive. You are hopeful that the three strategies together will eliminate most quality problems, although you don't know for certain.

Goal Planning Record

Subordinate:

Date of meeting:

Goal #1 and deadline:

Priority:
Action Strategy:

Notes:

Goal #2 and deadline:

Priority:
Action Strategy:

Notes:

Instructions for Observer

Use the observer's form to take notes on how well the goal-setting meeting was conducted. These notes will be used after the role play is finished to provide feedback to the student who played the role of the boss. Record whether each of the recommended steps was carried out, and take notes on effective and ineffective behaviors. If necessary, remind the role players that they are supposed to reach agreement on the quantity goal before going on to the quality goal.

Background Information

The boss is the vice president of a product division in a large multinational manufacturing company; he/she manages several facilities that produce paint and other types of protective coatings. The subordinate is the manager of a plant that makes paint. It is now January 15, and they are meeting to determine the performance goals for the subordinate. Goals are typically set for several aspects of plant performance, but this role play will concentrate on only two: quantity of output (measured in terms of gallons per day) and quality (percentage of defective batches).

Production for last year was 15,000 gallons per day, and the plant is currently producing at capacity. This level of output was the highest of the division's four paint plants. In an earlier meeting, the boss and subordinate had agreed to purchase two new mixing tanks to increase production output even more. The boss expects the new equipment to be installed and operational by March 1. He/she wants to see production increase to 18,000 gallons per day by March 15. The subordinate has some concerns about potential problems with installing the new mixing tanks on schedule, hiring workers to operate the equipment, and replacing worn valves in the older filling machines. He/she will propose a goal of 16,000 gallons per day to be achieved by April 15. If the potential problems can be dealt with adequately, this goal is too low and should be adjusted upward (17,000 to 18,000 gallons per day). However, the target date may need to be revised to sometime in April in order to allow for likely delays in hiring and training new employees and replacing the worn valves.

The percentage of defective batches of paint last year was 7% for the subordinate's plant. The average for the other three paint plants last year was 4% (the rate was 5% for one plant, 4% for the second, and 3% for the third). The boss would like to see the defective batch rate for the subordinate's plant reduced to 4% by the end of December. He/she believes this is a challenging goal, and to do more in one year may be unrealistic. The subordinate will propose a goal of 2%, which is unrealistically low. Resolution of the differences on goal level will involve discussion of the potential action strategies. It is likely that agreement will occur on a more realistic goal of 3 to 4 percent defective batches.

Observer Form

Record whether the "boss" did each recommended behavior and note any especially effective or ineffective aspects of the person's behavior.

1. Review purpose of the meeting with subordinate and show enthusiasm that it will be mutually beneficial.   YES   NO

   Notes:

2. Review the key results areas for which goals should be set and discuss relative priorities.   YES   NO

   Notes:

   Goal #1 (Quantity)

3. Review relevant data on prior performance and performance for any comparable units or employees.   YES   NO

   Notes:

4. Ask the subordinate to propose a challenging but realistic goal and an action strategy to achieve it.   YES   NO

   Notes:

5a. If the goal appears too easy, ask the subordinate to identify obstacles which prevent better performance or a shorter deadline, and ask the subordinate to suggest ways of overcoming these obstacles.   YES   NO

Notes:

6. If appropriate, suggest additional action strategies to improve performance, offer extra resources if justified by goal priority, and offer personal assistance if needed to implement the plans.   YES   NO

Notes:

7. Reach tentative agreement on a challenging but realistic goal and deadline and a tentative action strategy; record these and other agreements.
YES   NO

Notes:

Goal #2 (Quality)

3. Review relevant data on prior performance and performance for any comparable units or employees.   YES   NO

Notes:

4. Ask the subordinate to propose a challenging but realistic goal and an action strategy to achieve it.   YES   NO

Notes:

5b. If the goal or deadline appears too difficult, ask the subordinate to explain assumptions about causal effects, available resources, difficulty of overcoming obstacles, and estimated time needed to accomplish key action steps.   YES   NO

Notes:

5c. Discuss whether assumptions and predictions are realistic, and whether expected resources are feasible. Show appreciation for efforts to achieve difficult goals, but if necessary, reiterate the importance of realistic goals and plans.   YES   NO

Notes:

6. If appropriate, suggest additional action strategies to improve performance, offer extra resources if justified by goal priority, and offer personal assistance if needed to implement the plans.   YES   NO

Notes:

7. Reach tentative agreement on a challenging but realistic goal and deadline and a tentative action strategy; record these and other agreements. YES   NO

Notes:

8. Review all goals and plans for consistency, and make any necessary adjustments to reflect interdependencies among goals and differing priorities.   YES   NO

    Notes:

9. Summarize understanding of all goals and plans, and record any necessary changes in the written record.   YES   NO

    Notes:

10. Set date for first progress review meeting.   YES   NO

    Notes:

Action Planning

After completing this module a student will:

- *Understand why action planning is important.*
- *Understand the basic components of an action plan.*
- *Understand the procedures for developing an action plan.*
- *Understand how to evaluate an action plan.*

CONTENTS OF MODULE

- *Text: Action Planning*
- *Planning Exercise*
- *Case: Sterling Products*

Action Planning

When planning how to accomplish an objective or attain a goal, it is necessary first to identify potential strategies and select one that appears feasible and cost effective. This process is usually referred to as strategic planning or strategy formation. Action planning is a process of determining how to implement a strategy or carry out a project in an effective manner. In the case of action planning for a defined project such as building a new plant, developing a new product, or formulating a marketing campaign for a client, the project itself is the strategy for accomplishing some objective. This module will focus on the planning process that occurs after a general strategy has been selected or the basic nature of a project has been determined.

As defined here, systematic action planning includes four related phases:

1. **Programming:** Identify the action steps necessary to carry out the general strategy or project, and determine the optimal sequence for these action steps.
2. **Scheduling:** Estimate the amount of time needed to carry out each action step, and determine the optimal starting times and deadlines for each step.

3. **Budgeting:** Estimate the cost of each action step, including the cost of necessary resources and support services.
4. **Controlling:** Fix accountability for each action step and develop procedures for monitoring progress and detecting problems.

Why Action Planning is Important

There are many reasons why action planning is important for managers. The process of systematic action planning helps to identify better ways to accomplish an objective. Action plans result in better estimates of the time needed to carry out a strategy, thereby resulting in more realistic deadlines for carrying out projects and accomplishing objectives. Action plans help to avert delays caused by failure to carry out a critical action step, or failure to start the action step early enough. Action plans aid in estimating the likely cost of a proposed strategy, thereby enabling a manager to evaluate it by comparing costs with benefits. Action plans help to identify critical action steps where potential problems are likely to be most serious when implementing a strategy. Action plans make it easier to monitor progress when implementing a strategy or carrying out a project. Schedules, checkpoints, budget estimates, and so forth facilitate early detection of delays, problems, or cost overruns. Action plans facilitate the delegation of responsibility to subordinates. Finally, action planning facilitates coordination among managers at different levels, and laterally with peers.

Action Planning with Others

Action planning is not conducted in a vacuum. It is essential to coordinate action plans across levels of the organization, and among interrelated subunits. The action plans of a manager and subordinate are closely related. Subordinates help to implement a manager's action plans, and a subordinate's own action plans depend greatly on the plans developed by superiors. When it is appropriate for a manager's subordinates to develop action plans of their own, it is the manager's responsibility to review and authorize these plans. The manager should evaluate feasibility, cost effectiveness, and compatibility with his or her own plans and objectives. Typically, the manager will ask for additional information about aspects of the plan that are not clear or which do not appear feasible. As they discuss the proposed plans, the amount of resources and assistance that can be expected from the manager will be negotiated.

In general, it is desirable to consult with all of the key people whose support, cooperation, or authorization are essential for the successful implementation of a plan. These other people may include superiors, lateral peers, and outsiders such as clients, suppliers, and subcontractors. Objectives that involve several subordinates may be discussed in a group meeting.

Procedures for Action Planning

This section briefly describes procedures and guidelines for the four phases of action planning.

Program Action Steps

The process of identifying necessary action steps to implement a strategy or carry out a project can be described as a series of questions that must be answered. The questions are as follows:

- What activities must be carried out?
- What information must be obtained and from whom?
- What materials and supplies must be obtained and from whom?
- What equipment and facilities must be reserved or arranged, and from whom?
- What work must be subcontracted to outsiders?
- What work must be delegated?
- What personnel must be hired?
- What training and briefing of personnel is necessary?
- What sign-offs, permissions, or authorizations must be obtained, and from whom?
- Who needs to be kept informed about activities and decisions?

After the necessary action steps are identified and described in a clear, concise way, the next step is to determine the optimal sequencing for them. This step requires a deeper analysis of the connections and causal relationships among the action steps. Again, the analysis is facilitated by asking a series of key questions:

- What steps must be completed before another step can be started?
- What steps must be carried out at the same time to allow mutual adjustments to occur?
- What steps can be carried out independently?
- What steps are optional and can be skipped if there are delays?
- What steps are choice points for making choices among alternative paths?

If the optimal sequence of action steps is linear, a simple list of the necessary action steps in proper order is sufficient to describe it. However, if the sequence is complex and involves parallel paths, a type of flow chart called an "activity network" is useful (see Figure 7–1).

Programming is easier when the strategy or project is something that has been done before and the necessary action steps are well known. Thus, programming is facilitated by prior experience. When relevant expertise is lacking, it may be possible to obtain assistance from experienced co-workers, expert consultants, or printed materials with detailed instructions (e.g., "how to do it" books). Programming for a new strategy or task is much more difficult, and involves problem solving and logical analysis of action sequences leading to the desired outcome. In this case, programming is actually a continuation of the strategy formation process.

Schedule Action Steps

Scheduling is the determination of when each action step should start and end. The first step in scheduling action steps is to estimate how much time is required to carry out each action step. Key questions include the following:

- What was the average or typical amount of time required for each type of activity in the past?
- What unique conditions exist that may increase or decrease the time required to carry out an action step?
- What is the least amount of time an action step is likely to take if all goes well?
- What is the greatest amount of time each action step is likely to take if everything goes wrong?

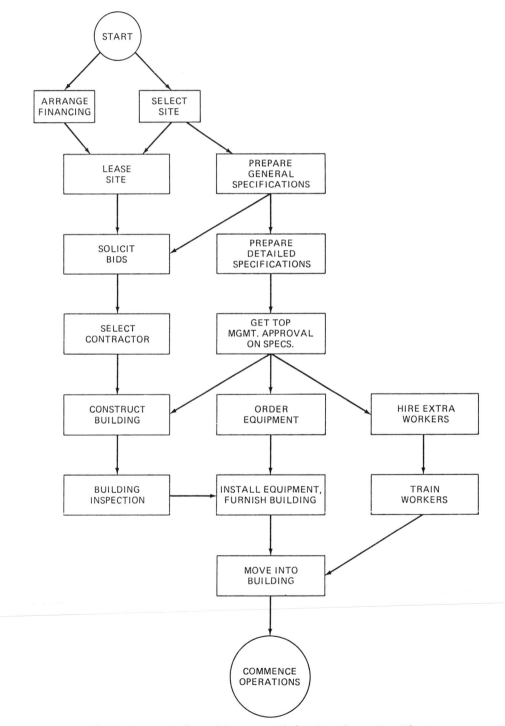

FIGURE 7–1 Sample Activity Network for Opening a New Plant

If it is difficult to estimate time requirements for an action step, the activity should be broken up into component steps for which estimates are likely to be easier. The estimated time for each action step should be listed in terms of days or fractions of days next to that action step on the activity list or activity network. Time estimates in action plans are very subjective and somewhat arbitrary. It is common to begin with the average time needed in the past for a particular type of activity, then make an adjustment for unique conditions. If problems and delays are very likely for an action step, additional slack should be built into the time estimate.

The next step is to determine when each action step should begin and end. A series of key questions can be asked to identify possible constraints on the scheduling of activities due to the availability of essential personnel, equipment, facilities, and supplies. These constraints affect the starting time for activities that involve them. It is common for projects to be delayed because a manager assumed an activity could occur at a time when the necessary equipment, support person, or facility was not available.

- Are there peak periods of utilization for equipment or facilities needed for the project or activity?
- Are necessary equipment or facilities already scheduled for other projects or activities that take priority?
- Are necessary equipment or facilities unavailable at certain times due to periodic maintenance, holidays, etc.?
- Are key personnel unavailable at certain times due to prior commitments?
- Are key personnel unavailable at certain times due to vacations and holidays?
- Are key personnel unavailable at certain times because they have different work schedules or are in different time zones?
- For outdoor activities, what weather conditions are desirable and when are these conditions most likely to occur?
- Are there predictable cycles for unavailability of essential supplies?

An activity list for a sequence of linear action steps can be converted into a "timeline" or "event calendar" by adding start and end times for each action step (see Figure 7–2). When there are not many action steps in the plan and most of the sequence is linear, an alternative approach is to use a regular calendar to list start and end times for

Project: Custom design product Y for client.
Deadline: October 18, 1988

Action Step	Time Required	Start Date	Deadline
1. Meet with client to determine specifications.	2 days	7-5	7-6
2. Develop preliminary plans.	5 days	7-7	7-13
3. Get approval of plans.	7 days	7-14	7-22
4. Develop prototype.	20 days	7-21	8-20
5. Test prototype.	5 days	8-22	8-26
6. Review tests with client.	1 day	8-29	8-29
7. Finalize design.	3 days	8-30	9-1
8. Start production.	30 days	9-5	10-14
9. Deliver product to client.	2 days	10-17	10-18

FIGURE 7–2 Sample Event Calendar

each action step. For a complex sequence of action steps described by an activity network, it is better to develop a "milestone chart" (see Figure 7–3).

The recommended procedure for determining start and end dates is the following: Begin with the last item in the sequence and use the estimated time necessary to perform that action step to determine the start date for it. Then use that start date to determine the deadline for the next-to-last activity. Repeat the process, working backward through the sequence of action steps until the starting time is determined for the first action step in the sequence. During the process, make any adjustments necessary for constraints, such as times when key personnel, equipment, or facilities are unavailable. This scheduling process is not as difficult as it may appear, and software is now available for personal computers to assist the planner in developing milestone charts.

Sometimes, after the total time for the project or action plan is determined, it becomes obvious that there is not enough time available to complete the project by the final deadline. In this case, it will be necessary either to revise the final deadline or modify the action plan to save time on some action steps. For example, it may be possible to start an action step earlier if it is not necessary to complete the preceding step first; or it may be possible to speed up an action step by using more resources, for instance, dividing up the work between two people rather than having only one person do it. Time estimates for each action step usually include some allowance for things that could go wrong. If it is essential to complete the project by a particular deadline, another alternative is to reduce the amount of slack time in the plan and manage it more closely in an effort to avoid any serious delays. Some plans in-

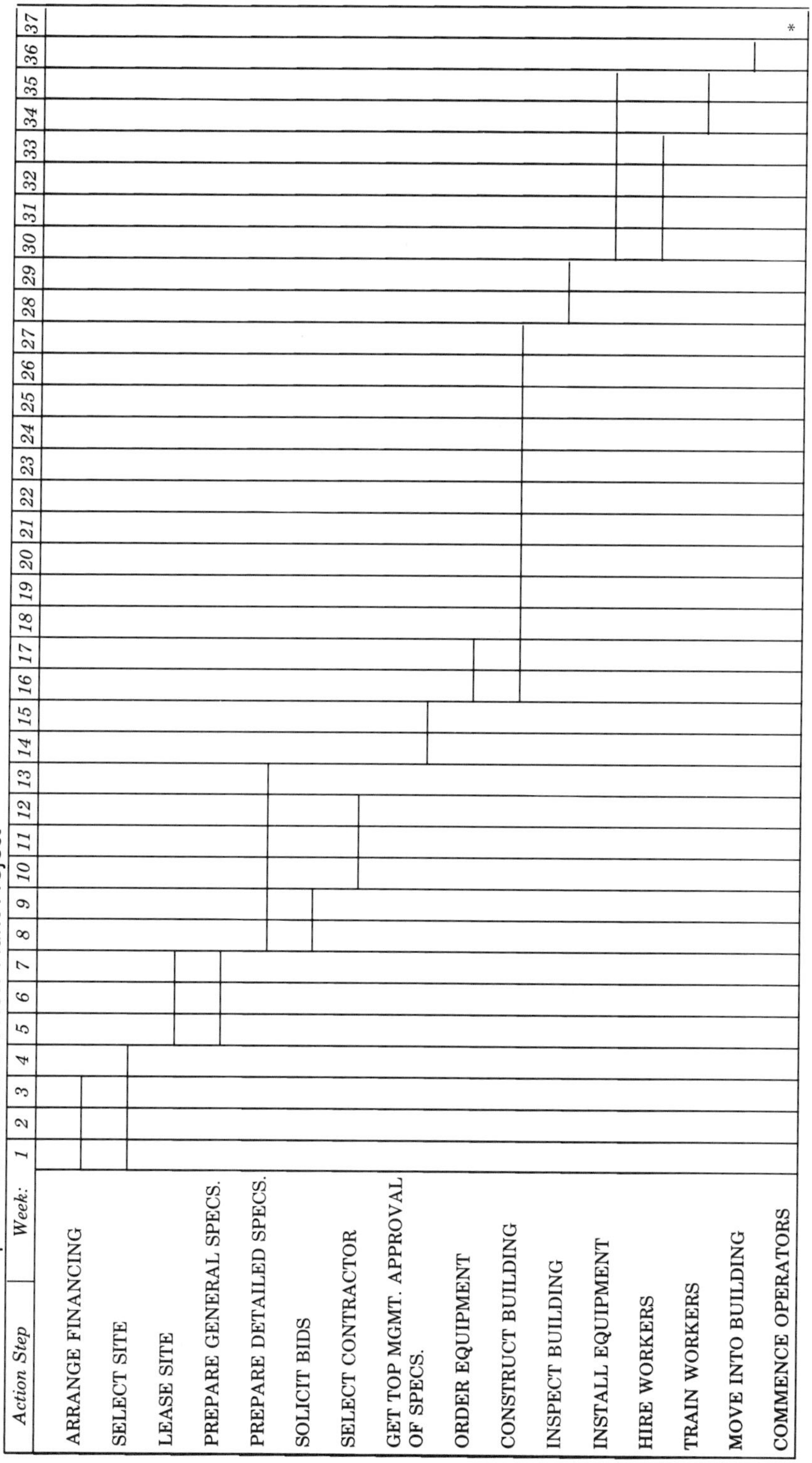

FIGURE 7–3 Sample Milestone Chart New Plant Project

clude built-in provisions for handling delays. These provisions include such things as optional action steps that can be omitted if necessary to save time, and choice points where a faster but more expensive path can be selected if the project is behind schedule at that time. Of course, there is no guarantee that delays can be avoided entirely, even with additional resources and closer management.

Determine Resource Requirements

The next step is to determine resource requirements for each action step in the plan. Resources include personnel, materials, supplies, support services, and expenses for purchase or use of equipment and facilities. There are many different approaches to budgeting for an action plan, and a number of subjective and arbitrary judgments are necessary. One of the decisions involves the treatment of indirect and overhead costs. Resource estimates may or may not include the cost of your own time and that of other employees, depending on the budgeting approach used by the organization. Similarly, resource estimates may or may not include overhead costs for use of the organization's existing equipment and facilities. Personnel costs may be specified only in hours, or hours may be used to compute the dollar cost for work on the project by the organization's employees. Regardless of which approach is used, some type of action plan work sheet like the one shown in Figure 7–4 is usually helpful.

Before costs can be estimated, it is necessary to make some decisions about who will carry out each action step. Some action steps will be done by you, some may be delegated to subordinates, some will require the assistance of other members of the organization, and some may be subcontracted to outside individuals or firms. Many action steps are likely to utilize existing supplies, equipment, and facilities, but the purchase, rental, or borrowing of some items may be necessary. It may be necessary also to hire more permanent or temporary employees. Making these decisions is likely to require investigation of costs for different options. This information can be collected at the same time as information about the availability of outside personnel, equipment, and facilities. When estimating costs, it is important to identify expenses requiring special authorization according to organization policy or because they exceed the limits of your budget authority. Necessary authorizations and approvals should be included as action steps in the plan.

The budgeting phase of action planning represents an important link with the regular budgeting process of the organization. It is important to consider the cost of each action step before making a final

FIGURE 7-4 Action Plan Work Sheet

Planner: _____ Eval. & Deadline: _____ Date: _____

What Will Be Done (Action Step)	Est. Days	When?		By Whom? (Accountability)	At What Cost?		Progress Check		
		Start	Deadline		Work Hours	Dollars	Started	Finished	Status

commitment to the action plan and deadline. After the total cost of the planned project or strategy has been estimated, a manager may discover that it exceeds the amount of resources previously allocated. Likewise, it may become evident that the costs of a project or strategy are not justified by the expected benefits. In either event, it will be necessary to consider ways to reduce costs. One possibility for reducing costs is to settle for a less ambitious deadline. Another way is to reduce the scope of the project or activity. If costs cannot be reduced sufficiently to justify the project or strategy, it will be necessary to reconsider alternative strategies, or to modify the objective.

Establishing Accountability and Controls

It is desirable to fix accountability for each action step to a single individual, even though more than one person is involved in carrying out the step. Individual accountability reduces problems that may arise due to diffusion of responsibility and role ambiguity ("I thought he was doing it"). In determining accountability, the following questions are helpful:

- Who has the necessary skills and expertise?
- Who will be available when the action step is scheduled to occur?
- Who is likely to have the necessary commitment?

Sometimes commitment is in doubt for the person who would normally carry out the action step. In this event, there are a number of options, some of which can be used simultaneously:

- Try to find someone more reliable and committed to carry out the action step.
- Build more slack into the schedule around action steps assigned to people who are unreliable.
- Give the person a deadline that is earlier than necessary.
- Monitor unreliable people more closely.
- Find a backup person who can step in and take over the action step if necessary.
- Identify alternative facilities, equipment, support services, suppliers, or subcontractors that can be used on short notice if necessary.

- Find ways to work around delays that may be caused by someone who is unreliable.
- Try to gain the person's commitment by using appropriate influence tactics.

Some possible approaches for gaining more cooperation and commitment are as follows:

- Explain how important the project or strategy is for the organization.
- Explain how the person will benefit from the project or strategy if it is successful.
- Involve others by asking them to review your tentative plan and suggest improvements, and by incorporating their ideas and giving credit for them.
- Make a personal appeal based on your friendship, or call in IOU's for past favors you did for the person.
- Make it clear that you have a legitimate right to expect the person's cooperation and assistance.
- Ask your boss to use his or her influence if necessary to get cooperation from someone whom you are unable to influence directly.
- For someone over whom you have no authority, try to get the action step incorporated into the person's own written goals and plans.

Effective management of an action plan requires appropriate monitoring of action steps. Even when the people who will carry out action steps are reliable, it is desirable to monitor their progress. Monitoring is facilitated by identifying appropriate dates for checking on the initiation, progress, and completion of scheduled action steps. You should not wait until the deadline for an activity to check if it has been started and is on schedule. Appropriate monitoring techniques may include written reports, meetings to review progress, visits to sites where activities are supposed to take place, and inspection of work samples. Costs should be monitored also in order to detect potential cost overruns, errors in payments, and possible misuse of funds. Expenses should be compared to budgeted amounts at appropriate points in the project.

Careful monitoring is essential for detecting any problems or delays. When a problem is discovered, it is important to deal with it quickly. Sometimes it is necessary to modify the schedule for all or part of an action plan to reflect unavoidable delays. Changes in scheduling are easier to make if done early, since people are less likely to have other commitments and more flexibility is possible. If it becomes evident that the final deadline for the project is unlikely to be met, it is important to inform people who will be affected as soon as possible.

Evaluation of Action Plans

The amount of detail necessary in an action plan varies with the nature of the project or strategy. More elaborate plans are appropriate for a project or strategy that is complex, important, and costly. Some projects or strategies are so simple and routine that they can be managed effectively with only a short activity list with some crude time estimates. It is important to identify the appropriate level of action planning. Insufficient plans are likely to result in failed or late projects or in cost overruns. Overly complex plans are likely to waste the manager's time, create unrealistic expectations, reduce flexibility, and encourage over-supervision. Although good data on managerial planning is not available, it is likely that most managers do too little action planning rather than too much. Descriptive research shows that managers tend to avoid formal planning in favor of spending time on solving immediate problems. In their daily activities, managers are often guided by informal agendas that are similar to plans, but these agendas usually lack the detail necessary to provide many of the benefits of proactive action planning.

Action plans should be evaluated by criteria related to the components of the planning process discussed earlier. To evaluate how feasible, comprehensive, and realistic an action plan is, the following questions are helpful:

- Are the action steps likely to lead to attainment of the plan's objective?
- Are all of the important action steps identified?
- Has the necessary sequencing of the action steps been determined?
- Is each action step described clearly without unnecessary details?
- Is each action step distinct from the others?
- Is each action step consistent with the law and with organizational policies and practices?
- Are the estimated times realistic?
- Is the final deadline realistic?
- Have resource requirements been estimated realistically?
- Do the benefits from the plan justify the costs?

- Has accountability for each action step been assigned to an appropriate individual?
- Has the cooperation of involved parties been insured?
- Have appropriate checkpoints and monitoring procedures been identified?
- Have likely problems and feasible remedies been identified?

References

Davies, E. W. (1983). *Project Management: Techniques, Applications, and Managerial Issues*. Institute of Industrial Engineers.

Kahalas, H. (1978). "A Look at Major Planning Methods: Development, Implementation, Strengths, and Limitations." *Long Range Planning*, August.

Knutson, J., & Scott, M. (1978). "Developing a Project Plan." *Journal of Systems Management,* October.

Martin, J. (1979). "Planning: The Gap Between Theory and Practice." *Long Range Planning,* December.

Meredith, J. R., & Mantel, S. J. (1985). *Project Management: A Managerial Approach*. New York: John Wiley.

Rolefson, J. F. (1975). "Project Management—Six Critical Steps." *Journal of Systems Management,* April.

Wiest, J. D., & Levy, F. K. (1977). *A Management Guide to PERT/CPM*. Englewood Cliffs, NJ: Prentice Hall.

PLANNING EXERCISE

Instructions

The purpose of this exercise is to give students an opportunity to carry out a relatively simple planning task using some of the methods learned in the planning module. The task demonstrates some of the types of judgments and analyses necessary to plan more complex projects and activities.

Assume that it is now March, and you have been asked by your boss to arrange a dinner dance for the approximately one hundred full-time employees of his department and their spouses. He has selected a site for the event, but there is still some flexibility on the date. If possible, your boss would like to have the event some evening during the first two weeks in June, but this is a time when this site is popular for weddings and receptions.

A separate caterer must be employed, since the site does not provide food service, only bar service for drinks. Your boss would like to have formal, printed announcements (with RSVP's) sent out three weeks before the event to get an accurate count of how many people will attend. Your boss wants to have a live band for entertainment. Assume that you have a limited budget and must check on prices for everything except the site.

In this exercise, you are asked to plan the dinner dance by carrying out each of the following steps:

1. There are four major subtasks (that is, site arrangements, dinner arrangements, entertainment arrangements, and invitations). Identify the component action steps for each subtask and list them in the proper sequence on the Activity List.

2. Next to each action step write your estimate of how long it would take to do that action step (hours or days).

3. Determine how much lead time is necessary for starting each action step. Assume 2 weeks turnaround for a print shop to print invitations. Identify any dependencies among action steps in different subtasks. A flow chart of action steps is optional; a flow chart is helpful, but it is possible to do the event calendar without making a flow chart.

4. Complete the event calendar by indicating the week in which each action step should occur. The event calendar should show all of the action steps for the four subtasks arranged in a logical sequence. Assume that the dinner dance will occur in the twelfth week after planning begins.

Activity List For Dinner Dance Plans

Site Arrangements

1. _____
_____

2. _____
_____

3. _____
_____

4. _____
_____

5. _____
_____

6. _____
_____

7. _____
_____

8. _____
_____

Dinner Arrangements

1. _____
_____

2. _____
_____

3. _____
_____

4. _____
_____

5. _____
_____

6. _____
_____

7. _____

_____

8. _____

_____

Guest List and Invitations

1. _____

_____

2. _____

_____

3. _____

_____

4. _____

_____

5. _____

_____

6. _____

_____

7. _____

_____

8. _____

_____

Entertainment

1. _____

_____

2. _____

_____

3. _____

_____

4. _____

_____

5. _____

_____

6. _____

_____

7. _____

_____

8. _____

_____

Event Calendar

Week 1 _____

_____

_____

_____

Week 2 _____

_____

_____

_____

Week 3 _____

_____

_____

_____

Week 4 _____

_____

_____

_____

Week 5 _____

_____

Week 6 _____

Week 7 _____

Week 8 _____

Week 9 _____

Week 10 _____

Week 11 _____

Week 12 Dinner dance is held.

Case: Sterling Products

The vice president for sales in Sterling Products, a large manufacturing company, set an objective to increase profits for the next year by 20%. The primary strategy for achieving this objective was to promote the company's premier brand, which yielded the highest profit margin. Marketing funds were shifted from other products to the premier brand, and a major promotional campaign was initiated. The sales representatives were encouraged to set higher individual goals for sales of the premier product. A memo was sent to inform the vice president for production about the sales forecasts for next year and to request that he or she go ahead with tentative plans to purchase new machines to increase production capacity for the premier brand.

The production department was under increasing pressure from the CEO to reduce costs for the basic, economy brand. Competitors were making major inroads into the company's market share for this product by offering a similar product at a lower price. The vice president for production set an objective for the coming year to reduce production costs for the economy brand by 10%. Production procedures were streamlined, and the economy brand was given priority scheduling to reduce overtime costs. Old equipment used for making the economy brand was replaced with new, more efficient equipment financed by funds that initially had been allocated to buy machines to make the premier brand. The vice president for production believed that the sales department had made highly unrealistic forecasts, and he didn't expect sales of the premier brand to increase very much. Even if sales of the premier brand did increase, he figured that production could be increased by working more overtime. Once the cost-cutting measures were implemented, the vice president for production sent a memo to the sales department telling them about the revised costs on the economy brand so that they would henceforth have more leeway to compete on price for sales of that brand.

When orders for the premier product suddenly increased, the production department could not meet the demand. As long delays developed in deliveries, sales were lost to competitors. Sales for the premier brand increased for the year, but they fell far short of the targeted levels. Furthermore, the cost per unit was higher than anticipated by the sales vice president, since the additional units involved considerable overtime. Thus, the profit objectives for the premier brand were not attained. Meanwhile, sales of the economy brand stayed about the same, since this product was de-emphasized by the sales force, even though it now could be priced more competitively. Although profits from both brands were up slightly, overall company profits would have been much higher if these self-inflicted problems had not occurred.

Questions for Students

1. What mistakes were made by the various parties in this case?

2. What things could have been done to avoid these problems and increase the likelihood of achieving higher company profits?

Monitoring and Reviewing Progress

LEARNING OBJECTIVES

After completing this module a student will:

- *Understand the purpose and importance of monitoring.*
- *Understand how often and when to schedule results review meetings with a subordinate.*
- *Understand how to prepare for a results review meeting with a subordinate.*
- *Understand how to conduct a results review meeting with a subordinate.*
- *Understand how to evaluate progress in relation to performance goals.*

CONTENTS OF MODULE

- *Text: Monitoring and Reviewing Progress*
- *Case: American Financial Corp.*
- *Case: Prompto Car Rental Company*
- *Progress Review Role Play*

Monitoring and Reviewing Progress

As noted in the module on managerial behavior, monitoring is one of the primary practices that determine how effective a manager is. Monitoring involves gathering information about the operations of the manager's organization or work unit and about relevant events in the external environment. Information is gathered about:

- The progress of the work.
- The success of projects or programs.
- The performance of individual subordinates.
- The quality of products or services.
- The concerns of customers and clients.
- Changes in the external environment such as market trends, economic conditions, government policies, technological developments, and actions of competitors.

The primary purpose of monitoring is to gather information necessary to formulate and modify objectives, strategies, plans, policies, and procedures. Monitoring provides the information managers need to guide their behavior toward subordinates, peers, superiors, and outsiders. When monitoring is insufficient, the organization is likely to experience failure to detect problems before they become serious—problems such as declining quality, low productivity, cost overruns, employee dissatisfaction, projects behind schedule, customer dissatisfaction, changes in customer preferences, and new technological developments that provide competitors with an advantage. Without adequate monitoring of subordinate performance, a manager is unable to provide appropriate recognition for achievements, to identify subordinates who need coaching or assistance in accomplishing their work objectives, to evaluate performance of subordinates accurately, and to have a sound basis for determining allocation of rewards such as pay increases.

Monitoring is facilitated by developing a network of contacts with people who can provide timely and relevant information about events affecting a manager's work unit. Monitoring is also aided by development of information systems and measurement procedures to provide relevant, accurate, and timely data on the quantity and quality of the work unit's products or services, the productivity of its employees, expenditures in relation to budgeted amounts, progress on projects in relation to target dates, and progress of subordinates in implementing action plans. Identification of relevant performance measures is discussed in more detail in the module on setting objectives.

Monitoring also depends on the quality of relations with subordinates. It is impeded when subordinates are afraid of informing their superiors about problems, mistakes, and delays. If subordinates are distrustful and withhold or distort information about problems, it is difficult if not impossible for managers to obtain the information necessary to manage effectively. Managers can use a variety of approaches to improve the upward flow of information, such as developing independent sources of information, increasing contacts with subordinates at various levels (e.g., management by wandering around), and reacting to problems in a constructive, non-punitive manner (e.g., helping subordinates learn from mistakes rather than punishing them).

Monitoring is necessary for all managers, but it is more important in some situations than in others. The following conditions increase the importance of obtaining timely and accurate information:

- Mistakes, quality problems, or accidents are likely due to inexperienced or unskilled subordinates, or due to the difficult nature of the work.
- Mistakes and accidents would be expensive or would endanger the health and lives of people.
- The work unit carries out long, complex projects requiring detailed planning and coordination.

- Subordinates have interdependent tasks requiring continuous coordination.
- The work unit's operations are interdependent with those of other units, and frequent coordination is necessary.
- Disruptions in the workflow are likely due to equipment breakdowns, accidents, technical problems, materials shortages, personnel shortages, bad weather, etc.
- There is danger of hostile actions of outsiders, such as terrorists, criminals, militant demonstrators, fanatics, and enemy military units.

Monitoring is most difficult when the work involves unstructured, unique tasks for which results can be determined only after a long time interval. For example, it is more difficult to evaluate progress in research and development than progress in sales or production. It is more difficult to evaluate the performance of a human resource manager than the performance of a sales manager. Difficulties in monitoring are increased also when a manager is geographically separated from subordinates, and when some subordinates work on different shifts.

Monitoring can take many forms, including observation of operations by a manager (e.g., visiting work facilities, walking around the office or plant), reading written reports, reviewing computer printouts or displays, inspecting the quality of samples of the work unit's products, surveying clients or customers to assess their satisfaction, and holding meetings after an activity or project is completed to determine what went well and what can be improved the next time. A common form of monitoring is the progress review meeting between a manager and an individual subordinate. Progress reviews are an essential component of management by objectives and other goal-setting programs. The remainder of this module text explains how to conduct progress review meetings in an effective manner.

Progress Review Meetings

Progress review meetings provide an opportunity for a manager and subordinate to review and discuss the subordinate's progress in relation to goals and action plans. The meetings are not a substitute for daily and weekly discussions about problems and issues in the work; rather, they provide a perspective on overall progress with respect to the various projects and activities carried out by the subordinate. Progress reviews are not intended to be performance appraisal sessions.

Rather, they are opportunites for exchanging information, providing feedback, clarifying expectations, providing coaching, and conducting mutual problem solving.

Having formal progress review meetings enables a manager to monitor a subordinate's progress and discover if the person is on target in progress toward achievement of performance goals. If any problems are detected, the meetings are useful for discovering causes and finding solutions. Thus, progress review meetings provide a variety of potential benefits:

- Facilitate correction of performance problems early before they get worse.
- Help a manager to determine if a subordinate needs additional coaching or assistance.
- Improve manager-subordinate communication.
- Provide an opportunity to review the feasibility of goals and actions plans and make revisions as necessary.
- Facilitate a manager's efforts to coordinate the activities of different subordinates.
- Provide information needed to evaluate whether a manager's own goals and action plans are realistic.

It is difficult to achieve an optimal balance between control and delegation. Progress review meetings enable a manager to monitor subordinate progress without having to supervise too closely on a day-to-day basis. The subordinate is given considerable latitude to deal with problems without interference, yet is free to ask for advice and assistance whenever it is needed.

Timing of Progress Reviews

The potential benefits will be realized only if progress reviews are held often enough. There should be at least four progress reviews during the year, at roughly 3-month intervals. Progress reviews may be held more often for a subordinate who has had unsatisfactory performance or is learning a new job. An alternative to more formal reviews is to hold informal reviews spaced between the regular formal ones, say at monthly intervals. The timing of review meetings depends partly on when performance data will be available, and when key action steps are scheduled for completion. Formal review meetings should be scheduled shortly after performance data is available. Informal reviews should be scheduled to coincide with the completion dates for key action steps, so that progress can be monitored more easily. Some projects or activities have obvious checkpoints for determining if progress is on schedule, such as those for which key action steps must be performed in sequence and completed on time if subsequent action steps are to be started on time. In general, the necessary degree of monitoring will depend on the competence of the subordinate and the nature of the work. More frequent monitoring is desirable when the subordinate is inexperienced, or when the task is very sensitive and mistakes would be very detrimental and embarrassing.

Preparation for Progress Review Meetings

At the time the next progress review meeting is scheduled, the manager should make sure the subordinate understands how to prepare for it. The subordinate should be reminded to gather relevant information on the current state of the quantitative performance indicators and the extent to which various action steps have been carried out. The subordinate should also note any new developments that are likely to affect future progress or performance. If there is a lot of detailed information, the manager may want to review a status report from the subordinate, prior to the meeting, summarizing progress to date. By the same token, if the manager has new information not available to the subordinate, this information should be passed on to the subordinate beforehand. It is especially important to communicate information about changes in plans, schedules, or policies that affect the subordinate's plans and action strategies. Such changes may include budget cuts, delays in implementing an action step, and revised deadlines, goals, or strategies by the manager or by other people with whom the subordinate must coordinate.

Identifying Reasons for Unsatisfactory Progress

How does one determine why progress for a goal or project is not on target? There are two general categories of reasons. First are situational causes, such as market conditions that are less favorable than anticipated, shortages in supplies, materials, or personnel, unexpected or unusual events (e.g., a major strike, an accident, a natural disaster, sabotage, lawsuits, new legislation or regulations), resource levels below budgeted levels due to last-minute cuts or shifts in priorities, and failure by people in other parts of the organization or by outsiders to carry out their part of a project properly and on time. Situational factors may make the goal and/or the timetable for implementing it unrealistic. Potential remedies for this type of problem include modifying the strategy for achieving the goal, changing the goal level, changing the deadline, and committing more resources. Sometimes it is necessary to use all of these remedies simultaneously.

Selection of an appropriate remedy should be done jointly by a process of discussion. It is important to be flexible about any necessary changes in goal level, timetable, action plans, or resource levels, but adequate consideration should be given to revision of action plans before lowering the goal, delaying the deadline, or committing more resources. When progress is not on target, some subordinates are likely to seek an easier goal, more resources, or more time, rather than having to find a better action plan or work harder to implement it. It is the manager's responsibility to keep goals and deadlines at a level that is challenging but realistic and cost effective. Of course, in the happy event that the situation is much more favorable than expected, and progress is far ahead of schedule, it may be appropriate to increase the goal, shorten the deadline, or reduce the level of resources.

Another reason for progress to be below target resides primarily in the subordinate and is due to deficiencies in subordinate skill or motivation. Examples of this type of problem include:

- Failure to carry out a major action step on schedule.
- Failure to monitor progress to detect a problem before it becomes serious.
- Poor judgment in deciding how to deal with a problem.
- Procrastination in dealing with a problem until it gets worse.
- Failure to notify superiors about a problem that requires their attention.
- Avoidable errors made in the performance of a task.
- Failure to follow standard procedures and rules.
- Unprofessional or improper actions.

Sometimes, the reason for below-target progress involves a combination of skill and situational factors. For example, an action plan may fail to achieve the desired results due to lack of knowledge about cause-effect relationships. Delays may occur because the subordinate did not allow enough time or start an activity early enough. Sometimes a subordinate has not had much experience with a particular type of activity and it takes much longer than expected. Sometimes delays are predictable but the subordinate, due to poor planning, fails to allow slack time in the schedule.

Reasons that involve deficiencies in subordinate skill or motivation are harder to detect than reasons due to the situation, because a subordinate is usually reluctant to admit mistakes and failures. However, it is important to identify these reasons for inadequate progress and take corrective action. The orientation of the manager should be to help the subordinate learn from mistakes and move on to correct them, rather than becoming angry and emphasizing blame. When probing to discover these causes, the manager can ask what types of things the subordinate would do differently with the benefit of hindsight, and what lessons were learned from the experience. If possible, ideas for corrective action should be suggested by the subordinate rather than by the manager. The manager should begin the discussion of corrective action by asking what the subordinate recommends, rather than by telling the subordinate what to do. The manager's contribution is to help the subordinate select an appropriate remedy and, if necessary, to suggest additional remedies that the subordinate does not consider.

Procedures for Progress Review Meetings

Procedures have been developed over the years by researchers and practitioners to improve the effectiveness of progress review meetings. The following sequence of procedures ensures that maximum results can be obtained in a minimum amount of time. The procedures improve communication, problem solving, and management of conflict, while avoiding wasted time, defensiveness, and hostility. The procedures allow both parties to concentrate on the purpose of the meeting and enhance mutual confidence that the meeting will be worthwhile. Each step in the suggested sequence builds upon the success of the earlier one. The wording assumes that you are the manager.

1. Review Purpose and Show Enthusiasm.

Begin the meeting by reviewing briefly the purpose and procedure to be followed. Your introductory remarks should emphasize the value of the meeting to both parties and the importance of open communication and joint problem solving.

2. Begin with a High Priority Goal.

In order to make the most efficient use of time, begin with an important objective or project. You should suggest the order of topics to be discussed and check to see if this is satisfactory to the subordinate. If the subordinate has any problems with this agenda, they should be discussed and resolved to your mutual satisfaction. A possible reason for changing the order is that two objectives are interdependent and they cannot be understood without reviewing them together.

3. Ask the Subordinate to Summarize Progress on the Goal.

To avoid defensiveness, it is best to ask the subordinate to review progress on an objective or project, rather than making your own judgment and announcing it to the subordinate. Ask the subordinate to present relevant information and make an initial assessment as to whether progress is on target or not on target. If there is agreement that progress is on target, provide appropriate praise and indicate that you are pleased with the progress.

4. Explore Reasons for Any Disagreement about Progress.

In most cases, a manager and subordinate will agree on the amount of progress. However, if there is a disagreement, it is important to explore it to identify the reason for the disagreement. Usually, disagreement is due to insufficient or ambiguous data, but it could be due to an initial misunderstanding about the expected rate of progress. The situation where you think progress is on target but the subordinate does not is easier to deal with than the opposite situation. You should keep in mind that improvement of performance is more likely if the subordinate agrees that progress is not on target. If disagreement is due to a misunderstanding, it should be cleared up. If it is due to insufficient information, it may be necessary to gather more information and review progress again for this objective at a later meeting.

5. Explore Reasons Why Progress Is Not on Target.

If there is agreement that progress is not on target, the reasons for the discrepancy should be identified. Both you and the subordinate should try to identify all of the reasons for delays, errors, or performance deficiencies in a careful, systematic manner, rather than jumping immediately to a discussion of corrective actions. Problems cannot be identified and resolved unless both parties are willing to share information openly without holding out on each other. Communication is more likely to be open if the discussion is kept as non-evaluative and unthreatening as possible. Causes should be analyzed in terms of events that were not anticipated, assumptions that were not accurate, action steps that failed to achieve their intended effect, or necessary actions that were not taken in time—not in terms of personal attributes such as poor judgment, irresponsibility, forgetfulness, or lack of motivation on the part of the subordinate.

6. Consider Potential Problems that Could Delay Progress.

Even when progress is on target, it is advisable to consider any recent developments or other information about possible problems in the near future that would delay progress or jeopardize the success of a project. If there is any indication of such problems, it may be advisable to monitor some trends and indicators more closely, plan ways to avoid potential obstacles, or develop contingency plans for responding to an unavoidable crisis.

7. Ask the Subordinate to Suggest Corrective Actions.

It is best to give the subordinate an opportunity to suggest corrective actions to deal with current or anticipated problems, rather than merely telling him or her what needs to be done. The subordinate should be encouraged to suggest a variety of possible actions that could be taken to get progress back on target or to avoid potential problems. In order to foster maximum creativity, all of the possibilities should be listed first, in a brainstorming fashion, before beginning to evaluate their feasibility. You should try to build on the ideas of the subordinate rather than merely pointing out limitations. In most cases, your own ideas for dealing with the problem can be presented as variations of the subordinate's ideas or as elaborations on them. Be alert for opportunities to provide assistance or facilitation to the subordinate by using your knowledge, influence, or contacts. Subordinates may be reluctant to suggest that you intervene on their behalf, because they may believe that it is an admission of weakness. For example, if a project is behind schedule because someone in another department failed to carry out a promise to provide necessary information, you can offer to try to get the information.

8. Record Level of Progress and Agreements on Action Steps.

It is useful to make notes describing progress on each goal and agreements reached on necessary action steps to deal with current or potential problems and obstacles. The notes may be made on a special form or review document if the organization has them. Any changes in goal level, deadlines, or action plans should also be recorded to facilitate mutual understanding of what is expected.

9. Summarize the Discussion.

After all goals have been reviewed, summarize the essence of the discussion, with special attention to any changes in goals, deadlines, or priorities, and major changes in action plans. This summarizing is usually done by the manager, but it can be done by the subordinate if desired. In the latter case, the manager should correct or add to the summary, as necessary. The purpose of a summary is to check for agreement and mutual understanding. As you end the meeting, it is useful to repeat your willingness to provide any necessary assistance or advice, and to indicate your availability to discuss any additional problems or complications that may arise. You may also want to set a tentative date and time for the next progress review meeting.

References

Caspe, M. S. (1979). "Monitoring People to Perform on Design and Construction Projects." *Project Management Quarterly,* December.

Giegold, W. C. (1978). *Management by Objectives: A Self-instructional Approach. Vol. 3: Performance Appraisal and the MBO Process.* New York: McGraw-Hill.

Hambrick, D. C. (1982). "Environmental Scanning and Organizational Strategy." *Strategic Management Journal,* 3, 159–174.

Kaplan, R. E. (1966). *The Warp and the Woof of the General Manager's Job.* Technical Report. Greensboro, NC: Center for Creative Leadership.

Livingston, J. L., & Ronen, R. (1975). "Motivation and Management Control Systems." *Decision Sciences,* April.

Meredith, J. R., & Mantel, S. J., Jr. (1985). *Project Management: A Managerial Approach.* New York: John Wiley.

Mintzberg, H. (1973). *The Nature of Managerial Work.* New York: Harper & Row.

Morrissey, G. L. (1977). *Management by Objectives and Results for Business and Industry*. Reading, MA: Addison-Wesley.

Newman, W. H. (1975). *Constructive Control*. Englewood Cliffs, NJ: Prentice Hall.

Weihrich, H. (1985). *Management Excellence: Productivity Through MBO*. New York: McGraw-Hill.

Case: American Financial Corp.

Betty Powell is the manager of human resources for American Financial Corporation, a large financial services company. When she arrived back in her office today after being away for a week, she discovered that a staffing report due the day before was still not finished. The report was for the vice president of the company's brokerage division. Just before she arrived back, the vice president called to ask where the report was.

Six weeks earlier, Betty had asked Don Adams, one of her subordinates, to write the staffing report. This is not the first time Don has missed a deadline. His work is very careful and meticulous, but he appears to be compulsive about checking and rechecking everything several times to avoid any mistakes.

Betty calls Don and asks him to meet with her immediately. When Don comes into her office, she greets him and asks him to sit down. The following dialogue occurs:

"Don, I understand the staffing report for the brokerage division is not completed yet. The division vice president needs that report to prepare his annual budget, and he is putting a lot of pressure on me to get it to him immediately. When I gave you this assignment, you assured me that six weeks was ample time to do it."

"I'm sorry that the report wasn't ready on schedule," Don responds, "but it turned out to be much more complex than I initially expected. I had to spend extra time verifying the figures from the branch offices, because they just didn't look right. Just when I thought . . ."

Betty interrupts, "Look Don, this is not the first time you have been late on an important project. You're supposed to be a professional, and professionals plan their work and get it done on time."

"It would not be very professional to do a report full of mistakes," replies Don. "It's important to me to do quality work that I can be proud of. It's not my fault that the branch managers don't keep accurate records."

"What types of mistakes did you find when you checked their records?" Betty asks.

"Well . . . I didn't actually find any mistakes," replies Don, looking embarrassed, "but after I entered the information into the computer and did the preliminary analysis, I discovered that the records were missing for one of the branch offices. I lost a week waiting to get the missing information but without it, the report would not provide an accurate picture of the division's staffing needs. It's a good thing I noticed . . ."

"Don, we have clerical workers to do things like checking records and making sure they are complete," Betty interrupts impatiently. "It sounds to me like you are not very efficient about managing your time. If you delegated some of these simple tasks to other people, you wouldn't get so far behind in your work."

"The clerical workers were tied up finishing the new employee manual," Don protests. "I don't get enough clerical help on any of my projects, and that's why they are sometimes late."

"Why didn't you inform me there were problems that might delay the report?" Betty asks, her voice showing she is becoming very annoyed. "I could have found you some clerical support."

Don is now becoming more defensive. "I tried to let you know last week, but you were on the West Coast doing the management training workshop. I left a message for you to call me."

"Don, you have an excuse for everything, and nothing is ever your fault," Betty says sarcastically. "You seem to be incapable of planning the action steps needed to do a project like this one. It doesn't take a lot of brains to realize that the records should be checked before beginning the data analysis. As for missing records, it wouldn't surprise me if they are buried somewhere under the piles of stuff laying around your office. You have the messiest office in the company."

Don looks sullen but does not reply. Betty continues her tirade.

"Don, your career in this company is going to be a very short one unless you get your act together. I want that report in my hands by noon tomorrow, and no more excuses."

Questions for Students

1. Evaluate how well Betty handled the progress review meeting. What things could have been done in the meeting to make it more effective?

2. What did Betty do wrong prior to the progress review meeting? What could have been done to avoid missing the deadline?

Case: Prompto Car Rental Company*

During its first year of operations, Prompto Rental Car Company had rapidly increasing revenues. Although profits are unusual in the first year of operations for many new firms, Prompto had a small profit. Scott, the vice president for Marketing at Prompto-Car, had lunch with his assistant, Karen, and announced some plans made by top management at a meeting earlier in the day.

"Karen, our little car rental company is ready to hit the big time. After one year of operation I think we are ready to compete with the likes of Budget Rent-A-Car and Thrifty. Our price structure is just too much for them to handle. Sometimes I even wonder how we can afford to rent cars at the prices we do.

"Let me tell you more about the expansion plans. I'm thinking of a computerized system for tying in with airplane reservations. The big three in the car rental business have gotten in bed with the airlines and I think we can, too. I'm even thinking of tying in with low-priced motels and hotels. A person renting from us can rent a car and sleep cheaper than he or she could by doing business with the majors. We may have to extend our line of credit to its outer limits to pull this off, but it will be worth it in the long run. We're poised for the big jump."

Karen replied, "Scott, it's curious that you should be talking about expansion at this time. I have some recent information that is hardly optimistic. It seems that business is taking a sudden downturn. Our rentals are off by 35 percent in the midwest, and down 25 percent in the east."

Scott countered almost defensively, "Hold on, there's been a slight downturn in the airline business lately. We're tied pretty much to their business cycle. It's nothing serious. In a couple of months, demand will be right back up, higher than ever."

"I have an idea," said Karen, "Let's call Bud, our midwestern regional manager, and see if he notices any real problems."

Over the telephone, Bud said angrily, "I wish I did know more about the problems. But it's me alone trying to cover ten states. Business doesn't look too good, but I can't be sure of the causes. I hear a few grumblings here and there about customer complaints. But customers would complain if we rented them Rolls Royces at 20 dollars per day. They would say the ash trays were dirty or the tires weren't properly inflated."

After Scott and Karen discussed Bud's comments, they agreed to obtain some first-hand information. Together, they paid a visit to the Metropolitan Airport to speak directly with a reservations clerk. Karen and Scott reassured the clerk, Melissa, that their mission was a genuine one; that they were making the visit to uncover problems, not to find out who should be blamed.

Melissa was surprisingly candid: "Quite frankly, we have more problems out here than you can expect a reservations clerk to handle. Customers may be willing to try us once because of our low prices, but we aren't getting much

* Adapted from Andrew J. Dubrin, *Fundamentals of Organizational Behavior: An Applied Perspective*. Elmsford, NY: Pergamon Press, Copyright © 1978.

repeat business. One experience with Prompto is about all most people can take."

"Why is that?" asked Scott.

"No offense, sir, but perhaps you should rent one of our cars and see some of the problems. People have complained to me about filthy ash trays, finding combs in the seat, broken windshield washers, unwashed cars, and cars that won't climb a hill. As instructed, I smile and say that we guarantee the problem will not happen again. But it's hard to be sincere, because I know the same problem, or worse, will show up again."

Karen interrupted: "How do you know that problem will repeat itself?"

"Simply because we don't have the employees we need to run this operation. Our two maintenance men are so overworked, I hesitate to ask them to take care of a problem. Besides that, we're kind of left to float on our own with very little supervision."

"Melissa, do you think you're exaggerating? Are our problems really that bad?"

"Yes, they are that bad," answered Melissa. "In fact the name Prompto-Car is a joke around the airport."

Questions for Students

1. What evidence is there in the case that the performance of this company is not monitored adequately by top management?

2. What additional types of information should have been collected regularly to give management a more accurate picture of how well the company is performing?

3. What is the link between monitoring and strategic planning in this case? In light of the new information, what should management do about their strategic plans for expansion?

PROGRESS REVIEW ROLE PLAY

Instructions

The purpose of this role play is to give students an opportunity to experience what it is like to conduct a progress review meeting with a subordinate. The role play also provides an opportunity to practice and strengthen skills that determine whether a progress review meeting will be productive.

For this role play, it is necessary to form three-person groups and determine for each group who will play the role of the boss, who will play the role of subordinate, and who will be the observer. Do not look at the materials or instructions for any role other than the one you have been selected to play.

If you have been selected to be the boss or subordinate, take about 10 minutes to read your role and plan what you will say. Students who play the role of the boss should use the meeting planner and record form. Students selected to be observers are provided with a form to take notes on how well the progress review meeting was handled. These notes will be the basis for feedback to the students who play the role of the boss.

Role For Boss

You are a middle manager in a public agency that provides financial assistance in paying for health-care expenses. Your subordinate is the supervisor of one of the departments in the agency. The major mission of that department is to determine applicant eligibility and process claims for health-care payment. It is now July 10, and you are about to hold the six-month review of the subordinate's progress on achieving performance goals for the current year.

One priority goal was to reduce the average time required to process claims, from 12 days to 7 days, by the end of the year. The major strategy for accomplishing this goal was the installation of a new, more effective computer system, which was expected to be operational by July 1. However, the computer system is still not operational, and the average time to process claims during June was still 11 days. You know that your subordinate has been having some difficulty getting necessary assistance from the computer systems department, but you are not sure what the problem is. You are on good terms with the head of that department, Jane Reynolds, although you rarely see her.

A second priority goal was a 20% reduction in errors by the end of the year in decisions about applicant eligibility for financial assistance. The action plan for this goal included two improvement projects. One project was to implement a new quality control procedure by June 1. This procedure includes some built-in checks to facilitate detection of errors made during the processing of applications. The new procedure became operational in April, and error rates for May and June were down by 10% compared to the rate for last year and for the first quarter of the current year.

The second improvement project is a short training course for employees to make them more aware of the typical sources of error in processing applications. You have considerable experience in the design of training, and you recommended that employees should be trained by working with simulated applications containing the types of client profiles most often involved in erroneous decisions. The employees would learn why the mistakes usually occur and how to avoid them. The schedule for this project called for your subordinate to set up the training course by September 1, and to train all of the employees in his/her department by November 1. You do not know how this project is progressing.

Progress Review Meeting: Preparation Notes and Record of Agreements

Goal 1: Reduce processing time for claims from 12 days to 7 days by the end of the year (12-31).
Date of this review meeting: July 10

1. Evidence of progress:

    Is progress on target? _____ Yes _____ No

2. Achievements to recognize?

3. Problems to resolve?

4. Changes in goal, timetable, or action plan?

5. Followup actions to take:
    Actions by your subordinate:

    Actions by you:

Progress Review Meeting: Preparation Notes and Record of Agreements

Goal 2: Reduce errors in applications 20% by the end of the year (12-31). Date of progress review: July 10

1. Evidence of progress:

   Is progress on target? _____ Yes _____ No

2. Achievements to recognize?

3. Problems to resolve?

4. Changes in goal, timetable, or action plan?

5. Followup actions to take:
   Actions by your subordinate:

   Actions by you:

Role for Subordinate

Your boss is a middle manager in a public agency that provides financial assistance in paying for health-care expenses. You are the supervisor of one of the departments in the agency. The major mission of your department is to determine applicant eligibility and process claims for health-care payment. It is now July 10, and you are about to meet with your boss for the six-month review of progress on your performance goals for the current year.

One priority goal was to reduce the average time required to process claims, from 12 days to 7 days, by the end of the year. The major strategy for accomplishing this goal was the installation of a new, more effective computer system, which was expected to be operational by July 1. However, the computer system is still not operational, and you are very frustrated by the delays, which you attribute to a lack of cooperation from the computer systems department. The manager of that department—Jane Reynolds—seems to give higher priority to other projects, and there seems to be a lack of commitment to your project. Twice in the last month, they have taken much longer than expected to do essential programming for the new computer system, and they have not even started the final testing and debugging sequence. You have told Jane how important this project is, but you don't seem to have much influence over her. Meanwhile, you have been able to make only small improvements in the average processing time for claims by eliminating some unnecessary procedures, which reduced the average time from 12 to 11 days. There is little else you can do until the new computer system is operational.

A second priority goal was a 20% reduction in errors by the end of the year in decisions about applicant eligibility for social services. The action plan for this goal included two improvement projects. One project, scheduled to be implemented by June 1, is a new quality control procedure that includes some built-in checks to facilitate detection of numerical errors made during the processing of applications. The new process became operational in April, and error rates for May and June were down by 10% compared to the rate for last year and for the first quarter of the current year. You are pleased with your progress in achieving this improvement, and you hope your boss appreciates that you were able to implement this project successfully and ahead of schedule.

The second improvement project is a short training course for employees to make them more aware of the typical sources of errors in processing applications. Your boss recommended that employees should be trained by working with simulated applications containing the types of client profiles most often involved in erroneous decisions. The employees would learn why the mistakes usually occur and how to avoid them. The schedule for this project called for you to set up the training course by September 1, and to train all employees in your department by November 1. The simulated applications are completed, but you are having some trouble figuring out how to use them in the training. Although you have some experience in coaching employees, you know very little about designing formal training. When your boss suggested the training course, you had no idea it would be so complicated. Your boss has expertise in training design and you are hoping he/she can give you some advice about setting up the course. However, you are a little hesitant to admit you don't know what to do.

Instructions for Observer

Use the observer form to take notes on how well the "manager" conducted the progress review meeting. These notes will be used after the role play is finished to provide feedback to the student who played the role of the boss. Record whether each of the recommended steps was carried out, and take notes on effective and ineffective behaviors.

Background Information

The boss is a middle manager in a public agency that provides financial assistance in paying for health-care expenses. The subordinate is the supervisor of a department in the agency. The major mission of the department is to determine applicant eligibility and process claims for health-care payment. It is now July 10, time for the six-month review of the subordinate's progress on attaining performance goals for the current year.

One priority goal was to reduce the average time required to process claims, from 12 days to 7 days, by the end of the year. The major strategy for accomplishing this goal was the installation of a new, more effective computer system, which was expected to be operational by July 1. The computer system is still not operational, and the average time to process claims during June was still 11 days. Progress is not on target for this goal.

A second priority goal was a 20% reduction in errors by the end of the year in decisions about applicant eligibility for financial assistance. The action plan for this goal included two improvement projects. One project was to implement a new quality control procedure by June 1. The new procedure was implemented in April, and the average error rate for May and June was down 10% from last year. The second improvement project is a short training course for employees to make them more aware of the typical sources of error in processing applications. The schedule for this project called for the subordinate to set up the training course by September 1, and to train all of the employees in his/her department by November 1. Simulated applications for the course are prepared, but the subordinate does not know the best way to use them in the training and is hoping for more guidance from the boss, who has expertise in training design. Progress is on target for this goal, but there is a problem that will jeopardize further progress if not resolved, namely the design of the training course.

Observer Form

Instructions

Record whether the "boss" did each recommended behavior, and note any especially effective or ineffective aspects of the behavior.

1. Review purpose of meeting with subordinate and show enthusiasm that it will be mutually beneficial.   YES   NO

   Notes:

2. Begin with a high-priority goal and ask the subordinate to review progress.   YES   NO

   Notes:

3. Probe to discover any underlying problems that are not acknowledged by the subordinate. Discuss and try to resolve any disagreement on progress.   YES   NO

   Notes:

4. If progress is clearly on target, provide appropriate praise. If progress is not on target, calmly express concern.   YES   NO

   Notes:

5. If progress is on target, ask if any new obstacles or problems are anticipated. If progress is not on target, ask the subordinate to identify obstacles preventing better progress.   YES   NO

   Notes:

6. Ask the subordinate to suggest ways to deal with any current or anticipated problems, and mutually discuss the options.   YES   NO

   Notes:

7. If necessary, revise the goal, deadline, or action plan, or offer to provide more resources or assistance. Record any agreements.   YES   NO

   Notes:

8. Turn to the next goal and ask the subordinate to review progress.
   YES   NO

   Notes:

9. Probe to discover any underlying problems that are not acknowledged by
   the subordinate. Discuss and try to resolve any disagreement on progress.   YES   NO

   Notes:

10. If progress is clearly on target, provide appropriate praise. If progress is
    not on target, calmly express concern.   YES   NO

    Notes:

11. If progress is on target, ask if any new obstacles or problems are antici-
    pated. If progress is not on target, ask the subordinate to identify obstacles
    preventing better progress.   YES   NO

    Notes:

12. Ask the subordinate to suggest ways to deal with any current or antici-
    pated problems, and mutually discuss the options.   YES   NO

    Notes:

13. If necessary, revise the goal, deadline, or action plan, or offer to provide
    more resources or assistance. Record any agreements.   YES   NO

    Notes:

14. Summarize overall progress and agreements reached, and repeat willing-
    ness to provide advice and assistance any time it is needed.
    YES   NO

    Notes:

15. Set a time and date for next (progess review or performance appraisal)
    meeting.   YES   NO

    Notes:

MODULE 9

Delegation

LEARNING OBJECTIVES

After completing this module a student will:

- *Understand different forms of delegation.*
- *Understand the potential advantages of delegation.*
- *Understand reasons why some managers avoid delegation.*
- *Understand what responsibilties to delegate.*
- *Understand procedures for effective delegation.*

CONTENTS OF MODULE

- *Text: Delegation*
- *Case: Henley Department Stores*
- *Case: The 60-hour Week*
- *Delegation Role Play*

Delegation

Delegation involves the assignment of new responsibilities to subordinates and additional authority to carry them out. It allows a subordinate more discretion and autonomy. Since the major work of managers is to accomplish objectives through the efforts of subordinates, skill in delegation is a major determinant of a manager's effectiveness. Students without managerial experience often fail to appreciate how difficult delegation is, and they do not understand the problems likely to occur when delegation is not carried out skillfully. This chapter will review varieties of delegation, advantages of delegation, reasons for lack of delegation, and guidelines for what to delegate and how to do it effectively. The concepts and guidelines presented in this chapter will help a manager to avoid some of the common pitfalls in delegation.

Varieties of Delegation

The term delegation is used to describe a variety of different forms and degrees of power sharing and task assignment. Understanding these variations makes it easier to determine how to delegate in a way appropriate to the situation. Major aspects of delegation include (Sherman, 1966; Webber, 1981):

- The variety and magnitude of responsibilities.
- The amount of discretion or range of choice allowed in deciding how to carry out responsibilities.
- The authority to take action and implement decisions without prior approval.
- The frequency and nature of reporting requirements.
- The flow of performance information.

In its most common form, delegation involves assignment of new and different tasks or responsibilities to a subordinate. For example, a person who was responsible for manufacturing something is given the additional responsibility of determining necessary materials and ordering them. Or the person is given the additional responsibility of inspecting the product he or she has made and correcting any defects. When new tasks are assigned, additional authority necessary to accomplish the tasks is usually delegated also. For example, the person who is given responsibility for ordering materials is given the authority to sign contracts with suppliers within specified constraints.

Sometimes delegation involves only the specification of additional authority and discretion for the same tasks and assignments already performed by the subordinate. For example, a sales representative is allowed to negotiate sales within a specified range of prices, quantities, and delivery dates, but cannot exceed these limits without prior approval from the sales manager. Delegation is increased by giving the sales representative more latitude in setting prices and delivery dates.

The extent to which a subordinate must check with the boss before taking action is another aspect of delegation. The lowest degree of delegation occurs when someone must ask the boss what to do whenever there is a problem. The amount of delegation is greater when the subordinate is allowed to determine what to do, but must get approval before implementing decisions. The most delegation occurs when the subordinate is allowed to make decisions and implement them without having to get prior approval. For example, a sales representative who was not allowed to make adjustments for damaged goods and late deliveries without checking first, is told to go ahead and resolve these matters on his or her own.

Reporting requirements are another aspect of delegation for which there is considerable variation. The amount of subordinate autonomy is greater when reports are required infrequently rather than frequently. For example, a plant manager must report production output and costs to the production vice president on a weekly basis rather than a daily basis. Autonomy is also greater when a subordinate is required to report only results, rather than reporting both the results and the procedures used to accomplish them. For example, a training director must report to the vice president for human resources the number of employees who were trained in each subject area and overall training expenses for the month, but not the types of training methods used, the number of trainers, or the breakdown of training expenses in different categories.

The flow of performance information involved in monitoring a subordinate's activities is also subject to variation. Subordinate autonomy is greater when detailed information about subordinate performance goes directly to the subordinate, who is allowed to correct any problems. A subordinate is likely to have less autonomy when detailed performance information goes first to the boss and is subsequently passed on to the subordinate. There is an intermediate amount of subordinate autonomy when detailed performance information goes to both simultaneously.

Potential Advantages of Delegation

Delegation offers a number of potential advantages if carried out in an appropriate and skillful manner by a manager.

Improved Decision Quality

One potential advantage of delegation, like other forms of participation and power sharing, is the improvement of decision quality. Delegation is likely to improve decision quality if a subordinate has more expertise in how to do the task than the manager has. Decision quality is also likely to improve if the subordinate's job requires quick responses to a changing situation and the lines of communication do not permit the manager to monitor the situation closely and make rapid adjustments. Since the subordinate is closer to the problem and has more relevant information about it than the manager, quicker and better decisions can be made by the subordinate. On the other hand, decision quality is not likely to improve if the subordinate lacks the skills to make good decisions, fails to understand what is expected, or has goals incompatible with those of the manager.

Increased Commitment

Another potential advantage of delegation is less resistance and greater commitment to implement decisions effectively. A subordinate who is responsible for making decisions is more likely to identify with them and consider them to be appropriate and justified than he or she would if the decisions were made by others. Since an unsuccessful decision reflects poorly on the competence of the person who made it, a greater effort is made to implement the decision effectively. However, commitment is unlikely to improve if delegation is seen as a manipulative tactic on the part of the manager, if the task is viewed as impossible, or if the subordinate does not consider the additional responsibilities to be appropriate and equitable.

Job Enrichment

Delegation of additional responsibilities and authority is a form of job enrichment that is likely to make a subordinate's job more interesting, challenging, and meaningful. Enriched jobs are sometimes necessary to attract and retain competent employees, especially when the organization has very limited opportunities for advancement to higher level positions. Giving junior managers more responsibility and authority, with a commensurate increase in salary, reduces the likelihood that they will be lured away to other companies in times of stiff competition for managerial talent. However, delegation will increase subordinate satisfaction only if the subordinate desires more responsibility and has the skills necessary to handle new responsibilities. In order for delegation to increase satisfaction, the subordinate must enjoy the experience of successfully accomplishing a challenging task. Constant frustrations due to a lack of sufficient authority and resources to carry out new responsibilities, or to a lack of ability, will decrease rather than increase job satisfaction.

Subordinate Development

Organizations need to develop managerial talent to fill vacant positions at higher levels of authority. Delegation can be an effective method of management development. Responsibilities similar to those in a higher position are delegated to a subordinate to develop the skills necessary to perform these responsibilities. When used for developmental purposes, delegation usually requires more coaching and monitoring by a manager. In this situation, it is evident that a subordinate does not have the necessary skills yet and must learn them while doing the new tasks or assignments. How the delegation is handled will determine how quickly and how much the subordinate learns.

Efficient Time Management

Delegation is one of the major methods of time management for a manager who is overloaded with responsibilities. By delegating less important duties and functions to subordinates, a manager frees additional time for more important responsibilities. Even when a manager could do the delegated tasks better than subordinates, it is a more efficient use of the manager's time to concentrate on those functions that will have the greatest influence on the performance of the manager's organizational unit. Without delegation, a manager is unlikely to have sufficient discretionary time to do some important tasks that require larger blocks of time and are not immediately urgent.

Reasons for Lack of Delegation

With all of these potential advantages from delegation, it would seem as if it should occur whenever appropriate. However, there are a number of reasons why some managers fail to delegate as much as they should (Newman & Warren, 1977; Preston & Zimmerer, 1978; Terry, 1972).

One reason is lack of confidence in subordinates. "If you want it done right, do it yourself" is an old expression that is still popular with many people. Some managers believe that they can do tasks better than subordinates, even when there is no factual basis for this conclusion. Lack of confidence may become a self-fulfilling prophecy. Subordinates may become apathetic and resentful if their development is stifled by excessive control and direction (Argyris, 1964).

A related reason for insufficient delegation is fear of being blamed for mistakes made by subordinates. Delegation is never absolute, because a manager continues to be responsible for the work activities of subordinates. In order to avoid the risk of mistakes, a manager may delegate sensitive tasks only to a few trusted subordinates, or not at all. Lack of delegation is especially a problem with managers who are insecure and managers who are perfectionists.

Failure to delegate may be the result of a strong need for power by a manager, sometimes combined with insecurity. Some managers desire to maintain absolute control over all aspects of their unit's operations, including decisions about work assignments, procedures, schedules, task goals, standards, allocation of resources, and personnel decisions. They enjoy the exercise of power over subordinates and the feeling of being indispensable. Delegation would require sharing power with subordinates. When subordinates are allowed to make decisions and handle problems on their own, it is likely to become evident that the manager is not indispensable. Furthermore, subordinates who demonstrate an ability to perform managerial responsibilities are seen as potential competitors for the manager's job.

Sometimes, failure to delegate is based on more justifiable reasons. If subordinates have interdependent jobs, extensive delegation makes it more difficult to coordinate the work. Examples of the types of work situations that have interdependent jobs include automobile assembly lines and product development teams. In this type of situation, power sharing by the manager of the work unit is more likely to take the form of consultation or group decisions than delegation to individuals. Delegation of authority is likely to result in subordinates doing things in different ways. When subordinates have similar jobs, any substantial amount of delegation would preclude the use of standardized facilities, equipment, procedures, and materials. Chain stores and restaurants such as MacDonalds are examples of organizations in which standardization limits the amount of delegation possible.

A final reason for lack of delegation is mistrust of subordinates. If a subordinate's values and objectives are perceived to be incompatible with those of the manager, little delegation of authority for decisions is likely to occur. Similarly, if subordinates are perceived to be lazy and unwilling to assume more responsibility, a manager is unlikely to use much delegation (McGregor, 1960). In many cases when a manager has a very negative perception of subordinate needs and values, this perception is very biased and inaccurate.

Guidelines on What to Delegate

The selection of tasks to delegate depends in part on the purpose of the delegation. Somewhat different tasks will be delegated depending on the purpose of the delegation.

1. Tasks that can be done better by a subordinate.

Some responsibilities can be done better by a subordinate than by you, because the subordinate has more expertise, because the subordinate is closer to the problem and can obtain more timely information about it, or because you simply do not have the time necessary to do the task properly. Such responsibilities are usually good candidates for delegation, regardless of the purpose.

2. Tasks that are urgent but not high-priority.

When the purpose is to reduce excessive workload, the best tasks for delegation are ones that are urgent but not high-priority. These are tasks that must get done quickly, and you do not have the time to do all of them. Some of these tasks may be things that a subordinate cannot do as well as you, but it is better for the tasks to be done by a subordinate than not at all. Delegation of these tasks frees more time for you to do high-priority tasks.

3. Tasks relevant to a subordinate's career.

If the purpose of delegation is to develop subordinate skills, the responsibilities must be ones relevant to the career objectives of a subordinate. Developmental delegation is likely to include special projects that allow a subordinate opportunity to struggle with a challenging task and exercise initiative and problem solving. Preparation of a subordinate to take over your job or advance to a similar job in another unit requires delegating some of your important managerial responsibilities, including ones the subordinate may not do as well as you. It is important to recognize that some of these delegated tasks may be irrelevant to the subordinate's current job, and in fact, may take time from the subordinate's regular work.

4. Tasks appropriate for the subordinate's ability and confidence.

Delegated tasks should be challenging for a subordinate, but not so difficult that the person has little hope of doing them successfully. The tasks should be difficult enough so that some mistakes are likely to occur, since mistakes are an integral part of the learning experience. However, the task should not be so difficult and important that mistakes will undermine the subordinate's self-confidence and ruin his or her reputation. Delegation for developmental purposes should be carried out gradually. As the subordinate learns how to handle initial responsibilities, additional ones are delegated.

5. Pleasant and unpleasant tasks.

Some managers keep all of the pleasant tasks for themselves and delegate only tedious, boring tasks to subordinates. Such tasks will not enrich subordinate jobs and are likely to reduce rather than increase subordinate job satisfaction. On the other hand, some managers with a martyr complex delegate only pleasant tasks and retain for themselves all the disagreeable ones. This approach leaves a gap in the development of subordinates and is likely to make the manager's job more stressful than it should be. Delegation should include both pleasant and unpleasant tasks. The unpleasant tasks should be shared by subordinates or rotated among them to avoid perceptions of favoritism and inequity in work assignments.

6. Tasks not central to the manager's role.

Tasks that are symbolically important and central to a manager's role should not be delegated. These responsibilities include such things as planning operations, allocating resources among subordinates, evaluating the performance of subordinates and providing feedback, making personnel decisions about pay increases and promotions for subordinates, directing the group's response to a crisis, and various figurehead activities for which an appearance by the manager is expected (Mintzberg, 1973). When it is necessary to develop subordinate skills related to these responsibilities, another form of participation such as consultation or group decisions can be used rather than delegation. For example, some planning may be carried out in planning meetings in which subordinates provide ideas and suggestions, but the responsibility for planning decisions is not given to individual subordinates. Likewise, a subordinate may be invited to help with the preparations and to accompany you to an important meeting with superiors or managers of other units, but the subordinate is not sent alone. However, in the special case of a subordinate with an appropriate managerial position (such as the assistant manager), even some delegation of central responsibilities may be feasible, especially for developmental purposes.

Guidelines on How to Delegate

The success of delegation depends as much on how it is carried out as on what is delegated. The following guidelines are designed to minimize problems and avoid common pitfalls related to the assignment of tasks and delegation of authority. The first set of guidelines are for the meeting in which delegation is carried out.

1. Specify responsibilities clearly and check for comprehension.

When delegating, it is essential to make sure the subordinate understands the new responsibilities. Explain clearly the results expected for a delegated task or assignment, clarify goals and objectives, and inform the person about any deadlines that must be met. Check for comprehension by asking if there are any questions, by questioning the subordinate about important aspects of the task, or by asking the subordinate to restate your expectations. For an inexperienced subordinate, you may want to ask the person to prepare action plans for you to review before they are implemented.

2. Provide adequate authority and specify limits of discretion.

Unless adequate resources are provided, the subordinate is unlikely to be successful in carrying out a delegated task. When assigning new responsibilities, determine the appropriate amount of authority needed by the subordinate to carry them out. Specify clearly the subordinate's scope of authority and limits of discretion. Authority includes the right to make decisions without prior approval and the right to reach agreements with other units in the organization or outsiders. Authority also includes the right to use resources such as funds, equipment, materials, personnel, facilities, and support services.

3. Specify reporting requirements.

It is important for a subordinate to understand the types of information that must be reported to you, how often reports are expected, and the manner in which progress will be monitored (e.g., by written reports, progress review meetings, presentations in department meetings). The frequency and timing of progress reviews will depend on the nature of the task and the competence of the subordinate. More frequent checking is appropriate for critical tasks with high exposure and high cost of mistakes, and for subordinates who lack experience and confidence. As a subordinate demonstrates competence in doing delegated tasks, the frequency of reporting can be reduced. Progress reports should emphasize results, but the means for accomplishing delegated tasks should not be ignored entirely. It is important to ensure that subordinates use procedures that are legal, ethical, and consistent with organizational policy.

4. Ensure subordinate acceptance of responsibilities.

If delegation is to be successful, the subordinate must accept the new assignments and be committed to carry them out. In some cases there is no problem with acceptance, because the assignments are interesting and important for the subordinate's career advancement.

However, a subordinate may be reluctant to admit doubts and concerns about new assignments. It is useful to allow the subordinate to participate in determining what tasks will be assigned and how much authority will be delegated. With developmental delegation, it is useful to discuss how the delegated tasks are relevant to the person's career advancement. If the subordinate lacks self confidence, it is helpful to express confidence in the person's ability to do a good job.

The next set of guidelines describes steps the manager should take after delegating responsibilities to a subordinate.

5. Inform others who need to know.

People who are affected by the delegation and people whose cooperation and assistance are necessary for the subordinate to do the delegated tasks should be informed about the subordinate's new responsibilities and authority. Unless informed about the delegation by you, these people may doubt the subordinate's authority and ignore his or her requests and directions. The people who need to be informed may include other subordinates, subordinates of your subordinate, peers in other units, outsiders such as clients and suppliers, and your boss.

6. Monitor progress at appropriate times in appropriate ways.

With delegated tasks, as with all tasks, it is important to monitor progress and provide feedback to the subordinate. If not in the delegation meeting, then soon after, you should decide what type of performance measures and progress indicators to collect. It is usually best to arrange for detailed information on performance to flow directly to the subordinate, with less detailed summary information coming to you at less frequent intervals. However, in the case of developmental delegation with an inexperienced subordinate, you may want to collect more detailed information more frequently, to enable you to check more closely on the progress of the subordinate.

7. Arrange for the subordinate to receive necessary information.

In addition to performance information, the subordinate will need various types of technical and general information to carry out his or her delegated tasks effectively. Keep the subordinate informed about changes that affect his or her plans and schedules. If possible, arrange for relevant technical information to flow directly to the subordinate, and help the subordinate establish his or her own sources of essential information.

8. Provide support and assistance, but avoid reverse delegation.

You should provide psychological support to a subordinate who is discouraged or frustrated, and encourage the person to keep going. For newly delegated tasks, it may be necessary to provide more advice and coaching about procedures for doing some aspect of the work. However, it is important to avoid reverse delegation where you reassert control over a task that was previously delegated. When a subordinate comes to you with problems, ask the person to recommend a solution. You can help the person evaluate whether the solution is feasible and appropriate, but your role should only be that of a resource person and consultant.

9. Make mistakes a learning experience.

It is important to recognize that mistakes are inevitable for delegated tasks and to be prepared to deal with them in an appropriate manner. Hold a subordinate accountable for his or her performance, but don't expect perfection, and don't expect a subordinate to do the task exactly the way you would have done it. Mistakes and failures should be treated seriously, but the response should not be one of criticism and blame. Mistakes should become a learning experience for both parties. Discuss the reason for the mistake and identify ways to avoid similar mistakes in the future. Provide additional instruction and coaching if it becomes obvious that the subordinate does not know how to do some essential aspect of the work.

Summary

Delegation is one of the most important functions carried out by a manager, and it is one of the major determinants of effective time management. Delegation is closely related to other managerial functions and practices, such as planning, organizing, directing, motivating, monitoring, informing, and developing subordinates. Thus, delegating necessarily involves many of the different skills and behaviors discussed in this book. Students will have an opportunity to practice selecting appropriate tasks to delegate in the Time Management Exercise.

References

Argyris, C. (1964). *Integrating the Individual and the Organization.* New York: John Wiley.

Heller, F., & Yukl, G. (1969). "Participation, Managerial Decision Making, and Situational Variables." *Organizational Behavior and Human Performance,* 4, 227–241.

Leana, C. R. (1986). "Predictors and Consequences of Delegation." *Academy of Management Journal, 29,* 754–774.

Maier, N. R. F., & Thurber, J. A. (1969). "Problems in Delegation." *Personnel Psychology, 22,* 131-139.

McConkey, D. (1974). *No Nonsense Delegation.* New York: AMACOM.

McGregor, D. (1960). *The Human Side of Enterprise.* New York: McGraw-Hill.

Mintzberg, H. (1973). *The Nature of Managerial Work.* New York: Harper & Row.

Newman, W. H., & Warren, K. (1977). *The Process of Management.* Englewood Cliffs, NJ: Prentice Hall.

Preston, P. & Zimmerer, T. W. (1978). *Management for Supervisors.* Englewood Cliffs, NJ: Prentice Hall.

Sherman, H. (1966). *It All Depends: A Pragmatic Approach to Delegation.* University, AL: University of Alabama Press, 1966.

Steinmetz, L. L. (1976). *The Art and Skill of Delegation.* Reading, MA: Addison-Wesley.

Terry, G. R. (1972). *Principles of Management.* Homewood, IL: Irwin.

Vroom, V. H., & Yetton, P. W. (1973). *Leadership and Decision Making.* Pittsburgh: University of Pittsburgh Press.

Webber, R. A. (1981). *To Be a Manager.* Homewood, IL: Irwin.

Whetten, D. A. , & Cameron, K. S. (1984). *Developing Managerial Skills.* Glenview, IL: Scott-Foresman.

Yukl, G. (1981). *Leadership in Organizations.* Englewood Cliffs, NJ: Prentice Hall.

Case: Henley Department Stores

Elizabeth Edwards is a store manager for Henley Department Stores, a large retail chain of stores in the northeast and midwest. She has been manager of a medium-sized store for nearly a year. Before that she was the assistant manager in another store for two years. Arriving at the store on Monday, Elizabeth is determined to make progress on her goal of improving store profits, which have dropped below average for the past six months. As she enters the store, she notices that the new window displays for the coming holidays have not been set up yet. Two weeks ago she delegated responsibility for these displays to her merchandise manager, Jeff Jorden. Well, she thinks, it is just like Jeff to screw up even a simple assignment like this one.

When she arrives at her office, Elizabeth greets her secretary, Mary Maxwell, and looks through her mail and telephone messages. One of the letters is from a customer complaining that Ms. Cooper, the new sales clerk in the woman's wear department, was very rude last week when the customer wanted to try on some clothing. Elizabeth asks Mary to go talk to the sales-clerk and reprimand her for being rude to a customer. Elizabeth frequently relies on her secretary to handle personnel matters of this nature. Mary has good administrative skills and has been a valuable employee. Elizabeth would like Mary to apply for a job as a department manager, but Mary likes her present job and does not want the added responsibility of a supervisory position.

Next, Elizabeth calls in Jeff Jorden, and in a very irritated tone of voice, asks him why the window displays are not set up yet. Jeff replies that employees in several departments are preparing the displays and they will be set up after Thanksgiving weekend, just as they were the year before. He adds that he did not realize Elizabeth was in such a hurry and wishes she had told him she wanted them set up earlier than usual. Just then the telephone rings, and, as Elizabeth picks up the phone, Jeff takes advantage of the opportunity to retreat back to his own office.

The call is from Brad Belmar, Elizabeth's boss. Brad asks her how she is progressing on a special sales report that he needs for a planning meeting the next day. Elizabeth assures him that the report will be sent by express mail at the end of the day. Hanging up the telephone, Elizabeth goes to the office where her three clerical employees work and asks them to gather the information needed for the report. She says that each of them should work on the report in between their other tasks. She tells them it is important to get the job done before the end of the work day.

Next, Elizabeth stops in to see Fred Franklin, the assistant store manager. Fred is the son-in-law of the executive vice president for Henley Stores, and Elizabeth suspects that he is being groomed for rapid advancement in the company. Fred has been an assistant manager for only six months, but Elizabeth views him as a potential rival for the position of store manager in a larger Henley's store currently under construction in the suburbs. Although Fred has an MBA degree (she has only a BA degree) and seems very capable, Elizabeth gives him mostly routine assignments that do not allow any opportunity to exercise initiative and impress higher management. She checks on him closely and insists on approving even small decisions. In the few instances where she has given him an important task with high visibility, she intentionally provided insufficient resources to do the task properly. Elizabeth asks Fred to report on a marketing project that he is doing for her. When Fred explains that he has made arrangements to try a new approach, Elizabeth gets upset and reprimands him for not checking with her beforehand.

Later in the afternoon, Elizabeth returns to the clerical section to get the information she needs to complete the sales report for her boss. When Elizabeth arrives, she learns that they are not finished yet. Randy Ross, one of the clerical employees, says that each of them worked on the task a little during the day, but they did not have much time to spare and there is still about an hour's worth of work to do. By this time, Elizabeth is really angry. This has not been her day. What is the matter with these employees? Don't they have any sense of responsibility when she gives them an important task like this one? She tells all three employees to drop everything and get the sales figures ready, even if they have to stay late.

Questions for Students

What specific mistakes did Elizabeth make in each of the following incidents, and how could she have been more effective as a manager?

1. Jeff and the holiday window displays.

2. Mary and the reprimand of the rude sales clerk.

3. The clerical workers collecting information for the sales report.

4. Delegation to Fred the assistant manager.

Case: The 60-hour Week*

Marvin felt a knot in his stomach when he glanced at his watch. It was already after 9 P.M. This was the third week in a row that he'd been working overtime every night, and the pressure was getting to him. When he got home, his wife was upset, and she let him know it.

"Who else is working there with you?" she demanded to know.

"No one," he admitted glumly, anticipating what was coming next.

"Why do you have to be the one who does all the work in that department?" she asked sarcastically.

"It's not work for the Customer Accounts Department," Marvin replied. "It's work for a committee that is looking into buying out another company."

He explained that his boss had personally asked him to serve on the committee and that it would make recommendations directly to the top management of Allied Industries.

"Look, Marvin, I know it's important work," she protested. "I just don't see why you can't do it during regular office hours."

"Because I still have to run the day-to-day operations of the Customer Accounts Department," he said patiently.

"But your department still runs when you're on vacation!" she reminded him. "Can't you pretend you're on vacation when you're working on this committee stuff?"

Marvin frowned deeply. His wife had made a good point. He thought for a while, then promised he would try to reassign some of his regular duties. The next day, Marvin made a record of everything he did. When he looked over his notes that evening, he was amazed to find how many of his duties could have been handled by his office workers. The next day he began delegating.

First, he asked Sylvia to make a series of phone calls, which he'd originally planned to to make himself, to sort out some inventory problems. After she asked a number of questions to clarify what was expected of her, Sylvia seemed confident and agreed to make the calls. Marvin urged her to be sure to tell him if she needed any help along the way, since he was still responsible if anything went wrong.

Marvin was even more cautious about assigning credit rating reports to Jane. Information in these reports was highly confidential, since any leak could violate the privacy of customers. It could also result in a bad credit reputation for a customer who had not had a final chance to make payments. Marvin had a lot of confidence in Jane and had shared confidential credit information with her in the past. Marvin carefully explained to Jane the importance of the assignment, and was very specific about how he wanted it done. He encouraged her to ask questions to be sure she knew what was expected. Marvin also explained that protecting the confidentiality of sensitive information would be an important factor in evaluating how well she did the job. Jane assured Marvin that she fully understood her assignment, but would need a partitioned office for privacy, which Marvin arranged.

* Adapted from W. J. Wasmuch and L. Greenhalgh, *Effective Supervision: Developing Your Skills Through Critical Incidents.* Englewood Cliffs, NJ: Prentice Hall, Copyright © 1979.

After Jane left, Marvin's secretary came into his office with her dictation notepad and reminded Marvin that he'd been putting off writing several letters. Marvin's mind was now back on the committee work, and he asked her to remind him what the letters were about. After she outlined what each letter ought to say, Marvin relized that she could compose such routine correspondence as well as he could. He asked if she would mind writing the letters herself.

"I wouldn't mind at all. I often have to rewrite them anyway, especially when your mind's on something else while you're dictating," she confessed, grinning.

"Then why have I been wasting my time dictating them in the first place?" Marvin asked.

"Beats me," she replied. "I guess you just got into the habit."

"Well, from now on, I don't want to be bothered with routine correspondence, since you probably do it better," he told her. "Don't even bring it to my attention unless there are special circumstances."

Marvin felt relieved as he turned back to his work for the committee. At ten minutes before five, the secretary brought in six letters for his signature. Marvin hurriedly glanced through the first letter and signed it, then automatically signed the others. He was out of the office by 5:30.

However, several days later Marvin received an angry telephone call from a long-time customer who had received one of the letters. His secretary had made a mistake that Marvin hadn't caught. Her letter implied that the customer was becoming a poor credit risk, when in fact there had been an agreement to delay payment until an insurance claim for a fire in his store was settled. There was actually a note to this effect in the file, but obviously his secretary had not checked the file. Rather, she had merely looked at how long the debt had been outstanding.

After explaining the error to the customer, amid many apologies, Marvin told his secretary what had happened. He wanted her to understand that the mistake could have been very costly. He also wanted to be sure that she, like himself, would learn from the mistake.

"In the future," Marvin told her, "I'll be sure to read each letter before I sign it if you will be sure to check all customer correspondence and credit information before drafting a letter. Is that agreeable?"

"You mean you still want me to write all your routine letters?" she asked weakly.

Questions for Students

1. Cite examples of effective and ineffective behavior by Marvin in delegating responsibilities to Sylvia, Jane, and his secretary.

DELEGATION ROLE PLAY

Instructions

The purpose of this role play is to allow students to practice the guidelines for delegating effectively. For this role play it is necessary for students to form three-person groups and determine for each group who will play the role of the boss, who will play the role of the subordinate, and who will serve as an observer.

All students can read the background information below, but do not look at the specific instructions for any role other than the one you have been selected to carry out. If you have been selected to be the boss (vice president of operations) or subordinate (store manager), take about 10 minutes to read your role and plan what you will say. Students selected to be observers should study the instructions for observers and the form for taking notes on the meeting. These notes will be the basis for feedback to the student playing the role of boss.

Background Information

Baxter Company is a retail discount chain with 20 stores in five states. The company was founded nine years ago and has been expanding rapidly. Most stores are located in suburban areas, some are in urban areas, and a few are in rural areas. The stores are all identical in appearance and layout. Merchandise is selected and purchased in large quantities by the headquarters buyers and stockpiled in the company's two warehouses. Each store receives an initial shipment of each item, then orders replacements as needed. All prices are set by headquarters marketing staff, and they also do the planning for all promotions and sales. Thus, all stores have the same prices, and the promotions go on simultaneously in all locations.

ROLE FOR BOSS

Vice President of Store Operations

Role for Boss

You are the vice president of operations for Baxter Stores. Top management has recently decided to experiment with decentralization of some important operating decisions. They feel that this change will improve sales and profits and reduce some bureaucratic problems such as promotions that some stores do not need or are not prepared to handle. A few stores have been selected to participate in this trial. These stores were selected because they have managers who appear to have the personality and ability required for an expanded managerial role. If the experiment goes smoothly, after one year the changes will be instituted in all the Baxter stores. At that time, a program of bonuses based on store profits will be instituted for store managers.

You are about to meet with one of your subordinates, who is the manager of store number 17. The purpose of the meeting is to explain how more authority for decisions will be delegated to him or her. The following changes will be made:

1. The manager of store #17 will be given responsibility for pricing decisions and will be able to adjust prices upward or downward on all items in his/her store. Prices can be increased by up to 25% above the list price recommended by the headquarters merchandise department, and they can be reduced down to the base cost of an item.

2. Store #17 will still receive shipments of standard items, but the manager will be given authority to spend up to 20% of his/her merchandise replacement budget on items purchased from other suppliers' lists rather than from the list of items available from Baxter warehouses. This flexibility will allow the store to obtain items that have special appeal in its local area. Monthly sales reports on special items must be submitted to the merchandise vice president.

3. The manager of Store #17 will be able to conduct promotions campaigns and special sales in addition to the ones initiated by headquarters. A promotions budget will be provided to pay for the cost of local advertising in newspapers and on radio and television. The size of this budget will be determined next week. Headquarters should be informed in advance of local promotions and sales, to allow coordination with store-wide promotions.

ROLE FOR SUBORDINATE

Manager of Store Number 17

Role for Manager of Store #17

You are about to meet with your boss, the vice president of store operations. You have heard through the grapevine that some major changes are in the works to decentralize operating decisions to the level of the store managers. You are very excited about this change, because you believe that your store could increase sales and profits if you had more discretion about store operations. You have been hampered in competing with other stores in the same area by lack of control over prices and choice of items to sell. You do not have much expertise about advertising campaigns and would need some instruction and advice from the experts at headquarters to help you learn how to plan promotions campaigns. You are hoping that greater responsibility for profits will also mean greater opportunity to earn bonuses based on store profits. You plan to ask your boss about this matter.

Instructions for Observers

Your job is to observe the role play and take notes on how well the student playing the role of boss followed the delegation guidelines presented in the module text. The relevant guidelines for this role play are listed on the observer form. Indicate whether the "boss" does each step and note examples of effective and ineffective behavior.

In preparation for the role play, read the background information and your copy of the role for the boss, so you can understand what information should be communicated to the subordinate during the delegating meeting.

Observer Form for Delegation Role Play

1. Specifies responsibilities and authority clearly.
Yes_____   No_____
Notes:

2. Checks for comprehension.   Yes_____   No_____
Notes:

3. Specifies reporting requirements.   Yes_____   No_____
Notes:

  4. Ensures subordinate acceptance of responsibilities.
  Yes_____   No_____
  Notes:

  5. Offers appropriate support, assistance, and resources.
  Yes_____   No_____
  Notes:

  6. Other observations.

MODULE 10

Time Management

After completing this module a student will:

- *Understand reasons for problems in time management.*
- *Understand the benefits of good time management.*
- *Understand common time wasters and how to avoid them.*
- *Learn guidelines for planning daily activities.*
- *Understand how time management relates to planning, setting objectives, and delegating.*

- *Text: Time Management*
- *Case: ABZ Corporation*
- *Time Management Exercise*

Time Management

Time is a scarce resource that must be managed well if a manager is to be effective. It is not possible to create more time, but most people can make better use of existing time. Time is "wasted" when it is used for things that are less important than other potential uses. The difficult part is not in finding time to do something, but rather in knowing what things are important enough to do. Some things are not important enough to be done at all much less in a careful, precise way; and doing them only steals time from more essential activities. The key to time management is knowing what you want to accomplish. A person with a clear set of objectives and priorities can identify important activities and plan the best way to use time. However, without clear objectives, no amount of planning will improve time management.

Sources of Problems in Time Management

Lack of clear objectives and priorities are not the only source of problems in time management. A number of normal human tendencies make it more difficult to manage time well, even when we have clear objectives:

- People prefer to do things that are interesting and pleasant before doing things that are tedious and unpleasant.
- People are able to do routine, repetitive activities in less time than they can do unusual, unfamiliar activities.
- People prefer to do easy things before doing things that are extremely difficult.
- People prefer to do things that will be completed and provide closure before doing things that will not.
- People tend to do things that are urgent before doing things that are not.
- Urgent things tend to be initiated by others rather than by ourselves.
- People tend to wait until just before a deadline to do a task.
- People do not have a very good awareness of how their time is used.
- People tend to equate activity with achievement.

Effective time management is also impeded by some basic paradoxes:

- People who are very busy cannot find time for planning that would save more time than it takes.
- People who mostly respond to urgent crises and problems insure that they will occur in the future, because they do not plan how to avoid them.
- People who will not delegate to inexperienced subordinates are unlikely to develop subordinates with adequate experience in activities that should be delegated.
- People who are able to find time to do things for others are likely to be asked to do even more things.
- People who tend to leave things out on their desk so they will not be lost or forgotten create such clutter that things are lost or forgotten.

Improving time management has a variety of benefits. The Pareto Principle says that 80% of effectiveness comes from 20% of what you do. Time management allows you to concentrate on the activities that are most important, thereby increasing your effectiveness. Greater effectiveness is likely to increase work satisfaction and chances for career advancement. Time management also reduces the frustrations and stress resulting from being overloaded with work. Lower stress and frustration, in turn, result in better physical and mental health. However, it is important to understand that time management does not mean doing everything faster and better, which would only increase stress and fatigue. Time management means doing fewer things but doing them well.

Common Time Wasters for Managers

Studies of managerial activities find some common time wasters, including the following:

1. Drop-in visitors.
2. Telephone interruptions.
3. Cluttered office.
4. Unessential tasks.
5. Unnecessary or over-long meetings.

The causes of each type of problem and some possible remedies are described in this section.

Drop-in Visitors

Casual visitors are probably the biggest time wasters for a manager. The nature of managerial work requires many brief contacts with a wide network of people, including subordinates, peers, superiors, clients, and other outsiders. However, the need to interact with many people frequently does not imply that a manager should be available at any time to anybody who wants to see him or her for any reason.

Some managers fail to screen visitors and prevent interruptions because of deep-seated fears and anxieties. Some managers may fear that without an "open door," visitors will be offended, important information will be missed, and open communication will be discouraged. For some managers, a strong need for affiliation and desire to socialize may be the cause of too much accessibility. In other cases, attributes of the physical environment or the organizational structure discourage privacy. Examples include lack of a separate office and lack of a secretary to screen visitors.

Some common remedies involve a variety of barriers, scheduling mechanisms, and screening mechanisms. Other remedies involve reducing the need for people to ask for information and advice. Frequent questions suggest a possible failure to clarify role expectations and disseminate relevant information to people. Still other remedies allow you to control the length of a visit and end it quickly.

- Have your secretary screen visitors, and provide enough guidance so that the secretary can make good judgments about who should gain access and who should be put off.
- Make yourself inaccessible during particular times of the week by closing your door or working in a more private location.
- Prepare polite excuses to discourage or shorten visits (such as, "I have to leave for a meeting," "I am expecting an important call," " I am in the middle of something that I have to finish right away, can I meet with you later?").
- Set up regular meetings each week with members of your work unit and encourage them to use these meetings for presenting appropriate problems, questions, and requests.
- Hold open office periods each week when you are available without an appointment for anybody who needs to see you for a few minutes.
- Clarify role expectations by setting specific goals and deadlines, giving clear instructions, and reaching agreement on action plans. Develop standard responses for types of crises and disturbances that can be handled directly by subordinates, making it unnecessary for them to ask you for instructions.
- Use non-verbal cues to signal that you are busy (for example, don't give eye contact to people who pass by or peer into your office; remain standing when an unannounced visitor comes to your door; hold the telephone in your hand as someone comes in, which shows you are about to make a call; look frequently at your watch to show that a meeting is running too long).
- Meet with people in their offices instead of yours.

These remedies are usually successful in reducing the number of announced visitors and keeping visits brief. However, these remedies should be used carefully and in a way that does not make you inaccessible to people who need to see you and with whom you need to maintain good relations.

Telephone Interruptions

The telephone is an important medium for communication by managers, and, in comparison to visiting someone or writing a memo, it can save time. However, telephones can become a major form of interruption if not controlled carefully. Reasons for problems with telephone interruptions are probably similar to the reasons for problems with drop-in visitors. Some managers are afraid of offending people or being unavailable.

It is much easier to deal with telephone interruptions than with unannounced visitors. Again, remedies involve a combination of better screening, better communication of role expectations and technical information, and increased alternatives for meeting with you.

- If you receive many calls that are not essential, have your secretary screen all of your calls. Provide enough guidance so that the secretary can make good judgments about who should gain access and who should be put off. For example, give the secretary a list of people who should be put through immediately. Have the secretary politely inquire about the identity of other callers and the nature of their business with you. If the secretary is in doubt about the relevance of a call, he or she should ask you before putting it through.

- Even if most calls you receive are important, you will want to ask your secretary to take your calls during special meetings or work sessions when you don't want to be interrupted except for an emergency or special person. If no secretary is available to take calls at these times, use an answering machine.

- Delegate responsibility for answering particular types of inquiries to your secretary or a subordinate to whom the call can be switched.

- If it is common to receive misdirected calls, keep handy a list of names and telephone numbers of the appropriate people who can provide information to a caller or deal with the caller's problem.

- Set aside some time periods each week when people know they can call you and get through.

- Prepare polite excuses to shorten calls (such as, "I can only talk for a minute now," "I have to leave for a meeting," "I am in the middle of a meeting, can I call you back later?").

- Clarify role expectations by setting specific goals and deadlines, giving clear instructions, and reaching agreement on action plans. Develop standard responses for types of crises and disturbances that can be handled directly by subordinates, making it unnecessary for them to ask you for instructions.

- Have materials and information ready for calls that you expect to receive, so you are prepared for them and do not need to waste time or call back. Being prepared also shortens calls that you initiate.

Cluttered Office

Clutter and disorganization in the office waste time. Things become lost, and time is lost searching for them. Items of paperwork are handled several times when they need to be handled only once. There are a number of causes of clutter and disorganization. Some people are afraid of losing or forgetting things, so they leave them on the desk where they can be seen. Some people leave things out because they don't want to look as if they are not busy. Sometimes clutter is the result of excessive paperwork; the sheer volume of paperwork that must be dealt with creates backlogs. Sometimes paperwork piles up because of indecisiveness; the person puts aside items of paperwork that could be dealt with immediately. Finally, some people are just habitually very messy and disorganized.

Remedies involve a variety of approaches, including better organization of files, decision rules for handling paperwork efficiently, efforts to reduce the amount of necessary paperwork, and better screening of paperwork by others.

- Set priorities on incoming correspondence and paperwork before you begin to deal with any items; correspondence can be sorted into general categories on a daily basis (first class mail and important internal memos that should be looked at today; miscellaneous memos and reports that should be filed or put aside until more time is available; junk mail and correspondence that should be discarded or redirected to others).
- If the flow of correspondence to you is excessive, and you have a very capable secretary or assistant, have the person screen and sort your correspondence for you.
- Try to handle items only once whenever possible; develop a set of decision rules to facilitate decisions about how to handle recurrent types of correspondence.
- Delegate responsibility for handling routine types of correspondence to your secretary and/or to subordinates.
- Set up an efficient file system with categories that are easy to remember and files that are easy to find.
- Periodically discard old records and files that are no longer relevant, or store them elsewhere.
- Reduce the amount of required reports and memos from subordinates, clients, and others, or set limits on how long these should be.
- Whenever appropriate, respond to memos or letters when you receive them by writing a short answer on the original document, rather than

waiting to prepare another memo or letter of your own. Also, use the telephone to save time when a formal, written response is unnecessary.

Unnecessary Tasks

Much time is wasted by some managers on tasks that are not important or that could be done as well by someone else. There are a number of reasons why some managers become overloaded with unnecessary tasks. One reason is the lack of clear objectives and priorities. As noted earlier, it is difficult to determine what tasks are important without a clear understanding of what you want to accomplish. Another reason is failure to delegate some of the work to subordinates. Reasons for failure to delegate are discussed in the module on delegation. A third reason for being overloaded with unessential tasks is inability to say no to requests. Some people are afraid of offending subordinates, peers, or the boss, and they lack the self-confidence and assertiveness to turn down requests. If the task is done well, the person who requested it is encouraged to ask for even more favors.

Possible remedies for this problem are directed at the causes:

- Prepare tactful ways to say no and use them. For example, say that you are very busy and would not be able to do a task until a time that you know is too late to be of any use to the person who requested it. Suggest other people who could do the task faster or better. Say that you could only do the task if the person does some of your work for you. Point out that an important task will be delayed or jeopardized if you do what the person requests. In the case of a request by your boss, you can ask the boss to decide which task is more important to him or her.

- Identify unessential tasks that can be eliminated. If necessary, get them removed from your list of required duties and responsibilities. To persuade your boss, show how resources will be saved or other benefits attained.

- Whenever feasible, delegate less important tasks to subordinates and your secretary.

- Put off any unessential tasks that cannot be delegated or eliminated, and do them in slack times, at times when you are too tired to do something important, or at odd times when you are waiting for someone.

- Procrastinate on routine but unnecessary tasks done for others such as peers. Sometimes when these things are not done, people will discover that they do not need them and stop asking for them.
- Use political power to get unessential tasks transferred to someone else or to another unit in the organization.

Unnecessary or Over-long Meetings

Meetings are an unavoidable part of the managerial job, but many of them waste time because they are unnecessary or take too long. Unproductive meetings occur due to a variety of causes, including lack of clear purpose, absence of key people, late participants, unprepared participants, unnecessary socializing, deviations from the agenda, interruptions, and lack of skilled leadership. Other approaches for making meetings more effective are discussed in the module on leading decision groups. Some possible remedies are the following:

- Determine who needs to be present for the meeting to be successful. Invite relevant people, but keep the group as small as possible.
- Prepare a clear agenda and distribute it in advance of the meeting.
- Inform people about what they need to do to prepare for a meeting, and make sure they receive any necessary information.
- Save time in meetings by assigning some preliminary tasks to be done by individuals outside of the meetings, such as preparing reports, analyses, and proposals, or gathering materials.
- Let people know that meetings will start on time, and be consistent about doing so. Set a good example by arriving at the meeting site on time.
- Arrange to hold meetings in a quiet location with adequate space and ventilation, and take steps to prevent unnecessary interruptions.
- Before ending a meeting, decide if and when a followup meeting should be scheduled. Assign clear responsibility to individuals for implementing decisions and/or making preparations for the next meeting.
- Prepare and distribute a summary after the meeting of what was discussed and decided, who was assigned which responsibilities, and the date, time, and location of the next scheduled meeting.

Other Causes of Poor Time Management

Time management is improved by dealing with common time wasters, but poor time management usually involves other deficiencies as well, such as inadequate planning, procrastination, and perfectionism. Ways to improve planning and avoid procrastination will be discussed next.

Planning Daily Activities

It was noted earlier that effective time management requires clear objectives, strategies, and priorities, which are determined through a process of long-term planning. Equally important are short-term plans to identify the action steps necessary to implement strategies and accomplish objectives. Other modules in this book describe how to set objectives and develop action plans to attain them. Formal time management systems focus on short-term planning, and they usually include weekly and daily planning forms for managers to schedule their appointments, meetings, and activities.

When planning daily activities, the first step is to make a "to-do list" for the day and assign priorities to each activity. A sample is shown in Figure 10–1. Priority A means an activity is urgent and important. Priority B means an activity is important but not urgent. Priority C means an activity is neither important nor urgent. Managers are instructed to use the prioritized activity list together with their calendar of required meetings and predetermined appointments to plan their day. Discretionary time should be used to carry out a mix of Priority A and Priority B activities in appropriate time periods. Some Priority C activities are handled at odd times or delegated to others. If there is insufficient time to do urgent activities with immediate deadlines, the manager should attempt to reschedule some activities that are less important, such as routine meetings. The task of juggling the various activities and deciding which to do is a difficult but essential component of managerial work.

Planning one's daily activities does not imply that a manager determines exactly what to do each minute of the day. Except for a few blocks of time set aside for longer cognitive tasks that require concentration (such as writing a report or preparing a budget or work schedule), most managerial work will involve interaction with other people. Sometimes structured interactions, such as pre-planned meetings or appointments with the key people, will be necessary. Related activities involving the same people can be grouped together. For example, a manager may meet with a subordinate to handle one item, then call in another subordinate or a peer to deal with another matter that involves all three people. Other activities on the manager's list or "mental

Item	Notes
Priority A: Must Do Today	
1. Prepare for staff meeting at 10:30	Find agenda, read info
2. Report on rush order to VP-Sales	Talk to assistant
3. Call supplier to check on new materials	
4. Prepare quality report for boss (overdue)	Get info from QC
5. Schedule dept. meeting for next week	Delegate to secretary
6. Plan production schedule for next week	Get work orders from PS
7. Schedule meetings for progress reviews with supervisors	Delegate to secretary
8. Set up meeting with boss to discuss budget	Review proposals
Priority B: Should Do If Time Available	
1. Prepare monthly production report	Get info from supervisors
2. Develop training schedule for machine operators.	Meet with assistant
3. Attend meeting of safety committee at 3:00 P.M.	
4. Meet with quality control mgr. to discuss new standards.	
5. Review performance reports for March	Get info from secretary
Priority C: Nice to Do If Time	
1. Read new technical report on PV machines	
2. Straighten out production files	
3. Meet with training director to discuss training needs	
4. Plan vacation schedules for summer	Get info from supervisors
5. Meet with R & D manager to get update on new products	

FIGURE 10–1 Sample Daily Activity Planner

agenda" can be attended to as opportunities arise. For example, a chance encounter with a peer may provide the opportunity to inquire about something the person is doing for you.

The planning of daily activities should take into account natural energy cycles and bio-rythms. Peak alertness and efficiency occur at different times of the day for different people. Some people function best in the morning, whereas others function best in the afternoon or are "night people." Peak periods should be used for difficult tasks and ones that require creativity. Simple, boring tasks should be scheduled for times of low mental and physical energy. Unimportant tasks, even if difficult, can be scheduled for times when a person is likely to be tired or at a low point in the energy cycle.

The planning of daily activities should also consider the fact that it is more efficient to do a series of similar tasks than to keep switching from one type of task to another. Sometimes it is possible to schedule similar activities (for example, making several telephone calls or writing several letters) for the same time during the day.

Procrastination and Perfectionism

Even when it is obvious that an activity is important, a person may choose to delay doing it in favor of a less important activity. One reason for procrastination is the fear of failure. People find excuses for delaying a task because they lack self-confidence or perceive the task to be impossible. One remedy for procrastination when there is a long and complex task is to divide the task into smaller parts, each of which is easier and less intimidating. It is best to start with an easy subtask if possible, but if not, a useful mental tactic to overcome initial resistance is to agree that you will work on the first subtask for an hour and continue only if it is going okay. Once part of a task has been done, the task is more likely to be finished than if never begun.

Another useful tactic is to set a definite deadline for beginning the task. However, it is important to avoid deluding oneself that a deadline is equivalent to actually starting the work. Some people even reward themselves just for setting a starting deadline. For example, having decided to begin a term paper on Monday, a student rewards himself by going boating on Saturday. Most likely the person is just reinforcing procrastination. Rewarding oneself is a useful tactic for encouraging additional progress, but rewards should occur only after part of the task is completed. In setting deadlines for difficult tasks, it is better to allow some slack and set a deadline that is earlier than the date when the task absolutely must be completed. Here again, however, having some slack should not become an excuse for not starting the task.

A useful tactic for avoiding procrastination over unpleasant tasks is to schedule them first thing in the day. Unpleasant tasks are more likely to get done if tackled first, before the daily stream of demands provides excuses to avoid them.

Some people begin a task, then delay completing it because they keep trying for perfection. Desire for perfectionism can be a virtue if a task is very important and it is possible to achieve perfectionism at a reasonable cost in time and resources. However, for many tasks, excellence is neither required nor justified. Extreme perfectionists are unable to establish priorities and allocate effort to different tasks commensurate with priorities. One possible remedy is to establish definite deadlines for activities and stick to them, regardless of whether the task is completed to perfection. Another approach is to establish specific quality standards to define excellence in a more realistic manner.

Analyzing Activity Patterns

It is difficult to improve time management without knowing how time is actually spent. Most managers are unable to estimate very accurately how much time they spend on different activities. Time management systems recommend that a manager should keep a daily log of activities for one or two weeks. The log should list each activity in 15-minute blocks of time. It is helpful to indicate the source of control over each activity (e.g., self, boss, subordinates, others, organizational requirements) and whether the activity was planned in advance or was an immediate reaction to requests and problems. Typical time wasters should be noted on the log (e.g., unnecessary interruptions, meetings that run too long, and failure to find things quickly). The time log should be analyzed to identify how important and necessary each activity is. Determine whether the activity can be eliminated, combined with others, or given less time. Identify whether too many activities are initiated by others, and whether adequate time is allowed for planned activities that are important but not urgent.

References

Douglas, M. E., & Douglas, D. N. (1980). *Manage Your Time, Manage Your Work, Manage Yourself.* New York: AMACOM.

Januz, L. R., & Jones, S. K. (1981). *Time Management for Executives.* New York: Charles Scribner.

Mackenzie, R. A. (1972). *The Time Trap.* New York: McGraw-Hill.

Schuler, R. S. (1979). "Managing Stress Means Managing Time." *Personnel Journal,* December, 851–854.

Webber, R. (1980). *Time is Money: The Key to Managerial Success.* New York: Free Press.

Case: ABZ Corporation

When Steve Arnold, a production manager at ABZ Corporation, drove into the parking lot Tuesday morning at 8:45, he was already forty-five minutes late for work. Steve had overslept that morning because he had been up late the night before finishing the monthly production report for his department. He parked his car and entered the rear of the plant building. Passing through the shipping area, Steve spotted his friend George Summers and stopped to ask how work was progressing on the new addition to George's house. George loves to talk about his home improvement projects, and it was another ten minutes before Steve could break away and continue on to his office.

Entering the office at 9:05, Steve greeted his secretary, Ruth Sweeney, and asked if there was anything urgent that needed his immediate attention. Ruth reminded him of the staff meeting at 9:30 with Steve's boss—Frank Jones, the vice president for production—and the other production managers. Steve thanked Ruth for reminding him (he had forgotten about the meeting) and continued on to his adjoining inner office. He went to his desk and began looking through the piles of papers to find the memo announcing the meeting so that he could find out what it was about. He vaguely remembered getting the memo last week, but had not had time to read it or look at the attached materials.

The phone rang and it was Sue Bradley, the sales vice president for ABZ Industries, who was inquiring about the status of a rush order for one of the company's important clients. Steve promised to look into the matter and get back to her with an answer later in the day. Steve had delegated the rush order last week to Lucy Adams, one of his production supervisors, and he had not thought about it since then. Stepping back into the outer office, Steve asked Ruth if she had seen Lucy today. Ruth replied that Lucy had been in earlier and then left without saying where she was going or when she would be back. Going back into his office, Steve rummaged through a pile of work orders on his desk, looking for the work order and also for the memo about the meeting. Finally, after fifteen minutes of frantic searching, he found his copy of the work order buried under some papers in the top drawer of his desk. The work order called for the delivery of some specially modified replacement parts to the client by Friday of the current week. It was now almost 9:30, and Steve had to go to the staff meeting. He made a mental note to check into the special order with Lucy later in the day.

The agenda for the staff meeting had not turned up during Steve's search for the work order, and he had no idea of what the meeting was about or how long it would last. It turned out that the meeting had been called by Frank Jones, Steve's boss, to discuss a proposed change in quality control procedures. All of the other production managers expressed concerns or made suggestions about how the improve the procedures. Steve was not prepared for the meeting, and he did not contribute much to the discussion except to say that he did not anticipate any problems with the proposed changes.

The meeting ended at 10:30, and Steve returned to his office, where he found Paul Chen, one of his production supervisors, waiting for him. Paul wanted to discuss a problem in the production schedules caused by a major equipment breakdown. Steve called Glenda Brown, his assistant manager, on the telephone and asked her to join them to help rearrange the production schedules for the next few days. Glenda came in shortly, and the three of them worked on the production schedules. While they were working, Steve was interrupted twice by telephone calls. One of the calls was from a credit company asking Steve to verify the employment of a machine operator in his department. The other call was from Steve's wife asking him to pick up some things from the store on the way home.

Work on revising the schedule was completed around 11:30, and as Paul and Glenda left, Ruth came in to announce that a Mr. Ferris was waiting and he claimed to have an appointment with Steve. Steve looked at his calendar but could not find any entry for the appointment. Since it was nearly noon, Steve invited Mr. Ferris to join him for lunch. Steve was tired of the food served in the company cafeteria, and he was never one to pass up an opportunity to have a nice business lunch that could be charged to the company.

Mr. Ferris drove them to a restaurant he liked on the other side of town where the food was good but the service slow. Steve ordered the luncheon special with a bottle of wine. Mr. Ferris was from one of the firms that provided materials used in the production process at ABZ, and the purpose of the meeting was to inquire about some changes in material specifications that had been requested by ABZ Industries. As Mr. Ferris talked, Steve realized that he would not be able to answer some of the technical questions, and he told Mr. Ferris that he would arrange a meeting with one of the engineers attached to his department.

When they returned to the the plant at 1:40, Steve introduced Mr. Ferris to an engineer who could answer his questions, then excused himself and walked back to his office. His secretary informed him that Lucy had returned and was out somewhere on the plant floor. Before he could go look for her, Steve's boss—Frank Jones—stopped in to ask about the quality figures he had asked Steve to assemble for him last week. Steve explained that he had given top priority to finishing the monthly production report the last few days and would do the quality information next. Frank Jones was clearly irritated, because he needed the quality data to finalize his proposal for new procedures, and he had made it clear to Steve that this task was more urgent then the production report. He asked Steve to get the quality data to him as soon as possible and left. Steve immediately called Glenda Brown, his assistant manager, and asked her to bring the computer printouts containing the quality data to his office. Steve thanked Glenda, and asked his secretary to hold his calls so that he would have some uninterrupted time to assemble the materials and write a short summary. This task was not difficult to do, but it took nearly an hour. By the time Steve gave the report to his secretary to send to his boss, it was 3:10.

Looking at his calendar, Steve noticed that he was already late for a 3:00 meeting of the plant safety committee. The committee meets weekly to review safety problems, and each department usually sends a representative. Steve rushed out to the meeting, which was held in another part of the plant. The meeting was very dull this week, because there were no important issues or problems to discuss. Drowsy from the wine and the big lunch, Steve was barely able to stay awake.

The meeting ended at 3:50, and as Steve walked back through his section of the plant, his assistant Glenda met him and asked for advice on how to handle a problem in assigning work for the next day. They discussed the problem for fifteen minutes, then Steve returned to his office at 4:05. As he entered his office, his secretary was just leaving. On the way out, she told him that Lucy had waited for him until her shift was over at 4:00, then left to go home. Steve knew that Lucy had a very long commute and did not like to stay late because she would get caught in heavy traffic. Steve decided he may as well leave also. He had promised his wife, who had to work late today, that he would stop at the store on the way home to pick up some things for her. As he drove out of the parking lot, Steve reflected that he was getting further behind in his work and was not accomplishing very much. He wondered what he could do to get better control over his job.

Questions for Students

1. What specific things did Steve do wrong, and what should he have done in each instance?

2. What are some things Steve can do to become more effective as a manager?

TIME MANAGEMENT EXERCISE

Instructions

The purpose of this modified in-basket exercise is to provide students with practice in thinking about priorities and planning activities for the next day. Assume you are a regional sales manager in a large corporation. You have been away on a business trip since Monday, and you have returned a day early. It is now 4:30 P.M. on Thursday, and you are in your office to look at your mail and plan some activities for the next day. Since you had expected to be away until Friday night, no meetings or appointments are scheduled for you at your office tomorrow. You have only half an hour to make your plans, because you have to meet your spouse for dinner.

The company has three major product lines, and each product line has several different models. Your regional sales office is housed in a company facility that includes other regional departments (e.g., personnel, accounting, distribution, maintenance), a large production facility, and a warehouse for company products. Your boss is the sales vice president for the company, and his office is at corporate headquarters in another state. You have 20 sales representatives who report to you, and an office staff of five employees who process orders sent in by the sales representatives. In addition, you have an assistant sales manager and a secretary.

Read through the items in your in-basket, then use the form to indicate the things you would plan to do tomorrow (Friday). Remember, you have only 30 minutes to make your plans. Your instructor will tell you when to begin.

In-basket Items

1. Memo from Barbara Sawyer, one of your sales representatives, asking for permission to attend a one-day course at corporate headquarters explaining the features of the new model of the copying machine. The course is next week, and she needs to have a decision by Monday. She notes that two other sales representatives from your office will be attending the course.

2. Letter from a major customer complaining about quality defects in the Model 1140 copier they purchased this year.

3. Note from your secretary reminding you that the monthly sales report is due at corporate headquarters this coming Wednesday.

4. Memo from Sharon Maroni, one of the sales representatives, asking for her company car to be replaced by a new one. Ever since it was rammed by a truck last month, the car keeps breaking down, leaving her stranded in remote areas.

5. Memo from the vice president for human resources, asking you to recommend somebody as a candidate for the new regional office in Alabama and provide background information on the person's qualifications. He wants each regional manager to identify the most promising candidate in his or her region. This information is needed in two weeks.

6. Note from your assistant manager requesting a meeting with you to discuss a new marketing proposal.

7. Note from your secretary informing you that your boss called and scheduled a meeting on Tuesday of next week to decide what the sales goals will be for your region.

8. Memo to all regional managers from the sales vice president requesting them to gather information about reasons for the recent decline in sales of Model 1140 copiers. The subject will be discussed at the meeting of regional managers in two weeks.

9. Memo from Lloyd Denton, one of your office staff, complaining about the parking situation. Since the expansion of the production facility into the employee parking lot, there are no longer enough spaces. The production employees start work earlier in the morning, and all the spaces are gone by the time the sales staff arrive. Parking is the responsibility of the facilities and maintenance manager.

10. Telephone message from a sales representative—Tom Jones—saying that a major corporation will order a large quantity of printers if we make some modifications. Tom wants to know if the changes are feasible and if the company is willing to make them. Call him back for details.

11. Letter from bank requesting verification of employment for one of your office staff. Employment verifications are handled by personnel.

12. Telephone message from George Palmer, one of your sales representatives, asking you to check into reasons for delay in delivery of printers to a customer who is threatening to cancel the order. Delivery is the responsibility of the distribution manager.

13. Letter from local resident complaining about the noise from the plant.

14. Memo from the training director at corporate headquarters, suggesting development of a training program for office staff in the new computer program being developed for processing orders.

15. Letter from a customer expressing appreciation that one of the sales representatives—Joe Owens—was so helpful in solving a technical problem for them.

16. Memo from the headquarters marketing department with a sample brochure attached for your review. No deadline given. It usually takes about half an hour to review a brochure and write comments.

17. Letter from an important customer inquiring about prices on the new FAX machines to be introduced next month.

18. Telephone message from a sales representative—Gwen Gordon—asking you to look into a mistake involving her health care benefits.

19. Expense authorization from a sales representative for your approval and signature. These forms are forwarded to accounting with your signature, and a copy remains in your sales office.

20. Telephone note about a call from a business reporter at a local paper wanting to interview you about the company's new FAX machine.

Plans for Tomorrow

Indicate what things you would do in each category. Indicate the priority in parentheses after the item, using the following ratings:

A High priority, both important and urgent, do tomorrow if possible.

B Moderate priority, important but not urgent, or urgent but only moderately important, do only if time available.

C Low priority, neither important nor urgent, or something that is the responsibility of someone in another unit.

Things to Check into Yourself

Responsibilities to Delegate (to Whom?)

Meetings or Appointments for Tomorrow (with Whom?)

Telephone Calls (to Whom, about What?)

Memos, Letters, or Notes to Write (to Whom, about What?)

Items to File, Hold, or Forward

Managing Conflict

LEARNING OBJECTIVES

After completing this module a student will:

- *Understand the advantages and disadvantages of conflict.*
- *Understand the conditions causing conflict.*
- *Understand different ways people respond to and cope with conflict.*
- *Understand the situations where each response is appropriate.*
- *Understand procedures for carrying out third-party interventions to manage conflict.*

CONTENTS OF MODULE

- *Text: Managing Interpersonal Conflict*
- *Case: Torando Electronics*
- *Case: Computer Peripherals, Inc.*
- *KB Sportswear Role Play*

Managing Interpersonal Conflict

A conflict is a dispute or struggle in which each party expresses hostility toward the other party and/or interferes intentionally with the other party's goal attainment. Conflicts can occur regardless of whether two parties have goals that are incompatible. Conflict occurs to some extent in all organizations and is a natural part of social relationships. Until recently, behavioral scientists assumed that conflict was an abnormal phenomenon with only negative consequences. Conflict was regarded as an evil to be eliminated whenever possible. However, now we know that conflict can have good consequences as well as bad ones, and the objective should be to manage conflict in such a way that the benefits are retained and the adverse effects minimized (Thomas, 1976).

Negative consequences of conflict are due primarily to the disruption of communication and reduction of cooperation and teamwork. When members of a group or organization have interdependent activities, performance will suffer if there is lack of cooperation and refusal to share information due to chronic conflict. The productive activity of each party will be reduced further by diversion of time and energy to "winning" conflicts. Individuals engaged in conflicts typically experience stress, frustration, and anxiety, which reduce job satisfaction, disrupt concentration on the work, and encourage withdrawal in the form of absenteeism or turnover. When conflict is excessive, the organization may be torn apart or immobilized, unable to take unified action in the face of threats from the external environment.

On the other hand, without some conflict an organization would not be able to maintain its vigor and adapt successfully to a changing environment. Adaptation requires changes in objectives, priorities, strategies, and procedures. Such changes create inconvenience, and they usually involve a redistribution of power and status. Many members of an organization will resist changes of this magnitude. Without overt conflict, these changes are unlikely to occur rapidly enough to ensure successful adaptation to external threats. In general, decisions involving conflict are less likely to reflect "stagnant thinking" or biased perceptions if forged from disagreement. Conflict often results in change and innovation. Although conflict is often a reflection of resistance by one party to innovations recommended by the other party, it may also be a source of motivation for both parties to seek innovative solutions that will resolve conflicts in mutually satisfactory ways.

Antecedent Conditions

Conflicts may be due to a variety of antecedent conditions (Robbins, 1974; Walton & Dutton, 1969). Many conflicts involve more than one antecedent condition, and the sources are not always mutually exclusive. Each antecedent condition will be described briefly.

Competition for Resources

One major source of conflict in organizations is competition for scarce resources such as budget funds, space, supplies, personnel, and support services (e.g., word processing, duplicating, data processing, equipment maintenance). The more scarce the supply of resources relative to the amount needed by the rival parties, and the more important the resources are to the parties, the more likely it is that conflict will develop and the more intense the conflict is likely to be. Cases of conflict resulting from competition over scarce resources can be found in most organizations. An example is a conflict between two sales managers over who will get priority in the scheduling of their product for production.

Task Interdependence

Conflict is more likely to develop between two individuals or groups who are dependent upon each other in some way for the successful performance of their tasks, than between parties with independent tasks. The task interdependence may be mutual or one-way, and the dependency may involve provision of supplies, information, assistance, or direction. The greater the difference in objectives and priorities for interdependent parties, the more likely conflict will develop and the more intensive it is likely to be. Conflict of this type is common between departments with different specialized functions, such as research and production, or sales and production. Strauss (1962, p. 164) provides an example from a study of purchasing agents: "Engineers write up the specifications for the products that the agents buy. If the specifications are too tight, or what is worse, if they call for one brand only, agents have little or no freedom to choose among suppliers, thus reducing their social status internally and their economic bargaining power externally. Yet engineers find it much easier to write down a well-known brand name than to draw up a lengthy functional specification which lists all the characteristics of the desired item." Disagreements may arise also because engineers are more concerned about the quality and reliability of an item, whereas purchasing agents are more concerned about low cost and quick delivery.

Jurisdictional Ambiguity

Jurisdictional ambiguity usually involves overlapping responsibility, and sometimes it involves gaps in responsibility. Overlapping responsibility is likely to result in conflict when one party attempts to assume more control over desirable activities, or to relinquish its part in the performance of undesirable activities. Conflict is likely also for joint activities when one party attempts to take all the credit for success or to blame the other for failure. Dutton and Walton (1965) describe a conflict between sales and production departments that was due in part to jurisdictional disagreement: When Sales wanted new product designs, Production resisted and found lots of reasons for not trying them. When Production attempted to avoid producing an order by claiming they did not have the necessary materials, Sales took the initiative in locating and ordering the materials. Production accused Sales of violating established procedures and overstepping its jurisdiction. As a result of the repeated conflicts, few new designs were developed, profitable orders were lost, crews were dismissed for lack of work, orders were not filled on time, and defective orders were shipped to customers.

Status Struggles

Conflict can result from a status struggle between two departments or two individuals when one party attempts to improve its status and the other party perceives this action as a threat to its position in the status hierarchy. Conflict can result also if workflow patterns are inconsistent with the status of the parties, such that a low-status party initiates action for a high-status party. Seiler (1963) describes what happened in one company where a low-status production engineering department initiated design and schedule changes for a production department that had equal or higher status: The production managers resented being told what to do and how to do it by engineers whose skills were no greater than their own. A great deal of time was wasted by production managers searching for errors in the engineers' drawings and preparing elaborate criticisms of these errors to embarrass the engineers.

Status conflict may be due also to perceived inequities in rewards, job assignments, working conditions, privileges, or status symbols. Inequity may be perceived when a person receives the same benefits and status symbols as someone with lower status; but there is even more inequity when the person with higher status receives fewer benefits than the person with lower status. When people believe that benefits and opportunities are fewer than what is fair for their status in the organization, frustration and resentment can lead to conflict with the manager responsible for these conditions, or with the people who are perceived to be getting more than they deserve.

Communication Barriers

Communication barriers include physical separation and lack of opportunities for interaction, either formally or informally. Another communication barrier is lack of a shared language and/or unfamiliarity with the technical language used by the other party. Communication barriers are seldom a major source of conflict, but they increase the likelihood that conflicts will develop from other sources. Insufficient communication can lead to pseudo-conflict by preventing agreement between two parties whose positions are actually compatible. Poor com-

munication can increase coordination problems and increase the likelihood of conflict between two parties with interdependent tasks. Seman-
tic difficulties and selective interpretation of information can
perpetuate misconceptions and encourage mutual distrust. For example, Robbins (1974) found that the animosity between a county welfare
department and other county agencies was directly attributable to
their ignorance about the welfare department's duties and contributions.

Open communication does not necessarily result in less conflict,
and sometimes it creates conflict that would not otherwise have occurred. It can reveal inequities or value differences between parties,
thereby stirring up resentment and hostility.

Values, Beliefs, and Traits

Underlying differences in values, beliefs, or personality may contribute to the development of conflict between people who must work
together. For example, competition between two people for resources,
status, or advancement is more likely to lead to conflict if both people
are very ambitious and have strong needs for achievement and power.
Conflict is more likely to occur between a manager and a subordinate if
the manager is very dominant and the subordinate has a strong need
for independence, or if the subordinate is very ambitious and the manager is insecure. Conflict is more likely between groups that differ in
religious, ethical, or cultural values and beliefs. Several aspects of personality are likely to increase the probability that disagreements will
result in open conflict. For example, disgreements due to differing values or objectives are aggravated when either party is intolerant, dog-
matic, and/or inflexible. Disagreements about the best way to accomplish an objective are aggravated when one party is narcissistic and
interprets dissent as personal rejection.

Reactions to Conflict

The parties to a conflict may react to it in a variety of ways (Robbins,
1974; Thomas, 1976). Withdrawal and smoothing are attempts to avoid
a confrontation over a conflict of interest. Accommodation is an attempt
to avoid or end conflict by giving in to the other party. Reactions such as
persuasion, forcing, bargaining, and integrative problem solving are
forms of confrontation with different consequences for how conflict is
resolved. Each type of conflict reaction will be described briefly.

Accommodation

Accommodation occurs when a person immediately gives in to another's requests or demands, even though the person would prefer to do something else. This response is also called submission, capitulation, or appeasement. It is important to remember that a conflict has occurred only if one party deliberately attempted to block the other's goal attainment, or if one party expressed hostility to the other during the interaction; it is not a conflict situation if a person willingly complies with a request without objection. Accommodation is most likely when maintaining a harmonious relationship is more important than getting one's way on a particular issue. Capitulation is also likely when the other party has an overwhelming power advantage and the yielding party sees no opportunity for avoidance or compromise. A danger posed by accommodation is that the other party will perceive the appeaser to be weak and will subsequently press for additional concessions. Accommodation in response to forcing can become a self-reinforcing pattern.

Withdrawal and Avoidance

One reaction to conflict is for either or both parties to withdraw from the relationship. For example, if two individuals are having a conflict, one party may leave the organization or transfer to another subunit in a different location. A related reaction is to remain in one's present position but avoid interacting with the other person. Avoidance can be an effective means of coping with conflict only if the parties have no need to interact to perform their work. However, if they have interdependent tasks that require coordination and cooperation, avoidance will seriously impair performance.

Smoothing and Conciliation

Another reaction is to "smooth over" the conflict and ignore it. There are a number of conciliatory actions a person can take to improve relations with the other side while avoiding confrontation over the conflict of interest:

• Tell the other party that you desire to improve relations.
• Offer compliments and show respect for achievements by the other party.
• Avoid making accusations, threats, or disparaging comments to the other party.

- Reinforce conciliatory actions by the other party by praising them and reciprocating.
- Emphasize the common characteristics and mutual interests of both parties.
- Make specific offers of assistance to the other party.
- Agree not to bring up differences in values or beliefs.

Smoothing may be an effective reaction to avoid escalation of conflict and improve relationships if the source of the conflict is not related to task performance. For example, if two persons have different political beliefs, religious convictions, or moral values and they get into frequent arguments, they can simply agree not to discuss these issues. However, like withdrawal, smoothing will not be effective if used to avoid confronting disagreements involving problems of coordination, sharing of resources, joint responsibilities, and other subjects related to the performance of both parties. Such problems are likely to grow worse rather than disappear if ignored.

Persuasion

One approach for confronting conflict is to attempt to change the other party's position through use of rational persuasion. Some common types of persuasive tactics include the following:

- Provide factual evidence supporting your position.
- Discredit information supporting the opponent's position.
- Point out errors in the logic of your opponent.
- Point out possible costs and disadvantages of the other party's proposals that may have been overlooked.
- Point out how your proposals will benefit the other party.
- Show how your proposals are consistent with prior precedent, prevailing norms, or accepted standards of justice and equity.

The success of a persuasive appeal depends on the credibility of the person making it and on the willingness of the other party to consider factual information relevant to the disagreement. A persuasive appeal is more likely to be successful if the parties have compatible goals but disagree about the best way to attain these goals. If the parties have incompatible goals, persuasive appeals are likely to be ignored or discounted. Persuasive tactics are more effective if they do not threaten the ego or status of the other party. For example, rather than accusing the other party of being ignorant or malicious, simply provide evidence showing that your position is more likely to benefit both parties. A direct attack on the other party's position is less likely to succeed than an indirect approach, such as presenting facts that are likely to lead the other party to reach the desired conclusion.

Forcing

Another form of confrontation is the use of pressure tactics in an attempt to force the other party to give in. Pressure tactics in a conflict situation include threats, punishments, and positional commitments.

A threat is an explicit or implicit warning that failure to comply with a demand will result in some undesirable consequences for the other party. A threat is more likely to be effective if the other party perceives it to be credible. Credibility is dependent both on the capacity to carry out a threat and the willingness to do so. Thus, a party may attempt to demonstrate capacity and willingness at the time the threat is made. For example, a labor union may publicize the fact that it has an adequate strike fund to support workers in the event of a strike, and members may be asked to authorize a strike even before negotiations begin, to convince management that the threat of a strike is real.

One approach for demonstrating to the other party that threats should be taken seriously is to apply a small amount of coercive power to give the other party a "taste of what will happen" if your demands are not met. For example, a labor union may initiate a work slowdown for a short period of time in one plant of a large company to show management they are serious about demands for better working conditions. Management may close one of several plants to show the union that they are serious about moving production overseas if labor does not make wage and work rule concessions. Another variation of this approach is to apply the full measure of one's coercive power with the condition that it will end as soon as the other party gives in to some specific demands. For example, an organization may suspend rebellious members until they agree to perform their assigned duties.

Threats and punishment samples will not necessarily have the desired effect. Although some people are influenced by them, others refuse to be intimidated. When each party has the capacity to cause adverse outcomes for the other party, use of threats is likely to be met with counter-threats, and aggressive acts are likely to result in an escalating spiral of aggression and counter-aggression.

A positional commitment is a statement by one party that the other party must give in or face the consequences of a deadlock. This tactic is used during bargaining. Examples are "non-negotiable demands" and "take it or leave it" final offers. A positional commitment is most likely to succeed if the party making it can show that further concessions would cost more than would be gained by a settlement. However, a positional commitment will not succeed if the demanded settlement is unlikely to satisfy the other party's minimal aspirations. Thus, successful use of this tactic requires one to estimate how much the other party is willing to concede rather than fail to achieve an agreement, then demand this much and no more.

Forcing is seldom the best way to resolve a conflict. It often creates resentment in the weaker party, who is likely to respond with passive resistance rather than enthusiastic commitment. The weaker party may be able to sabotage a plan by doing only what is specifically required and showing no initiative in dealing with unanticipated problems. Forcing may also lead to withdrawal by the weaker party. However, forcing is more effective than avoidance if the conflict involves interdependent activities and the performance of both parties depends on resolution of their disagreement.

Bargaining

Bargaining can be defined as a process of exchanging concessions until a mutually acceptable compromise is identified. Usually, the goal of each party is to obtain the maximum possible benefits under the circumstances, without concern for the benefits obtained by the other party. Experienced bargainers usually begin by demanding more than they really expect to get, and they realize that some concessions will be necessary in order to avoid a deadlock. However, the necessity of making concessions presents a dilemma when each party is trying to avoid any sign of weakness. If a party concedes too easily, it is likely to appear weak and the other party will be encouraged to demand more and offer less. Pruitt (1972) provides some examples of exchange-oriented tactics that can be used in an attempt to cope with this dilemma:

• Make a small unilateral concession and state that further concessions will not be made unless the other party makes a significant concession first.

• Suggest a specific exchange of concessions that would be acceptable to you.

• Informally signal a willingness to make a concession later if the other party makes one now.

- Propose that a mediator be obtained to help find an acceptable compromise.

Exchange-oriented tactics often involve "tacit communication" in which one party signals a willingness to be flexible without actually making an explicit offer or promise. This type of tacit communication encourages the other party to make a concession by implicitly promising that it will be reciprocated. There is less danger of appearing weak, because a tacit proposal can be denied later if it fails to elicit a positive response from the other party. However, since tacit communication is intentionally ambiguous, it may be overlooked or misunderstood by the other party.

Bargaining can be an effective method for resolving some types of conflicts. In order to result in an agreement rather than a stalemate, there must exist at least one settlement that provides each party enough benefits to satisfy minimal aspirations. However, even if a mutually acceptable compromise exists, it may not be discovered during the bargaining process if the prevailing climate is one of distrust, hostility, and inflexibility. Bargaining is not a feasible approach for some types of conflict situations. It is not likely to occur if each party is firmly convinced that they are right and the other side is wrong, if they do not trust each other, and if they have no way to ensure that an agreement will be observed.

Even when bargaining is feasible, a compromise agreement sometimes fails to deal with the underlying problem in a rational manner consistent with the long-term interests of both parties. For example, two departments in an organization were competing for control over a new production process. The conflict was resolved by an agreement to divide up the new machines and personnel equally between the two departments. The cost of running duplicate operations eventually became excessive, and the departments had to compete continually for the available work. The compromise turned out to be unsatisfactory for both parties and unprofitable for the organization.

Integrative Problem Solving

Integrative problem solving is an attempt to find a settlement that satisfies the needs of both parties. The conflict is defined as a mutual problem, and the parties cooperate in searching for a mutually satisfactory solution. Each party tries to understand the conflict from the other party's point of view and to discover what needs of the other party must be satisfied by any settlement. There is an open exchange of information about facts, needs, and feelings. An example in integrative problem solving is the type of labor-management negotiations called "productivity bargaining" that occurs in some companies. In return for increases in pay or benefits, the union cooperates with management in revising work rules and procedures to reduce costs and improve productivity and quality.

A number of integrative tactics and procedures have been proposed by Blake and Mouton (1984) and Walton and McKersie (1965):

• Definition of the problem should be a joint effort, and ample time should be allowed to explore the problem in the absence of excessive pressure for a quick settlement.

• Problems should be stated in terms of specifics rather than abstract principles, and points of initial agreement in the objectives, priorities, and beliefs of the parties should be identified along with the differences.

• The parties should work together in developing alternative solutions. If this is not feasible, each party should present a range of acceptable solutions, rather than promoting a single solution that is best for them.

• When there is a solution that maximizes joint benefits but favors one party or the other, some way should be found to provide special benefits to the other party to make the solution equitable.

• All agreements on separate issues should be considered tentative until every issue is resolved, since some issues are interrelated and cannot be settled independently in an optimal manner.

Most of the procedures used for integrative problem solving are incompatible with the kinds of tactics employed in forcing or bargaining. Positional commitments and specific hard demands are inconsistent with a flexible, exploratory approach to problem solving. Threats and punitive actions are inconsistent with the creation of an atmosphere of trust and cooperation. Deception and bluffing are inconsistent with open disclosure of needs and preferences and sharing of factual information. Thus, the use of forcing and bargaining tactics is likely to undermine any efforts to carry out integrative problem solving.

The success of integrative problem solving is not ensured by the use of any particular set of procedures. It is an orientation rather than a set of tactics, and its success depends on the mutual cooperation and creativity of the parties (Walton & McKersie, 1965). The effectiveness of integrative problem solving ultimately depends on the nature of the conflict situation. This approach is most appropriate when there exists a solution that would be optimally beneficial to both parties. If no such solution exists, the parties may end up with a "split the difference" compromise similar to that commonly resulting from bargaining. Another condition that facilitates the effectiveness of integrative problem solving is a high level of mutual trust. A party is unlikely to reveal its true preferences and minimal needs if it expects the other party to take advantage of this information and to provide inaccurate information in return. Some of the conciliatory tactics discussed earlier are helpful for creating a climate of trust favorable to integrative problem solving.

Third-party Interventions

The discussion of approaches for handling conflict has focused so far on conflict situations directly involving a manager. In this section, the focus shifts to the situation where the manager attempts to manage conflict between two other parties, such as two subordinates, a subordinate and a peer, or a subordinate and a client. Three major approaches are examined.

Mediation

Mediators try to help the two parties resolve a conflict in a constructive manner. Unlike an arbitrator, who hears both sides then makes a decision, the role of a mediator is to help the parties find a mutually agreeable solution. Success is more likely if the mediator is perceived to be impartial and trustworthy. One potential contribution of a mediator is the re-establishment of communication that has broken down. A mediator can encourage the parties to resume face-to-face negotiations. If two parties refuse to talk directly to each other, a mediator can transmit offers and messages back and forth. Another contribution is the facilitation of bargaining between two parties when it has become deadlocked. The mediator can test potential compromises by asking one party what would be expected in return for a specific concession by the other party. Since the discussion involves hypothetical exchanges rather than formal offers, the feasibility of different compromises can be tested without either party appearing weak or too eager for an agreement. Thus, a mediator can help one side retreat from a positional commitment without losing face.

A mediator can facilitate integrative problem solving in several ways. One way is to aid in collecting and clarifying factual information when facts are ambiguous and the parties disagree about them. Another way is to help each party gain a better understanding of their own preferences among different potential settlements. Sometimes the two parties will give a trusted mediator information that they are unwilling to disclose to each other. A mediator with accurate information about each party's needs and preferences may be able to discover an integrative solution that was not obvious to the opposing parties.

Process Consultation

The intervention of a mediator improves the prospects of a settlement, but mediation is not always successful. The focus of mediation is on the issues, not on the underlying relationship between the parties. Sometimes there is so much distrust and hostility in the relationship that a constructive settlement cannot be achieved until the relationship is improved. Process consultation is a form of third-party intervention that is directed at improving the relationship and developing the capacity of the parties to resolve conflicts by themselves (Blake & Mouton, 1984; Walton, 1969). The parties may be individuals or groups.

One objective in inter-party process consultation is to help each party understand how they are perceived by the other party. A variety of procedures can be used. One procedure is to have each party prepare a written description of how they perceive themselves and how they perceive the other party. The descriptions include goals, intentions, attitudes and behavior relevant to the relationship between the parties. The parties exchange descriptions, and each party examines the discrepancy between their self-image and the image of them held by the other party. They also examine the discrepancy between their image of the other party and that party's self-image. A meeting is held separately with each party to discuss the misperceptions and diagnose the reasons for the underlying hostility in the relationship. Next, the parties are brought together to exchange and discuss their diagnoses. At this meeting, procedures that facilitate active listening, such as use of restatement, help to ensure that each party listens carefully and understands what the other party is saying. Any non-productive reactions such as threats, blaming, and derogatory comments are discouraged. Issues that need to be resolved are identified, and the actions needed to deal with these issues are planned. In the case of groups, joint committees may be formed to work on the issues and make recommendations for dealing with them.

For individuals, a more informal approach is common. Written descriptions may be used, or the process consultant may simply get the two people together to explore their perceptions and attitudes. One procedure is to ask one person to describe what the other does that is annoying and to explain why it causes problems. The discussion focuses on behavior rather than intentions or traits. During this description, the other person is not allowed to interrupt. When the person is finished, the other party must restate what was said in his or her own words. Then the other party has a turn, and the process is repeated. Each person is asked to select one or two negative behaviors pointed out by the other person and agree to work on these to improve relations. Each person is asked to describe specific actions or changes he or she will make. Then a followup meeting is scheduled at an appropriate time to review progress and select additional ways to improve relations.

Organizational Changes

One way to reduce conflict is to make organizational changes that will reduce the antecedent causes of conflict. For example, incentives for competition can be eliminated and replaced by incentives for cooperation. A compensation system based in part on joint performance of a task fosters cooperation and development of mutual respect and appreciation between people who must work together to achieve important objectives. Task interdependence can be increased or decreased by reorganization of the workflow. Jurisdictional ambiguity can be reduced by providing clearer job descriptions and procedural guidelines. Communication barriers can be reduced by providing more opportunities for interaction, reducing physical separation, and providing training in common languages, including technical jargon. Status differences can be made less salient by removing obvious but unnecessary status symbols, such as different uniforms, separate dining areas, special parking places, and required use of special titles or forms of address.

Guidelines for Third Parties

The following guidelines summarize third-party interventions that do not involve changes in the organization. The actions are divided into problem-oriented actions designed to facilitate discovery of a mutually satisfactory solution to the immediate problem, and relationship-oriented actions designed to improve the relationship between parties. Which specific actions are appropriate for any particular conflict will depend upon the nature of the situation and how serious and prolonged the conflict has been.

Problem-oriented Actions

- Encourage shared definition of the problem by asking each party to explain how it is viewed, using situational terms instead of personal terms where someone is at fault.
- Provide factual information relevant to the problem or help to verify it.
- Encourage both parties to disclose their real needs and priorities.
- Encourage the parties to identify shared objectives and values.
- Encourage generation of integrative solutions after the problem is defined.
- Suggest helpful compromises or integrative solutions not obvious to the parties.
- Check to ensure commitment of both parties to any agreements.

Relationship-oriented Actions

- Remain impartial and show acceptance and respect toward both parties.
- Discourage non-productive behavior such as threats, insults, stereotyping, and exaggerations (for example, "You people always . . .").
- Ensure that each party has ample opportunity to speak and that nobody dominates the conversation.
- Encourage active listening (e.g., no interruptions, restatement of the other party's position).
- Use humor to reduce tension.
- Ask each party to describe how they view the other's behavior and intentions, then ask the other party to restate this perception.
- Then ask each party to describe their own behavior and intentions and to compare their self-perception to the way the other party perceives them.
- Then ask each party to select one or two things they will change to improve relations.

Summary

Conflicts have both positive and negative consequences in organizations. Conflicts are caused by a variety of factors, and more than one is often present in a conflict situation. It is easier to handle conflict, either as an involved party or as a third party, when the reasons for the conflict are known. Reactions to conflict take many forms, including accommodation, smoothing, withdrawal, persuasion, forcing, bargaining, and integrative problem solving. The appropriateness of each reaction depends on the nature of the conflict. Procedures have been developed to facilitate the efforts of third parties to help resolve conflict between groups or between individuals. Major forms of third-party intervention include mediation and process consultation.

The success of a manager in handling conflicts depends in part on skills in diagnosing the reasons for conflict and skills in selecting an appropriate response. However, success also depends on communication skills, influence skills, problem-solving skills, delegation skills, and skills in leading meetings. These skills are the subject of other modules in this book.

References

Blake, R. R., & Mouton, J. S. (1984). *Solving Costly Organizational Conflicts*. San Francisco: Jossey-Bass.

Brewer, M. B., & Dramer, R. M. (1985). "The Psychology of Intergroup Attitudes and Behavior." In M. R. Rosensweig and L. W. Porter (eds.), *Annual Review of Psychology, Vol. 36*. Palo Alto, CA: Annual Reviews, pp. 219–243.

Brown, L. D. (1983). *Managing Conflict at Organizational Interfaces*. Reading, MA: Addison-Wesley.

Dutton, J. M., & Walton, R. E. (1965). "Interdepartmental Conflict and Cooperation: Two Contrasting Studies." *Human Organization*, 25, 207–220.

Pruitt, D. G. (1972). "Methods for Resolving Differences of Interest: A Theoretical Analysis." *Journal of Social Issues*, 28, 133–154.

Robbins, S. P. (1974). *Managing Organizational Conflict: A Non-traditional Approach*. Englewood Cliffs, NJ: Prentice Hall.

Seiler, J. A. (1963). "Diagnosing Interdepartmental Conflict." *Harvard Business Review*, 41 (September-October), 121–132.

Strauss, G. (1962). "Tactics of Lateral Relationship: The Purchasing Agents." *Administrative Science Quarterly*, 7, 161–186.

Thomas, K. (1976). "Conflict and Conflict Management." In M. D. Dunnette (ed.), *Handbook of Industrial and Organizational Psychology*. Chicago: Rand McNally.

Walton, R. E., & Dutton, J. M. (1969). "The Management of Interdepartmental Conflict: A Model and Review." *Administrative Science Quarterly*, 14, 73–84.

Walton, R. E., & McKersie, R. B. (1965). *A Behavioral Theory of Labor Negotiations*. New York: McGraw-Hill.

Walton, R. E. (1969). *Interpersonal Peacemaking: Confrontation and Third Party Consultation*. Reading, MA: Addison-Wesley.

Case: Torando Electronics*

The prototype project development department of Torando Electronics Company played an essential role in the development of the product lines sold by the firm. The department consisted of 12 engineers and 35 technicians who worked on the first floor of the plant. Each project usually had at least two engineers and five technicians working together under the direction of a project supervisor.

When each project was started, the engineers submitted a written work order, and the department manager would assign the technicians to work with the engineers. Upon completion of each project, a quality control assessor would inspect the work. The engineers were recognized by the top management of the company as having the expertise to submit top-quality work orders, and in only a few instances were their requests rejected. The engineers were college graduates and were paid on a salary basis.

Most of the 35 technicians had previously worked as assembly workers at Torando, and they knew plant operations very well. They were paid on an hourly basis, and most of their pay raises were based primarily on seniority. The majority of technicians worked the day shift, although some had to work the other two shifts. Seniority was used to schedule the shift workers.

The technicians interacted with each other off the job, either through activities such as softball, bowling, card games, or professional football parties on the weekends during the season. The technicians ate lunch and took coffee breaks together.

The engineers rarely, if ever, spent any off-the-job time with the technicians. They had an engineering office where they took coffee breaks and often met after work to schedule some activity for the evening.

Rudy Garcia, the new department manager, was concerned about the strained relationship that existed between the technicians and engineers. He noticed the engineers complaining about the slowness and poor quality of work being done by the technicians. These complaints were occurring regularly. It was also obvious to Rudy that the productivity of the department was extremely low compared to similar departments in other plants of the company.

Because of the perceived problems in the department, Rudy started to investigate the relationship between the engineers and technicians. For two weeks he talked to a number of the technicians and most of the engineers to learn more about the interaction between the two groups. He found that the technicians believed that the engineers requested work orders for projects that were poorly developed. The technicians also believed that their suggestions on how to accomplish projects were never followed.

Rudy discovered that the engineers believed that they were part of the management team and needed control over the technicians. The engineers believed that the technicians were feared by management because they were unionized. In addition, the engineers thought that the technicians were "drag-

* Adapted from James L. Gibson, John M. Ivancevich, and James H. Donnelly, Jr., *Fundamentals of Management*. Dallas: Business Publications, Inc., Copyright © 1975.

ging their feet" and passively resisting any suggestions or recommendations initiated by the engineers.

After his preliminary investigation of the situation, Rudy concluded that immediate action had to be taken. He wanted to be fair but firm in his efforts to minimize or resolve the friction.

Questions for Students

1. What conditions contributed to the conflict between engineers and technicians? Consider each of the following conditions:

   Competition for Resources

   Task Interdependence

   Jurisdictional Ambiguity

   Status Struggles

   Communication Barriers

2. What actions could Rudy take to improve relations between the engineers and technicians? Consider each of the following types of intervention:

Mediation

Process Analysis

Organizational Changes

Case: Computer Peripherals, Inc.*

Gary Anderson, the director of manufacturing at Computer Peripherals, Inc. began to observe a disruptive amount of conflict between two of his key subordinates, Tony Bianco, the manager of Production, and Laird Howard, the manager of Quality Control. He decided to intervene in this problem by conducting a three-way conference among himself and the two managers. Gary hoped his two managers would develop a clear perception of the problem, which would lead to a resolution of the conflict.

Gary: I've asked you two fellows to meet with me because I think your differences are getting out of hand. You're both wasting a lot of time sending angry memos to one another. And I think you're both creating morale problems. Just today one of our hourly employees told the plant personnel manager that the feuding between Production and Quality Control is causing production delays.

The way I want to handle this is for you two to arrive at a better understanding of the reasons behind your conflicts. I'm not going to be an arbitrator or a judge. My role is to get you guys to work things out for yourselves. From the looks on your faces, it seems that I'd better give you some more structure. Tony, I'll ask you to go first. Look at Laird and tell him what he's doing that's bugging you. Be candid and thorough. We'll both remain silent while you're talking. Then Laird will get his turn.

Tony: Laird, I don't think I have anything against you personally. I just don't like the way you're doing a lot of things. In fact, Laird, you're getting out of hand. Let me go over the points that come to mind. At the top of my list is the fact that you're too picky. You look for defects too small for almost any customer to be concerned about. One example is last month you wrote a report saying our high-speed printer will hit a double strike once in 150,000 strokes. Who cares? The printer sells for $3,000, not $300,000.

Another problem I see is that you act like quality is a game. You and your crew are forever playing "gotcha." Instead of getting pleasure out of finding a zero-defect product, you get your jollies out of finding defects. I hate that gleam you get in your eyes when you tell the rest of the management team about quality defects you've discovered.

I also don't like the idea of you being so sneaky and indirect. When you find a problem, I wish you would tell Production first. Instead, you pussyfoot around the plant telling other people. The other departments learn of these alleged defects before we do.

Maybe the biggest problem is that you're losing your perspective. In your eyes, quality is king and queen. You seem to forget that unless we produce and sell a product, there would be nothing for your department to inspect. I think you're too power hungry.

---

* Adapted from Andrew J. Dubrin, *Contemporary Applied Management: Behavioral Science Techniques for Managers and Professionals*. Dallas: Business Publications, Copyright © 1985.

Gary: Thanks for being so candid. I can see Laird sitting on the edge of his chair, eager to let you know how he sees things.

Laird: I won't dignify some of your charges with a rebuttal. Besides, the way I understand the ground rules of this meeting, right now I'm just supposed to give you my impressions of your behavior. Above all, Tony, I believe that you give only lip service to product quality. If the president and Gary weren't so solidly behind quality, I think you would have our department report to you. You would keep it under your thumb by converting the department back to a quality-control inspection operation.

One of the reasons I think you're not really interested in quality is that you believe we don't have a quality problem until we receive a customer complaint. I remember distinctly you refused to listen to our advice on those daisy-wheel printing discs until returns from the dealers started pouring in. You told Gary you complied, but you really didn't.

And talk about power plays, you're the department that is trying to grab all the power and the glory. I have heard you downplay the importance of the quality department more than once. I heard that you tried to have the job of your department secretary upgraded one notch higher than that of our department secretary.

Tony, maybe the underlying problem is that you are too sensitive to criticism. The job of the quality department is to needle Production from time to time. You're just too thin-skinned.

That's all I have for now.

Gary: Now let's see how well each of you were communicating and listening. Tony, state in your own words what criticisms you heard Laird make of you. Then, Laird, you do the same.

Tony: Laird thinks I'm a power-crazy fool from Production. Seriously, Laird has these negatives about me. He thinks I'm not truly interested in manufacturing and won't accept his recommendations. He thinks that I want too much power for our department and that I'm thin-skinned.

Laird: Tony has some issues in relation to me that I didn't realize existed. He thinks I'm too perfectionistic and that I'm playing games with him instead of only pointing out true quality problems. He believes that I embarrass his department by telling other departments before I notify him, and that I place too much importance on product quality.

Gary: The fact that you can both see clearly what each other thinks is a good starting point. The next step is to take action, to grant some concessions to the other side. Tony, let's begin with you. What changes can you make to decrease the conflict between you and Laird?

Tony: Since I think I pay much more than lip service to quality, I see no need for changes there. Yet, I will make a deliberate effort never to downplay the contribution of the quality department to our overall manufacturing effort. And I will try to be more open to the suggestions Laird's group has to offer.

Gary: Laird, I'd like you to react to Tony's comments, and then specify what changes you think you can make.

Laird: I would be very satisfied if Tony would make the changes he just spelled out. I don't think we're being too picky, but I guess I do act a little too triumphant when we find errors. Perhaps I'm like a dentist who gets a thrill out of discovering a cavity. I will tone down a bit there. Also, I'll make certain that if we discover any quality problems, I'll discuss them with Tony first. I do feel a little guilty about having been loose-tongued on that matter in the past.

Gary: I think we've made a good start toward resolving these problems. Let's all get together for lunch in about a month to review progress on these matters.

Questions for Students

1. Describe effective behaviors displayed by Gary in dealing with the conflict.

2. Evaluate the likely success of the intervention.

3. What other techniques or approaches could have been used?

KB SPORTSWEAR ROLE PLAY

Instructions

The purpose of this role play is to give students an opportunity to experience what it is like to be in a conflict situation involving management issues. The role play involves three parties: the president of KB Sportswear, the vice president for sales, and the vice president for production. The conflict involves the two vice presidents. The person playing the role of company president has an opportunity to practice techniques for third-party interventions. An observer may be used to take notes on how the conflict was handled. Do not look at the materials for any role other than the one that you are selected to play.

If you are selected to be one of the vice presidents, read the background information and the information for your role. Try to imagine how the person would actually feel in that situation and try to act accordingly. However, at the same time, be willing to respond to any sincere efforts to find a satisfactory solution to the problem that is the major source of the conflict.

The person selected to play the role of the company president should read the background information and the role for president. If an observer is used, the person who acts as observer should use the form provided to take notes on the conflict process.

Your instructor will provide additional information on procedures for the role play.

Background Information

KB Sportswear is a small company that manufactures clothing used in sports and recreational activities, including ski apparel, jogging outfits, swim wear, tennis outfits, and clothing for hunting and fishing. The company's sportswear is manufactured at two small plants just across the border in Mexico. KB sells its sportswear to a variety of department stores, sporting goods stores, and clothing stores, including small, individually owned stores as well as large chain stores.

The sportswear markets serviced by the company are increasingly dominated by fads and fashion trends. Items such as ski jackets and sweaters and jogging outfits are purchased more for general use, not just for use in a sports activity. In any given year, some styles and patterns for a particular type of sportswear are likely to be more popular than others. The stores typically order only a limited quantity of various items, then place followup orders for particular styles that are selling well. Since most sportswear is seasonal and fashions change from year to year, it is very important for stores to receive quick delivery on these reorders. Otherwise, they miss opportunities for profitable sales and may be stuck with inventory that cannot be sold except at greatly reduced prices at post-season sales.

The company has a sales force of twenty sales representatives, each with a different territory. The sales representatives work on a commission basis. Since one basis for making sales is the promise of quick delivery, there is intense pressure from the sales representatives to get a reorder filled quickly.

Orders made by the stores are placed with the sales representatives or sent by mail directly to the headquarters sales office in Los Angeles. Because of the urgency for quick deliveries, reorders are usually called in to the sales office by the sales reps, or by the customers themselves. A credit check is made on the customer by the sales office before an order is sent to the headquarters production office. Depending on the results of a credit check, the customer may be required to pay in advance before an order is filled.

By the time most reorders come in, the plants are usually in the middle of producing items for the next season. If this production is disrupted, the line of sportswear for the next season will not be ready on time. Thus, production scheduling is very important.

During the past year, average delivery time for reorders has increased from four weeks to six weeks, and relations between sales and manufacturing have deteriorated over this issue. The president, Paul (Pauline) Campbell, has called a meeting with the sales vice president, Carl (Carla) Jackson, and the production vice president, Luis (Louise) Sanchez, at company headquarters in Los Angeles to attempt to resolve the conflict.

ROLE FOR KB PRESIDENT

Paul (Pauline) Campbell

Role for KB President, Paul (Pauline) Campbell

You have been the president of KB Sportswear for the last five years. The company has been growing steadily in sales, and its lines of sportswear are now being sold in most parts of the United States. However, the problem of delivery delays on reorders threatens to cut into sales, and may have done so already. You believe that the company has enough plant capacity to produce all of the sportswear that it can sell this year if the production scheduling problems can be worked out.

There are several constraints on solving the problem. The company cannot afford to maintain large inventories of items if it is going to be stuck with many unpopular lines that do not sell. KB cannot afford to build or buy another plant at the present time, although in another year or two it may be feasible. If absolutely necessary, it is possible to subcontract some work to other companies. However, subcontracting production would increase costs, which are now at minimum levels, and would not necessarily guarantee any faster delivery of reorders. You hope that you can help to resolve the conflict between Sales and Production and get them to cooperate in discovering how to reduce delays in delivery of reorders.

ROLE FOR VP-SALES

Carl (Carla) Jackson

Role for VP-Sales, Carl (Carla) Jackson

You are glad that this meeting is being held so that you can express your growing frustration with the production people. Don't they understand that without Sales there wouldn't be any company? Nearly half of KB's sales are accounted for by reorders. You are proud of your record in increasing sales over the last two years, but the same kind of increase will not be possible in the next two years if delays in deliveries continue to get worse. Even now, some potential sales are being lost to other companies who guarantee faster delivery. Once a company gets a bad reputation about late deliveries, it becomes difficult to obtain any business from the large stores who are your most important customers.

Several of the sales reps have complained to you that the production people are uncooperative. When the sales reps try to find out about an order, they usually can't get a definite answer. How can they make sales if it is impossible to tell a store how long it will take to get a reorder? You heard through the grapevine that one of the sales reps stopped in at the plant last week to check on a special order and was told never to come back.

You believe that Production is entirely at fault for the problem of slow deliveries on reorders. All they seem to care about is saving a few dollars on production costs. The production scheduling doesn't seem to make any sense. Sometimes a sales rep has to wait five weeks for a reorder, and other times the same type of order is filled in two weeks. Why can't Production fill all of the reorders in two or three weeks? You wonder why things are so screwed up in Production. Are the managers down there in those Mexican plants taking too many siestas?

In addition, your sales reps complain that Production doesn't seem to have any sense of priorities. A reorder for a small store is sometimes filled before a reorder for a major customer like a department store chain. If Production cannot do all of the reorders quickly, then they should expedite reorders for the major customers and let the less important customers wait longer.

You believe that the production mess can be straightened out with better management. However, if it is not possible to speed up deliveries with the present facilities, then the company should build another plant or subcontract the reorders to other companies. Most of KB's lines could be made anywhere in the world, such as in Korea or in Singapore.

ROLE FOR VP-PRODUCTION

Luis (Louise) Sanchez

Role for VP-Production, Luis (Louise) Sanchez

You have been looking forward to this meeting, because it is about time something was done about the sales representatives. All they seem to care about is making fat commissions. They make unrealistic promises of fast delivery to stores, then they expect miracles from Production to bail them out. They have become especially obnoxious lately in pestering the plant managers or anybody else they can talk to about reorders. Production people are constantly getting telephone calls from one sales rep or another checking on reorders. Some sales reps attempted to influence a plant manager to give them favorable treatment. You heard that last week one sales rep even came to the plant and offered a bribe for doing his order first. The manager threw him out and told him never to show his face in that plant again!

You are proud that production of sportswear by KB has been increased substantially, while unit costs have been kept below the industry average. It is this success that allows the company to remain competitive in its pricing of sportswear. However, you cannot keep production costs down if you have to keep interrupting the high-volume work on next season's lines to make small batches of reorder items. Don't the sales reps understand that you can't shut down regular production every time they have some little ski shop in Vermont that wants a dozen ski jackets? If the sales people could tell you sooner which items are selling well, rather than waiting for actual reorders, you could build up larger inventories of the "hot" items.

You are aware that the delivery time on reorders has gotten worse, but it is not your fault. As sales have increased in the last two years, the two plants have come close to full capacity, making the scheduling of production for reorders even more difficult than before. Your plant managers usually delay production on reorders until there is enough volume of a particular type of item to make it economical to interrupt the regular production. Only very large reorders that don't have to be combined with other orders get processed quickly.

Delays in delivery of reorders are due also to the tougher requirements for credit checks instituted last year by the headquarters sales office. Before you can fill a reorder you must wait for a credit check on the customer to be completed, even for major department stores worth many times more than KB Sportswear. Relaxing these requirements would help speed up deliveries on at least some of the reorders.

Instructions for Observer

Note any examples of effective behavior in the following categories by the person who plays the role of company president. Make a checkmark if behavior is observed. Use notes as basis for your feedback.

Problem-oriented Actions

_____ 1. Encourages shared definition of the problem by asking each party to explain how it is viewed, using situational terms, not personal terms.

_____ 2. Provides factual information relevant to the problem or help to verify it.

_____ 3. Encourages both parties to disclose their real needs and priorities.

_____ 4. Encourages parties to identify shared objectives and values.

_____ 5. Encourages generation of integrative solutions after the problem is defined.

_____ 6. Suggests helpful compromises or integrative solutions not obvious to the parties.

_____ 7. Checks to ensure commitment of both parties to any agreements.

Relationship-oriented Actions

_____ **1.** Remains impartial and shows acceptance and respect toward both parties.

_____ **2.** Discourages non-productive behavior such as threats, insults, stereotyping, and exaggerations (e.g., "you people always . . ").

_____ **3.** Ensures that each party has ample opportunity to speak and that nobody dominates the conversation.

_____ **4.** Encourages active listening (e.g., no interruptions, restatement of the other party's position).

_____ **5.** Uses humor or smoothing to reduce tension.

_____ **6.** Asks each party to describe how they view the other's behavior and intentions, then asks the other party to restate this perception.

_____ **7.** Asks each party to describe their own behavior and intentions and to compare their self-perception to the way the other party perceives them.

_____ **8.** Asks each party to select one or two things they will change to improve relations.

MODULE 12

Leading Meetings

LEARNING OBJECTIVES

After completing this module a student will:

- *Understand the potential advantages and disadvantages of group decisions.*
- *Understand procedures for presenting a problem to a group.*
- *Understand common errors in problem analysis by groups and how to avoid them.*
- *Understand procedures for reducing inhibition and facilitating generation of creative ideas.*
- *Understand procedures for evaluating alternatives and reaching consensus.*

CONTENTS OF MODULE

- *Text: Leading Decision Groups*
- *Case: Mainline Food Service*
- *New Product Decision Role Play*
- *New Machine Decision Role Play*
- *Problem Solving Role Play*

Leading Decision Groups

Many of the important decisions in organizations are made by groups rather than by individual managers. There are several potential advantages to group problem solving and decision making:

- Group decisions allow a pooling of relevant knowledge and ideas are distributed widely among different people.
- Group decisions are appropriate to avoid concentrating power for making a particular type of decision in a single individual.
- Group decisions allow responsibility to be diffused among several people, thereby facilitating some types of unpopular decisions such as budget cutbacks and disciplinary actions.
- Group decisions help members understand the nature of the problem and the reasons for the final choice of a solution; this understanding helps members implement the decision effectively.
- Group decisions are likely to result in higher commitment by group members to implement them, as compared to decisions made by a single manager without participation by people who must implement them.

On the negative side, group decisions have some potential disadvantages as compared to decisions made by an individual manager:

- Group decisions usually take longer to make than decisions made by a single manager, and the cost in terms of participant time is greater.
- A group will not necessarily make a better decision than a single manager who has all of the relevant information and knowledge needed to make the decision, and in some cases the group decision will be inferior.
- When group members have objectives and/or priorities that are different from those of the manager, the resulting decision may be self-serving and contrary to the best interests of the organization.
- When group members disagree among themselves about objectives and priorities, they may settle upon a poor compromise decision rather than openly confronting the conflict and trying to find an optimal solution that satisfies each party's concerns.
- When a group has a strong commitment to existing policies, members tend to support each other in defensive avoidance of evidence that these policies are no longer adequate.

Whether a group decision is superior to an individual decision by a manager depends on the internal group processes that occur during decision making. There are a number of ways in which the group leader can facilitate systematic analysis of problems, contribution of ideas by group members, clarity of communication among members, and constructive resolution of disagreement. Guidelines and procedures are presented for several phases of the group process, including presentation of the problem, problem analysis, solution generation, and solution choice.

Presentation of the Problem

The manner in which a problem is presented can either hinder or facilitate group problem solving. A presentation that is vague and ambiguous creates confusion, misunderstanding, and possibly even anxiety. A presentation that implies the group is to blame for the problem stimulates defensiveness. A presentation that implies a favored solution by the leader tends to discourage consideration of other solutions and may engender resentment by group members. Maier (1963, p. 76) offers several recommendations about the way a problem should be presented to the group.

1. Be brief.

In most cases, it is possible to present the problem in five minutes or less. It is common for leaders to spend too much time introducing the problem before inviting discussion. Long introductions give the impression that the leader is trying to sell a particular point of view. Another disadvantage of long introductions is that they usually create confusion and misunderstanding. Too much information at one time "overloads" people, and they are unable to digest all of it. The leader should briefly introduce the problem, then pause and wait for the group to respond. If the problem statement is not clear, someone will ask questions indicating a lack of understanding. At that point, the leader can make a more detailed description of the problem or call upon an expert member to do so. Sometimes, the group will request the leader's opinion about the cause of the problem. If this occurs, the leader should point out that the purpose of the meeting is to obtain the group's ideas, not to promote his or her own ideas.

2. Share essential information.

When the problem is presented, essential facts known to the leader should be reviewed briefly, including how long the problem has been evident, the nature of the problem symptoms, and what if anything has been done about the problem up to that time. The amount of information that should be presented depends on the nature of the problem and the group's prior information about it. The leader should be careful to present facts with as little interpretation as possible. For example, if the problem is how to increase sales, it is better simply to review sales figures for each district than to make judgments such as "sales are terrible in the central district." If there are definite constraints on solutions available to the group, such as spending limits or legal restrictions, these should also be mentioned briefly when the problem is presented.

3. Use situational terms.

The problem should be stated in situational terms rather than in behavioral terms, to avoid the implication that certain persons are behaving improperly. A situational description is less likely to threaten group members and make them defensive. Instead of making an accusation, the leader asks for help in solving a mutual problem. Examples of behavioral and situational problem statements are as follows:

- How can we get people to stop their excessive use of the duplicating machines? (Behavioral)
- How can we reduce duplicating expenses? (Situational)

4. Avoid suggesting causes or solutions.

The problem statement should not suggest the reasons for the problem or possible solutions to it. This kind of statement would limit the consideration of different problem diagnoses by the group. Instead, the problem statement should be worded in a way that encourages exploration of a variety of causes and a variety of possible solutions. Examples of restrictive and less restrictive problem statements are the following:

- How can we introduce incentives to increase employee productivity?
- How can we increase employee productivity?

The first problem statement implies that the cause of low productivity is poor motivation, whereas the second statement leaves it up to the group to discover the cause of low productivity and generate solutions.

5. Invoke mutual interests.

The problem statement should incorporate mutual interests of group members. Problem solving will be more effective if the members are interested in the problem and perceive that its solution will benefit them as well as the organization. Consider the following examples:

- How can we hold down production costs?
- How can we protect our jobs by keeping production costs below those of competitors?

The second problem statement will be more effective with group members who are not initially concerned about holding down production costs, because it indicates how the problem is relevant to their interests.

6. Specify one primary objective.

The problem statement should specify only one major objective. Other objectives should be regarded as secondary, and any benefits and costs relevant to these objectives should be treated as positive or negative by-products of achieving the primary objective. This guideline is intended to facilitate diagnosis of the problem and simplify the evaluation of solutions. Consider the following example:

• How can we reduce errors and delays in deliveries to customers?

Two objectives are stated, but it is not clear which one is paramount. It is also unclear whether there is one complex problem or two unrelated ones. It is easier to make an initial problem diagnosis for each objective, to see if errors and delays have different and completely unrelated causes and need different kinds of solutions. If a common cause is found for the two problems, then they can be solved together.

Problem Diagnosis

After the problem is presented to the group, the next step is to determine the cause of the problem. There are basically two different kinds of problems: "control-deviation problems" and "goal-attainment problems."

In a control-deviation problem, the objective is to restore conditions to a previously satisfactory state. For example, some equipment that was operating properly suddenly starts having defective output. The cause of a control-deviation problem is determined by a logical analysis of data on the exact nature of the deviation from normal, satisfactory conditions and the exact timing of the deviations (e.g., when did they start, how often do they occur, how long do they last?). The main reason for holding a meeting to solve a control-deviation problem is that the leader does not have all the information needed to determine the nature and cause of the problem. In making the problem diagnosis, the leader should have the group follow a systematic procedure to describe the deviations and identify single or multiple changes that occurred prior to the onset of the deviations (Kepner & Tregoe, 1981).

In a goal-attainment problem, a new or higher goal has been established, and the problem is how to attain the goal. The problem is caused by obstacles that prevent the goal from being attained in some easy, obvious manner. The meeting is held because the leader does not have all the relevant information about the nature of the problem, and the group has the collective knowledge to diagnose the problem and generate more creative solutions than the leader could do alone.

Several common errors occur in problem diagnosis, regardless of whether the diagnosis is made by an individual or a group. These common errors include:

- Confusing facts with opinions or assumptions.
- Confusing symptoms with causes.
- Looking for scapegoats to blame.
- Proposing solutions before the problem is clearly understood.
- Defining the problem in a way that implies a choice must be made between two particular solutions.

The leader can help the group avoid making these types of errors by following the following guidelines.

1. Encourage alternative problem statements.

As a first step in problem diagnosis for a goal-attainment problem, Maier (1963) recommends that the leader should stimulate group members to express different conceptions of the problem. Since a complex problem has many elements to be considered, alternative problem diagnoses help to identify different parts of the problem and suggest different ways of solving it. For control-deviation problems, only one description of the problem is needed, but it is worthwhile to consider more than one potential cause of the problem. To avoid dominating and inhibiting the group's thinking, the leader should refrain from offering ideas of his or her own about the nature of the problem until other group members have presented their ideas.

2. Evaluate alternative problem statements.

Comparison of alternative problem statements is easier if members are encouraged to provide supporting facts and explain the logic behind their inferences and hypotheses. In making this comparison, it may be possible for the group to agree which problem statement is the most accurate and useful one. However, for goal-attainment problems, it is not absolutely necessary for the group to agree on a single problem statement. In some cases, where there is disagreement about the nature of the problem, it is advisable to adjourn the meeting so that members can collect additional information needed to understand it. In other cases, where additional information is unnecessary or unavailable, the group can select one problem statement that appears especially promising and consider possible solutions in an effort to make further progress. Sometimes in the course of exploring solutions the understanding of the problem will change (Gordon, 1961).

Solution Generation

As in problem diagnosis, the leader should be careful to avoid dominating the discussion and imposing his or her own ideas and preferences on the group. Effective leaders make sure that the discussion remains focused on the problem, that everyone has an opportunity to participate, that members are not inhibited or defensive, that enthusiasm is maintained, and that new ideas are protected and nurtured.

Creative idea generation is a vital element of problem solving for goal-attainment problems. It is important for development of alternative problem definitions and for development of potential solutions to the problem. The contribution of ideas by group members can be inhibited in many ways. Much of the problem stems either from domination of the discussion by certain individuals or from members' fears that their ideas will be evaluated unfavorably. The following guidelines and procedures help to reduce inhibition and facilitate idea generation in groups.

1. Focus on the present.

A common problem in decision groups is to get bogged down in discussing what should have been done in the past instead of what can be done in the present. The leader should discourage retrospective critiques except when they clearly provide insight about promising solutions for the immediate problem. It is desirable to learn from mistakes, but current problems must be solved in the present, not in the past.

2. Encourage novel solutions.

Some groups have a tendency to focus on solutions that have been used in the past, instead of attempting to create novel solutions. Group members should be encouraged to consider solutions other than those that have been used previously. One approach is to ask each member to write down one new solution.

3. Separate idea generation and evaluation.

Research on problem solving in groups has found that idea generation is less inhibited when it is separated from idea evaluation (Maier, 1963). Based on this research, some new procedures were developed to reduce inhibition and facilitate idea generation.

Brainstorming is a procedure wherein members are encouraged to suggest any idea about the problem that comes to mind. The ideas are written on a blackboard or flip chart, and no positive or negative evaluation of ideas, including scowls, groans, sighs, or gestures, is permitted. Contribution of ideas is supposed to be completely spontaneous, and members are encouraged to build on each other's ideas. It was hoped that with brainstorming, inhibition would be reduced by deferring evaluation of ideas; domination would be reduced by making contributions brief and spontaneous; and creativity would be increased by mutual facilitation of ideas and a climate of acceptance for strange and novel ideas. However, brainstorming is only partially successful. It improves idea generation in comparison with a regular interacting group, but some inhibition continues to occur.

The nominal group technique (Delbecq, Van de Ven & Gustafson, 1975) was developed to improve upon brainstorming as a method for reducing inhibition. Members of the group are asked to write their ideas on slips of paper without discussing them. A period of from five to fifteen minutes is usually required to write ideas, and the leader insures that there is no talking during this time. The next step is a round-robin contribution of ideas; each member in turn is asked to contribute one idea. As an idea is suggested, it is written by the leader on a blackboard or flip chart. No evaluation or discussion of ideas is permitted during the posting. As the round robin continues, some members may pass if they have no additional ideas differing from those already posted. Ideas not on a person's original list may be suggested also, and members are encouraged to build on each other's ideas. After all ideas are posted, the leader reviews the list and asks if there are any questions, statements of clarification, or statements of agreement or disagreement regarding the relevance of an idea to the problem.

Solution Evaluation

When alternatives are not evaluated carefully, the result is likely to be a poor quality decision. Alternatives are evaluated in terms of their likely consequences. Sometimes adverse consequences are not foreseen when an alternative is intially proposed. Sometimes a proposed solution would create new problems that are worse than the original one.

When a solution is selected without due consideration to the cost of implementing it, the cost may prove to be greater than the benefits. Common problems in evaluating alternatives include incomplete participation, groupthink, and hasty decisions.

Just as group members may be inhibited during problem solving, they may be inhibited about contributing their opinions and knowledge during solution evaluation and choice. Incomplete participation sometimes results in a "false consensus." When some members loudly advocate a particular solution, and other members remain silent or fail to take a position, the silent ones are usually assumed to be in agreement. In fact, silence may indicate dissent rather than agreement. A false consensus will result in a lower quality decision if the inhibited members have important information indicating that the alternative favored by the more vocal members is in fact deficient. This information is likely to be suppressed by members who are afraid to openly oppose the vocal minority, especially if the leader, or other high-status persons, supports the dominant position. A false consensus will also lead to a low level of decision acceptance by members of the "silent majority."

Highly cohesive groups sometimes foster a phenomenon called groupthink (Janis, 1972). Spurred by their strong attraction to the group and identification with it, members typically overestimate the group's potential for taking effective action and underestimate the obstacles related to a risky course of action. Several related processes strengthen the illusion of invulnerability. First, strong cohesiveness causes group members to avoid open disagreement about a course of action that is the initial favorite. In the group discussion, members are inhibited from expressing doubts or disclosing negative information by the desire to avoid disrupting the illusion of harmony. In the rare event that doubts are expressed by someone, other members apply social pressure on the person to cease being a dissenter and to go along with the majority preference. Negative information is discounted in various ways, such as by attacking its validity or questioning the credibility of the source. If a plan of action involves dubious ethics, belief in the group's inherent morality tends to cause members to conclude that the actions are justified by the objectives. The potential for failure is discounted by the group's tendency to exaggerate its own capabilities and to stereotype and ridicule competitors and opponents. When groupthink prevails, the group usually fails to consider a wide variety of alternatives; it ignores negative information and exaggerates positive information; and it fails to devote adequate time to consideration of the potential risks and costs of the preferred alternative. The result is often a disaster that could have been avoided.

A "hasty decision" is one made without an adequate evaluation of the available alternatives. In the case of groupthink, the evaluation is superficial because nobody is willing to criticize the alternative preferred by a majority of the members. However, even when a group has critics who are not inhibited, a strong majority coalition may ram through a decision before the critics have an opportunity to explain its weaknesses and gather support. The pressure of time is another reason for hasty decisions. They often occur when a meeting is about to end, and members desire to resolve matters quickly so they can adjourn and avoid another meeting.

The following guidelines help to avert the three types of process problems and facilitate careful consideration of the positive and negative aspects of each alternative.

1. Allow ample time to evaluate consequences.

The leader should plan meetings so that enough time is available to explore the implications and consequences of each alternative. If an important decision is being considered and the meeting must end before solutions can be properly evaluated, the leader should try to postpone the decision until another meeting. If an immediate decision is not necessary and it is obvious that more information is needed, the leader may want to adjourn the meeting and arrange for additional information to be obtained.

2. Facilitate participation.

The leader can do much to facilitate complete participation by engaging in appropriate gatekeeping behavior. Each member should be encouraged to contribute to the evaluation of solutions, and members should be discouraged from dominating the discussion and using social-pressure tactics, such as threats and derogatory comments, to intimidate persons who disagree with them. The leader should be careful to continue discussion long enough to provide minority factions with ample opportunity to influence the decision.

3. Encourage positive restatement and idea building.

One of the most useful techniques for nurturing new ideas is to ask group members to restate another member's idea and find something worthwhile about it before saying anything critical. The procedure works even better when a member who points out a deficiency or limitation of another's idea is required to suggest a way to correct the deficiency or overcome the limitation. This approach emphasizes careful listening and constructive, helpful behavior.

4. List advantages and disadvantages.

The two-column procedure is recommended by Maier (1963) when there is no single solution that is clearly superior to all of the others, and each solution has both positive and negative features. The procedure is feasible only if the number of solutions under consideration is small. If more than four solutions are available, the list should first be reduced, otherwise the procedure will be too time-consuming. Each solution is written on a blackboard or flip chart. Under each solution, the leader makes two columns and labels one "advantages" and the other "disadvantages." Then the leader asks members to work together as a group in exploring the advantages and disadvantages of each alternative. The alternatives can be discussed one at a time, or they can all be discussed together. The important point is to involve every group member in the identification of both the advantages and the disadvantages of each alternative. The procedure is intended to avert the usual tendency people have to support their preferred alternative and criticize competing ones. As the group members point out advantages and disadvantages, the leader abbreviates each comment and writes it in the appropriate column. After the posting of comments is completed, objections to any items are considered by the group, and those that lack factual support or are irrelevant can be deleted.

5. Identify costs and benefits.

Cost-benefit analysis is appropriate when the consequences of each solution are fairly certain, and it is possible to make reasonably accurate estimates of the benefits and costs involved. The analysis consists of identifying benefits and costs in monetary terms, using cost accounting and other quantitative techniques. It is important for the leader to insure that this analysis is as objective as possible. The analysis should be conducted in a systematic manner, and care should be taken to avoid biasing estimates of costs and benefits to support a preferred solution. After the alternatives have all been analyzed, the group selects the best one by using whatever economic criterion seems most appropriate (such as, maximize net benefit or maximize return on investment).

7. Assign devil's advocates.

When a preliminary evaluation of alternatives reveals that one alternative is strongly favored and there is danger of a groupthink type of decision, the leader should try to postpone the decision until a later meeting and assign one or more group members to serve as a "devil's advocate" to investigate possible weaknesses of the proposed solution (Janis, 1972). The process can be formalized by having one part of the group prepare a formal proposal supported by all of the key underlying assumptions, facts, and data. Then the devil's advocates prepare a formal critique and present it to the group. In making the critique, the devil's advocates examine all of the assumptions, facts, and recommendations in the proposal, looking for weaknesses such as faulty logic, doubtful inferences, questionable assumptions, overlooked information, biased forecasts, and misinterpreted data. Finally, the group considers whether the proposal can be revised to deal with the criticisms in a satisfactory manner. If not, the group may try to generate additional solutions or postpone the decision.

Solution Choice

During the process of evaluating solutions, some groups become polarized into two opposing factions, each strongly committed to its own preferred alternative. When polarization occurs, each faction tends to ignore the good features of the opposing position. Discussion is focused on differences between positions, while similarities are ignored. As each faction concentrates on attacking the weaknesses of the opposing position, emotional debate replaces objective analysis. Each faction selects different facts or makes a different interpretation of facts to support its own position. Loud arguments are likely to ensue as people struggle to be heard or interrupt opposing speakers. Since members are not listening carefully to opposing speakers, they seldom understand what is being said (Blake, Shepard & Mouton, 1964).

Polarization may lead to a number of undesirable outcomes. One possible outcome is a prolonged stalemate in which the group is unable to reach a decision. Another outcome is a forced decision in which the politically stronger faction imposes its choice on the weaker faction. If this happens, it is unlikely that members of the weaker faction will be committed to implement the decision. Another possible outcome is that the two factions will agree on a compromise decision that is only marginally acceptable to either faction, in which case there is unlikely to be much commitment to the decision (Schein, 1969).

The following guidelines were developed to help group leaders avoid polarization and facilitate a decision resulting in member commitment.

1. Equalize participation.

When it is time to make the final choice among alternatives, participation can be equalized by a formal voting procedure. Voting can be done by a show of hands, by going around the group to hear each member's preference, or with a secret written ballot. The secret ballot is appropriate if there is indication that members will be inhibited about revealing their real preferences. A voting procedure is easy to use when there are only a few alternatives, but it is not very effective when there are many alternatives. As the number of alternatives increases, it is more and more likely that the votes will be widely distributed among them without a clear majority or even a strong plurality for any one alternative. Rather than go through successive ballots when there are many alternatives, it is better initially to reduce the list by having each member write his or her three most preferred alternatives on a slip of paper, after which the leader posts the tally for each alternative. After the list is reduced to the three or four most popular alternatives, it then becomes feasible to make the final choice with a regular voting procedure (Maier, 1963).

2. Encourage consensus.

Voting is a common procedure, but whenever feasible, the leader should encourage the group to try to reach a consensus rather than deciding on the basis of a simple majority. A consensus occurs when all members of the group agree that a particular alternative is acceptable to them, even though it is not necessarily the first choice of every member. A consensus decision usually generates more commitment than a majority decision, but more time is typically needed to make such a decision and a group consensus is not easy to achieve. When the group has a large majority in support of one alternative, but there are still a few dissenters, the leader should carefully weigh the possible benefits of winning them over against the cost of spending additional discussion time. If adequate time has already been devoted to discussion of alternatives, it is usually not worthwhile to prolong the discussion merely to persuade one or two stubborn members. In this situation, the leader should take the initiative and declare that a group decision has been reached.

3. Discourage polarization.

Polarization can sometimes be prevented by an alert leader who is sensitive to its early signs. The leader can try to reduce tension and hostility by use of conflict management behavior, such as discouraging derogatory comments, pointing out areas of agreement, and interjecting some humor into the discussion. Misunderstandings due to poor listening can be minimized by restating comments or asking a group member to restate the comment made by someone in the opposing faction. The leader can point out to the group that they appear to be drifting toward polarization and ask them to discuss ways to avoid it. When there are rival alternatives, and the group is having difficulty reaching agreement, the leader should help reduce tension and hostility, and try to develop an understanding and appreciation of both alternatives. One approach is to get members to participate actively in developing a supporting case for each alternative.

4. Encourage an integrative solution.

An integrative solution may involve either a composite solution using the best features of the rival solutions, or a completely new solution that both factions can agree is superior to the initial solutions. One way to begin this procedure is to examine both alternatives closely to identify what features they have in common as well as how they differ. This comparison leads to a better understanding and appreciation of the opposing alternatives, especially if all group members become actively involved in the discussion. The leader should encourage participation, keep the discussion analytical rather than critical, and post the results of the comparison to provide a visual summary of the similarities and differences.

5. Encourage experimentation.

When a group is sharply divided in support of competing alternatives, it is sometimes feasible to conduct a limited test of one or both of the alternatives to evaluate their likely consequences. Whether such a test is feasible will depend on time pressures, the cost of experimentation, and the possibility of conducting a limited, reversible trial for either alternative. Experimentation is highly desirable when it is likely to provide accurate information about consequences, and different estimates of the consequences are the primary source of the disagreement over which alternative is better. The most direct procedure is to conduct a limited test of both alternatives simultaneously, then compare the results. It is also possible to use a sequential strategy in which only one alternative is tested initially. If the consequences are satisfactory to both factions, the other alternative does not need to be tested.

6. Hold a "second chance" meeting.

For controversial, important decisions, it is useful to hold another meeting after the group reaches a preliminary consensus on the best alternative. This "second chance" meeting allows members time to re-consider the evidence and express any lingering doubts before making a final decision. A related option is to postpone the final decision until a completely independent decision group makes a separate recommenda-tion, or outside consultants provide an independent report on the feasi-bility of various alternatives (Janis, 1972).

7. Clarify responsibilities for implementation and followup.

After the group decides what alternative to select, the job of the leader is not finished. Before the meeting ends, the leader should make some provisions for implementing the decision. Necessary action steps should be specified and responsibility for each action step assigned to individuals. If a followup meeting is needed, the preparations needed for that meeting should be determined and responsibilities assigned. The date and time should also be determined, if possible, when every-body is present. Finally, after the meeting, the leader should distribute a summary of what was discussed and decided, and what responsibili-ties were assigned to which people.

Summary

The success of a decision group depends to a large extent on the leader's skill in facilitating the group discussion, recognizing process problems, and dealing with these problems. The contribution of the leader is not to solve the problem or find the best alternative. Rather, the leader should introduce the problem, keep the discussion on track, and ensure that the group follows an efficient and systematic process, utilizing available information and ideas, and selecting a feasible alternative that it is committed to implement. However, it is important to remem-ber that these leadership functions need not be performed only by a single person. In mature groups, leadership functions are usually shared by members, rather than being concentrated in a single person (Bradford, 1976).

References

Blake, R. R., Shepard, H. A., & Mouton, J. S. (1964). *Managing Intergroup Conflict in Industry.* Houston: Gulf Publishing.

Bouchard, T. J. (1971). "Whatever Happened to Brainstorming?" *Journal of Creative Behavior, 5,* 182–189.

Bradford, L. P. (1976). *Making Meetings Work.* La Jolla, CA: University Associates.

Brilhart, J. K. (1986). *Effective Group Discussion.* Dubuque, IA: W. C. Brown.

Delbecq, A. L., Van De Ven, A. H., & Gustafson, D. H. (1975). *Group Techniques for Program Planning: A Guide to Nominal and Delphi Processes.* Glenview, IL: Scott-Foresman.

Gordon, W. J. (1961). *Synectics.* New York: Collier Books.

Janis, I. L. (1972). *Victims of Groupthink.* Boston: Houghton-Mifflin.

Kepner, C., & Tregoe, B. (1981). *The New Rational Manager.* Princeton, NJ: Kepner-Tregoe.

Maier, N. R. F. (1963). *Problem-solving Discussions and Conferences: Leadership Methods and Skills.* New York: McGraw-Hill.

Schein, E. (1969). *Process Consultation: Its Role in Management Development.* Reading, MA: Addison-Wesley.

Tropman, J. E. (1980). *Effective Meetings: Improving Group Decision Making.* Beverly Hills, CA: Sage Publications.

Case: Mainline Food Service*

Ralph Benson, president of Mainline Food Service, Inc., looked forward with anticipation to his Monday morning staff meeting with his five key subordinates. After the usual exchange of pleasantries, Ralph introduced the major topic of the meeting. "I'm glad you could all be here today. We have some heavy thinking to do. The way I see the problem, Mainline Food Service needs to diversify a bit. For more than thirty years we've been offering vending machine service on a nationwide basis. As you all know, this is a tough, competitive business with very slim profit margins. Because of the many cost-cutting procedures I've suggested—sometimes over your objections—we've been able to stay profitable. Nevertheless, it's obvious to me that we need to diversify. As I see the problem, we should be using some of our capital to get into the restaurant business. The purpose of today's meeting is to decide what type of restaurant business we should enter."

Naomi Miller, manager of customer service, spoke first: "Ralph, you've made the assumption that we should be entering the restaurant business. Isn't that kind of limiting our choices? Suppose I said we should be opening up a chain of garden stores? Why are we restricting ourselves to restaurants?"

"Naomi, enough of your philosophizing," replied Ralph. "It only takes common sense to realize that a company in the food business should stick to the food business."

Ralph asked for somebody to make the first specific suggestion about restaurants. Buzz Owens, institutional sales manager, complied.

"Let's go all the way, Ralph. I'm suggesting we open up a chain of ten posh restaurants called the Executive Club. You could only eat there if you had a membership card that cost about fifty dollars per year. All our waitresses would be well spoken and physically attractive. Grand dining has sort of slipped by the wayside, but I think there is still a big demand for that kind of fine, elite restaurant."

"Buzz, I would hardly call that a novel idea. It's been tried many times in the past and failed," answered Ralph. "Does anybody have a novel idea?"

Chuck Adams, manager of vending operations, spoke next: "Ralph, you asked for a novel suggestion, so I'm taking you at your word. My brainstorm for a new restaurant chain would be to set up a franchise of fast-food restaurants called Jet Service. Each restaurant would have a fiberglass front that would look like the nose cone and cockpit of a Boeing 747. The help would all wear airplane personnel uniforms. We'd have travel posters on the walls, and jet-turbine-shaped salt and pepper shakers. Even our rest rooms would be styled after those found in an airplane."

"Thanks so much, Chuck. If we ever merge with Eastern Airlines or Pan Am, I'll be back in touch. Maybe you need an airplane trip yourself. Maybe you've been working too hard! Next suggestion please."

John Rubright, operations manager, looked around at his colleagues self-consciously before making his suggestion. "Ralph, I've given a lot of careful

* Adapted from A. J. Dubrin, *Human Relations, A Job Oriented Approach.* Reston, VA: Reston Publishing, Copyright © 1978.

thought to our problem. I detect a new era of conservatism and nostalgia sweeping the country. I'm recommending that we open a chain of simple country restaurants called GOFF. That stands for Good Old Fashioned Food, get it? We would have knotty pine chairs and tables and our help would wear colonial uniforms."

"Thanks for the suggestion," said Ralph, "It's not half bad, but it seems to me that type of restaurant has been tried in New England for many years, and it stands no chance of succeeding. We haven't heard yet from Dinah Malone. As director of Quality Control, she should have a good idea about the restaurant business."

"My idea is so basic that it might be dismissed as too simple," said Dinah. "Yet I think I'm onto something very important. The United States is tired of McDonald's and the like, but most people can no longer afford to eat in first-class restaurants. I'm saying let's bring back the old-fashioned aluminum-exterior diner. But let's do it in a big way, with smiling porters and authentic railroad whistles. Let's call this chain, 'Dinah's Diner.'"

"I could see why you would want a chain of restaurants named after you, Dinah, but is the Ford Motor Company bringing back the Model T? Maybe we've gone far enough in today's meeting. Let's all try again next Monday. During the week, try to be at your creative best. I'm eager to get some new suggestions."

As the last person left the room, Ralph said to his secretary, "Why can't our people be more creative?"

Questions for Students

1. What mistakes were made by Ralph in presenting the problem to the group?

2. Describe the things Ralph does that discourage creativity.

3. What could Ralph do to facilitate creative suggestions by the group?

ROLE PLAY EXERCISE: THE NEW PRODUCT DECISION

Instructions

The purpose of this role play is to give students an opportunity to experience what it is like to participate in a group that must make an important managerial decision. The role play also provides an opportunity to practice and strengthen skills that determine whether a decision group will be productive.

For this role play, students will be formed into five-person groups, and each group member will be assigned a different role. An observer may be assigned to record the process of each group. Do not look at the materials or instructions for any role other than the one you have been assigned. Your instructor will give you more information about how to do this exercise.

Background Information

ABCO is a large manufacturing company that makes chemicals, solvents, and various kinds of compounds. The company is financially sound, but sales have been stable in the last year without any increases. The Product Research Department has developed a new bonding agent, and the executive group is meeting now to decide whether to begin marketing and production of the new product. The executive group includes:

Chris Jones, President
Jerry (Gerry) Brown, VP-Research
Joe (Jo) Alvares, VP-Production
Lynn Johnson, VP-Marketing
Sam Goldstein, VP-Finance

ROLE FOR CHRIS JONES

ABCO President

Role for Chris Jones, ABCO President

You have been president of ABCO for three years. Under your leadership the company has been turned around from a condition of falling profits to one of modest but stable profits. You have aggressively encouraged expansion of research and development so that the company can remain competitive in an era of rapid technological change. Future growth for ABCO is dependent on sales of new or improved products, since demand for existing products is not increasing much and there is considerable foreign competition.

You have called the meeting for today to evaluate the prospects for the new bonding agent developed by ABCO's research scientists. ABCO holds patents on the basic process used to make the bonding agent. The specialized equipment needed to produce the new compound is available for purchase. The testing device necessary for quality control is made only by Eureka Corporation, one of your competitors, but you do not anticipate any problem in leasing their test device.

You hope that the executive group will be able to reach a decision on the best course of action to follow.

ROLE FOR JERRY (GERRY) BROWN

VP for Research

Role for Jerry (Gerry) Brown, VP-Research

You have been vice president of research and development at ABCO for ten years. Before Chris Jones took over as president of the company, the Research Department was hampered by inadequate budgets. The company did not invest enough of its profits in development of new products, and this was a major reason for loss of sales to domestic and foreign competitors. However, now there are several research projects underway, and the new bonding agent is farthest along toward final development. Product testing research has been going on for several months, and the results show that the new bonding agent is superior to any existing product on the market. In fact, the bonding agent is so strong and versatile that it can be used to bond materials that formerly had to be welded or fastened together mechanically. Nevertheless, just this week one of your junior scientists ran some tests that indicated the new compound may break down after a period of time when subjected to high temperatures, especially if the compound contains any impurities not detected and removed during production. More research is underway to determine the exact conditions under which problems may occur. You are hopeful about the prospects, because a successful new product would help your department get the larger research budgets you believe are necessary for ABCO to remain competitive in coming years.

ROLE FOR JOE (JO) ALVARES

VP for Production

Role for Joe (Jo) Alvares, VP-Production

You have been vice president of production for six years, during which time you have been very effective in minimizing production costs in order to keep ABCO competitive. The bonding agent developed by the Research Department is the first new product to come along in several years. In your opinion, going ahead with production would create some technical problems, but nothing insurmountable. Production of the bonding agent would require purchase of some new equipment which could not be used for existing products. The production equipment could be installed in six to eight weeks after it is delivered. A special quality control device to test for impurities could be leased from Eureka Corporation. Some new production employees would need to be hired, and anyone involved in making the new bonding agent would have to be trained to safely handle the extremely hazardous chemicals involved in the production process, in order to avoid accidents or an explosion. You enjoy the challenge of bringing a new product into regular production, and you are looking forward to getting started with pre-production planning as soon as possible.

ROLE FOR LYNN JOHNSON

VP for Marketing

Role for Lynn Johnson, VP-Marketing

You have been vice president for marketing for two years, having been promoted to the position when your predecessor left for another job. You have been anxious to show what you can do to improve sales, but you have been frustrated by unfavorable market conditions and ABCO's lack of exciting new products. Now it looks like the company has finally come up with a winner. The new bonding agent could be sold to a variety of different industries, including home appliances, automobiles, building construction, aircraft construction, and military weapons systems. Your staff has projected a rapid sales growth for the new product, and it could become one of ABCO's most important products within a few years. You have just learned from reliable sources that Eureka Corporation, one of ABCO's competitors, is working on a similar product based on a different compound. You are concerned that any delay would mean losing the advantage of being first on the market with a new kind of product. You would like to begin planning a major marketing campaign for the new product as soon as possible.

ROLE FOR SAM GOLDSTEIN

VP for Finance

Role for Sam Goldstein, VP-Finance

You have been the vice president for finance at ABCO for five years and have worked for the company for nearly twenty years. ABCO badly needs a successful new product. Sales have leveled off in recent years, and competition keeps getting more intense. Just before this meeting, your staff gave you the financial projections for the current year, and profits are expected to decline by 10 percent. If the new bonding agent could be put on the market quickly, profits could be up again by the end of next year. You have already investigated the cost of purchasing new equipment to produce the bonding agent. The specialized production equipment would be very expensive, and the company would have to increase its long-term debt in order to finance the purchase. However, you are convinced that it would be an excellent investment. Production costs for the new product would be slightly higher than for other compounds currently made by ABCO, but because it is a unique product with no competitors, it could be sold at a premium price, yielding large profits. You strongly favor going ahead with marketing and production of the new product.

ROLE PLAY EXERCISE: THE NEW MACHINE DECISION

Instructions

The purpose of this role play is to give students an opportunity to experience what it is like to participate in a group that must make an important managerial decision with incomplete information. The role play also provides an opportunity to practice and strengthen skills that determine whether a decision group will be productive.

For this role play, students will be formed into five-person groups, and each group member will be assigned a different role. Do not look at the materials or instructions for any role other than the one you have been assigned. An observer may be assigned to record the process of each group. If so, observer materials will be provided by the instructor. Your instructor will give you more information about how to do this exercise.

Background Information

Genco is a medium-sized manufacturing company with several plants. The company has received a larger than usual volume of new orders for its products. To fill these orders, it is necessary to acquire another machine to increase production capacity at one of the plants. There are three types of machines that would provide the necessary increase in production capacity for the coming year: the Martin 350, the Decker 200, and the Borg 900. The plant currently has four Decker 200 machines which were purchased three years ago.

The plant manager, Chris Erickson has scheduled a meeting with four subordinates to decide what type of machine to acquire. The subordinates are:

Terry (Terri) Miller, day-shift production supervisor

Marty (Marti) Smith, night-shift production supervisor

Michael (Michele) Jones, maintenance supervisor

Andy (Andrea) Williams, purchasing manager

ROLE FOR PLANT MANAGER

Chris Erickson

Role for Plant Manager, Chris Erickson

You have called this meeting to decide which type of machine to acquire. You do not know much about the machines and must rely on the advice of your four subordinates. You are aware that they have strong preferences in this matter, but you are hopeful that the meeting will result in general agreement on which machine best meets the needs of Genco. In any case, some decision must be reached today.

The lead time needed to get a machine installed and into production is around six weeks, and your boss wants you to decide today either to purchase one of the machines or to lease one for a year. It is an important decision because the machines are expensive and they differ in cost, reliability, flexibility, energy efficiency, and other factors relevant to company profits. The machines are usually operated for eight years before being retired. In the last two years, cost of machines has averaged around 10% of annual production costs, with cost of energy to operate the machines 3%, cost of materials 35%, direct cost of labor 40%, and overhead costs 12%.

ROLE FOR PURCHASING MANAGER

Andy (Andrea) Williams

Role for Purchasing Manager,
Andy (Andrea) Williams

You have been purchasing manager at Genco for five years. You favor the Decker 200 machine for several reasons. First, it is the cheapest of the three machines to purchase. Since the company already has four of the Decker machines, it could get a good deal on a fifth machine. In talking to the sales representatives for each type of machine, you have recently learned that it would cost only $100,000 for a new Decker 200, versus $125,000 for a Borg 900 and $115,000 for a Martin 350. The Borg and Martin can be purchased or leased, but the Decker can only be purchased.

The firm that makes the Decker provides excellent service to its customers. When there is a maintenance problem that cannot be handled by Genco, they will send someone out quickly to service the machine. You believe that it is appropriate to reward them for their low cost and excellent service record by giving them the order for the new machine. You distrust the Martin machines because, prior to getting its current machines, Genco had some of the earlier models of the Martin and they proved very costly to operate.

ROLE FOR MAINTENANCE SUPERVISOR

Michael (Michele) Jones

Role for Maintenance Supervisor, Michael (Michele) Jones

You have been a maintenance supervisor at Genco for two years. The plant where you worked prior to joining Genco had both the Martin 350 and the Borg 900 machines, so you have some basis for comparing them. The Martin 350 was less complicated and easier to maintain. It had a better record for reliable operation without breakdowns, and when a breakdown occurred, it was easier to repair. The average downtime due to breakdowns was only 15 minutes per eight-hour shift, versus 30 minutes for the Borg 900. Average downtime for the Decker 200 machines here at Genco has been 20 minutes. Breakdowns cause lost production, production delays, and higher labor costs, because operators must be paid when waiting for their machine to be repaired. Direct labor costs represent 40% of the total cost of production, so downtime is an important consideration. You strongly prefer the Martin 350. It is greatly improved over the earlier model of the Martin, and you believe that it is superior to the Decker 200 and the Borg 900.

ROLE FOR DAY-SHIFT PRODUCTION SUPERVISOR

Terry (Terri) Miller

Role for Day-Shift Production Supervisor, Terry (Terri) Miller

You have been a production supervisor at Genco for eight years and have had extensive experience working with machines of this type. You are very satisfied with the four Decker 200 machines owned by Genco. Prior to the time these machines were purchased, the plant had some older models of the Martin machine. Those machines had some defects that the manufacturer was never able to remedy completely. In contrast, the Decker 200 does exactly what it was designed to do without any serious problems. It is a great little machine. Having five machines of the same type would make it easier to schedule production. Moreover, since the present employees already know how to operate a Decker, less training would be necessary. You don't know much about the Borg 900, but you have heard that it is a difficult machine to operate and that it requires highly skilled personnel.

ROLE FOR NIGHT-SHIFT PRODUCTION SUPERVISOR

Marty (Marti) Smith

Role for Night-Shift Production Supervisor, Marty (Marti) Smith

You have been a production supervisor at Genco for three years. You favor the Borg 900 machine because it has greater capacity and more flexibility than the Decker 200 or the Martin 350. The standard production output when there are no breakdowns is 20% higher for the Borg than for the other two machines, which are roughly equal to each other in output. Because the Borg 900 is more flexible, it would enable the company to do some types of jobs that are not possible now with the existing machines. The Borg is a complex machine that requires more skill to operate. However, the company that makes the Borg provides a three-day training course for operators at no extra cost. The training is conducted after the machine is installed, and it emphasizes preventative maintenance and use of operating procedures that minimize unnecessary breakdowns. This new training program has been found to reduce machine breakdowns by at least 50% for operators who have been trained. Despite the complexity of the Borg, it is an energy efficient machine with a per unit operating cost 15% lower than the Decker 200 and 10% lower than the Martin 350. The Borg can be leased with an option to buy after one year at a cost reduced by the amount of the lease.

PROBLEM SOLVING ROLE PLAY EXERCISE

Instructions

The purpose of this role play exercise is to give students an opportunity to experience what it is like to participate in a management group that is struggling to understand the reason for a complex and serious problem. For this exercise, students will be formed into five-person groups, and each group member will be assigned a different role to play. The information available to the group is sufficient to diagnose the cause of the problem. One or two additional students may be assigned to a group as observers to record the group's problem solving processes.

Do not look at the materials or instructions for any other role than the one you have been assigned. During the role play, you may communicate any of the information in your role materials orally to other members of the group, but do not show your written role to them. Observers are not supposed to talk to group members during the role play. Your instructor will provide more information about group assignments and procedures for doing this exercise.

Background Information

Simmons Electronics is a small manufacturing company that makes specialized electronic components for aerospace companies. Simmons has a major contract to manufacture a guidance system unit for missiles. Simmons assembles the guidance system units, using some components that are made by the company as well as some components that are purchased from other companies. The completed units are shipped to the client where they are subjected to extensive tests under simulated conditions. Any units that fail these tests are returned to be reworked. The rework process involves elaborate checking and costs almost as much as the initial production. Moreover, only one or two reworks a month can be done without disrupting regular production.

Production on this project started in July. It is now the first week in December, and the company is behind schedule in deliveries of acceptable units. The table below shows the number of units needed, produced and delivered, accepted, reworked, and delinquent for each month of production.

	July	Aug.	Sept.	Oct.	Nov.	Dec.	Jan.	Feb.	March
Amount needed	20	20	20	20	30	30	30	30	30
Amount produced	20	20	20	20	30				
Amount accepted	19	19	20	20	25				
Amount reworked	0	0	1	1	0				
Amount delinquent	1	2	1	0	5				

The project manager for the guidance system project has called a meeting of the key managers involved in the project to identify the cause of the problem and find a solution. Attending the meeting are the following people:

Project Manager
Production Manager
Engineering Manager
Purchasing Manager
Human Resource Manager

ROLE FOR PROJECT MANAGER

Role for Project Manager

It is your responsibility to supervise the guidance system project, coordinate the contributions of different departments, and keep the project on schedule. The guidance system units are produced on two assembly lines. Assembly Lines 1 and 2 are used during the day shift. The day shift has been working at full capacity since the project began, and it produces twice as many units as the night shift. There are twice as many employees on the day shift as on the night shift.

The project has had a troubled history. The production schedule now in effect provides for only the minimum number of units needed each month. If any units are rejected by the client, the project will fall behind schedule. As the summary table shows, some rejections occurred in July and August. That problem was traced to the equipment used in adjusting the tracking sensors on Assembly Line 1. This adjustment is a critical step in the production process, since proper adjustment is essential for the guidance system to perform adequately. The problem was solved in September by purchasing better equipment that allowed the tracking sensors to be adjusted to the specific tolerances. By the end of October, the project was back on schedule. Then, in November, rejects started occurring again, this time more drastically. The reason for the recent rejects is not known, and people have different opinions about the likely cause.

You have called a meeting of managers who have the information needed to identify the cause of the problem. Your task is to run the meeting in an efficient manner. The group has 30 minutes to discover why the reject rate has increased and to find a solution.

ROLE FOR PRODUCTION MANAGER

Role for Production Manager

It is your responsibility to supervise the manufacture of components and the assembly of the guidance units, using components made in house and components purchased outside. The production process was initially done by 20 employees on the day shift, on Assembly Lines 1 and 2. Then in January, when production was scheduled to increase by 50%, a night shift of 10 workers was added, using Assembly Line 2. Some day-shift workers were moved to the night shift, because it was necessary to have some experienced workers on both shifts to operate critical equipment and to help train the new workers.

Starting the night shift has not been as smooth as you had hoped. There have been more problems at night, including fights and accidents. For example, there was one incident the first week where a careless worker ran his forklift into the electrical transformer and cut off the supply of power to the entire plant. Production was disrupted for two hours until repairs could be made. The transformer is still not working properly, and some of the heavy machinery in the plant that is operated only at night causes power surges when it is turned on and off. The night shift has been supervised by your assistant production manager, who formerly ran Assembly Line 2 on the day shift. You wonder if he has enough experience to deal with the special problems on the night shift. You are considering moving to the night shift yourself for a while to get things under control.

ROLE FOR ENGINEERING MANAGER

Role for Engineering Manager

One of your responsibilities is to supervise the adjustment of the tracking sensors after the components for the guidance system are assembled. The adjustment is done with some specialized equipment that is extremely sensitive. Each assembly line has its own machines for adjusting tracking sensors. New equipment was purchased in August for Assembly Line 1, because the old equipment did not allow adjustments to be made to the necessary tolerance levels. The deficiency in this equipment was the cause of the rejected units in July and August, both of which were produced on Assembly Line 1. No units were rejected on Assembly Line 1 after the new equipment was installed.

You have investigated the source of the rejects in November. They all occurred for units produced on Assembly Line 2 on the night shift. As in the case of the earlier rejects, you suspect that the cause may have something to do with the equipment used to adjust the tracking sensors. Although the present equipment on Assembly Line 2 allows operators to set tolerances to specified levels, it is several years old and may not be as reliable as it used to be. You favor replacing it with new equipment like that purchased for Assembly Line 1. In the meantime, Assembly Line 1 will be used for aspects of the rework that must be done on a regular assembly line to be safe.

ROLE FOR PURCHASING MANAGER

Role for Purchasing Manager

Your responsibility is to purchase the materials, components, and equipment used in production of guidance system units and other products. You are very pleased with the success of the equipment you purchased for Assembly Line 1 to replace the old equipment that caused the rejects in July and August. Although the new equipment was very expensive ($40,000), it has several advantages: it allows closer tolerances to be set; it is faster; it provides better protection against voltage surges; and it is easier to maintain. However, in comparison to the older equipment, the new equipment requires more skill, so it is important to use experienced and responsible workers to operate it.

You suspect that the new rash of rejects may be due to the use of inferior materials in producing the tracking sensors. The current supplier of materials for the guidance system project was selected because the supplier has a good reputation and the lowest price. However, you have subsequently heard that the supplier is having financial problems, and you wonder if the quality of their materials has suffered as a result. To test the materials would take a couple of weeks. You know of an alternative supplier, but the materials would cost about 40% more if purchased from that company.

ROLE FOR HUMAN RESOURCE MANAGER

Role for Human Resource Manager

It is your responsibility to hire and train workers for company projects, to manage the pay and benefits system, and to handle day-to-day union matters and grievances. You have been very busy during September and October helping to prepare for the initiation of the night shift. The night shift was staffed by 6 of the day shift workers and 4 new workers. An additional 6 new workers were hired for the day shift to replace those who were moved to the night. You hired the ten new workers and supervised their initial training. Additional on-the-job training of new workers is being provided by the experienced workers on both shifts.

The employees who moved from the day shift to the night shift were very unhappy about the change, because they do not like working nights. It is difficult to adjust to a different work schedule, and there are a number of things that make the work more tedious and unpleasant at night. The workers miss seeing their friends who are still on the day shift. It is much noisier due to some heavy equipment in another part of the plant that is only operated at night. The company cafeteria is not open at night, and only vending machine food is available. A couple of the workers who were switched have been complaining to the union that they should get extra pay for having to work at night.

You have just learned that the defective units were all produced by the night shift. You suspect that the quality problems in the guidance units may be related to dissatisfaction among the workers who were moved from the day to the night shift. Workers who are upset are likely to be less careful about quality.